I0878578

THE MEMORY OF THE HOLOCAUST IN AUSTRALIA

The Memory of the Holocaust in Australia

Editors
Tom Lawson
James Jordan

VALLENTINE MITCHELL
LONDON • PORTLAND, OR

First published in 2008 by Vallentine Mitchell

Suite 314, Premier House,
112–114 Station Road,
Edgware, Middlesex HA8 7BJ

920 NE 58th Avenue, Suite 300
Portland, Oregon,
97213-3786

www.vmbooks.com

British Library Cataloguing in Publication Data

ISBN 978 0 85303 794 1 (cloth)
ISBN 978 0 85303 795 8 (paper)

Library of Congress Cataloging-in-Publication Data:

A catalog record has been applied for

This group of studies first appeared in a special issue of *Holocaust Studies: A Journal of Culture and History*, Vol.13/2–3 [ISSN 1359-1371] published by Vallentine Mitchell & Co. Ltd.

Printed by Biddles Ltd., King's Lynn, Norfolk

Contents

To the Memory of Frank Cass
1930–2007

Introduction

TOM LAWSON and JAMES JORDAN

Most readers of this volume will be familiar with the 'strange case of Helen Demidenko', but it is worth repeating. Demidenko's award-winning novel *The Hand that Signed the Paper* was well received in Australian literary circles in the mid-1990s as an account of the horrors of the Second World War, and by implication the Holocaust. Demidenko's narrative of Ukrainian perpetrators of atrocity against Jews, and their post-war journey to Australia, made genuine efforts to understand and interrogate the motivations behind participation in mass-murder in the context of war. Yet Demidenko's attempts to understand the 'cycle of violence' between Jews and Ukrainians were also underpinned by familiar antisemitism. The book suggested that Jews had, in effect, controlled the Bolshevik domination of the Ukraine, and as such the genocidal famine of the 1930s. When Nazi forces wrested Ukraine from Bolshevik control, the Jews put to death by Nazi death squads, abetted by Ukrainian volunteers, were, Demidenko implied, the authors of their own misfortune and victims of a form of genocidal accounting.[1] The furore provoked by Demidenko's adoption of many of the tropes of Nazi antisemitism only intensified when it became clear that her claims to have written the book from if not personal then at least familial experience as a Ukrainian immigrant to Australia were proved to be false: Demidenko was in fact the British-born Helen Darville.

Darville's attempts to assume a false ethnic identity remain unfathomable, but the affair as a whole represented a particularly *Australian* example of the echoes of the Holocaust in the contemporary world, and as such the global significance of Holocaust memory. Australia is an immigrant community that accommodated (both the actual as well as the imagined) perpetrators and victims of Nazi persecution in the aftermath of the Second World War. As such, Nazi persecution has been present (if not acknowledged) in Australian society, in many forms, for the past 60 years. The collection that follows is a series of essays concerned with the ways in which Australian society as a whole and particularly Australian Jewish communities have both avoided and confronted this shadow of the Holocaust.

Darville's links to the politics of the Holocaust did not end with *The Hand that Signed the Paper*, however. In 2000 she was appointed as the correspondent for *Australian Style* magazine at the libel trial brought by Holocaust denier David Irving against Penguin books in London. Her political leanings were again made abundantly clear when she supported the 'Churchillian' Irving in her account of the trial in which he was found to be a liar and a Nazi.[2] The ability of both Darville and the Holocaust to make the news in Australian society was again confirmed when her reportage was itself the subject of critical coverage in the Australian daily press.[3]

Darville's presence at the Royal Courts of Justice in early 2000 is indicative of the genuinely global role that the Holocaust and its memory play in contemporary politics and society. Darville, a British Australian, was reporting on a libel trial brought by a man who has spent significant portions of his life in Germany and Austria, against an American Jewish author and her publishers over allegations that he falsified evidence found in Russian and German archives, in books published throughout the world which are particularly praised in contemporary Iran, about events on continental Europe, for an Australian magazine. The reverberations of the Holocaust seem to know no boundaries.

It is the shape and impact of those reverberations in Australian politics and society, and particularly amongst Australia's Jewish communities, which are the subject of this collection of essays. Together they demonstrate the degree to which the memory of the Holocaust is both collective – in that its development, shape and texture is comparable throughout, at least, Western societies – and highly singular – in that the form that the Holocaust takes in a society is often determined by the cultural and political contexts of that individual case, from the micro to the national level. As such *The Memory of the Holocaust in Australia* can be read as *both* part of the effort to discern the global memory of the Holocaust and as questioning the validity of such a project.[4] The essays here confront, within the Australian case study, many of the questions which dominate Holocaust memory studies, ranging from the attempt to plot the historical narrative of the development of Holocaust consciousness since 1945, through discerning the role that the *Shoah* plays in articulating Jewish identities both historically and in the contemporary world.

While the contexts of Holocaust memory are in some ways universal, memories are in the very first instance personal. Konrad Kwiet's rendering of the narrative of Bully Schott's life and especially his incredible survival from the Nazi 'Final Solution' acts as a useful reminder of this and appears as the first essay in this volume. Kwiet makes clear that Bully was sceptical of the whole notion of collective memory and the scholarly discourse surrounding it. Such scepticism highlights the problematic relationship between the individual and the collective in studies of Holocaust memory – Bully Schott stands as an example of the attempt made by many survivors to protect their memories from the scholar's desire to place them inside a general context. The present volume has no pretensions as to its ability to resolve those tensions and presents Bully's story as a counterweight to the generalisations that follow – perhaps to be borne in mind when reading the rest of the essays which do attempt to analyse the 'aftermath' in a manner that may not have met with Bully's approval.

Yet Bully's life also acts as an example as to why the Holocaust and its memory is an issue for communities so geographically removed from the killing fields. Bully Schott's experiences intersect with many of the questions that dominate the landscape of Holocaust history. To name just a few: the relationship between ordinary Germans and Jewish victims – Bully was protected by non-Jewish Germans; the question of what constituted Jewish resistance; the so-called grey zone which so many of the victims of the Holocaust inhabited – Kwiet describes Schott's involvement in the death of a fellow victim; and the difficulties that the past created for the present of a migrant – Bully encountered perpetrators of the Holocaust as well as its victims when building a new life in Australia. As such Bully was a personal example of the presence of the Holocaust in Australian society. That Bully's own experience of Holocaust memory seems to have, even indirectly, been shaped by the politics of the Cold War also highlights the external pressures placed even on individual memories. Konrad Kwiet describes, for example, that Bully's migration to Australia rather than Israel was to avoid being recruited as a Soviet spy.

Bully's death and as such the loss of his personal memories – only the fragments that he committed to paper or in interview remain – highlight another issue common to many of these essays, that of the future of Holocaust memory. There is a developing sense that we have reached, and perhaps have passed, a watershed in the memory and memorialisation of the Holocaust. Reactions against an apparent surfeit of Holocaust memory are common – most famously of course Norman Finkelstein's *Holocaust Industry*.[5] There is also a growing sense that the changing present, and especially the emergence of new enemies for the West in the so-called 'war on terror', challenges the utility of the Holocaust as the example of the ultimate atrocity.[6] But more than this of course – and again Bully Schott's story is a moving example – as time moves on the wartime generation is inevitably dying out, and such personal connections to the Second World War and the Holocaust are being lost. As both Amelia Klein and Sharon Kangisser Cohen demonstrate in their essays, we are fast approaching the end of the survivor generation and thus must face manifold questions about how the *Shoah* is represented, about who 'owns' the past, and the mechanisms through which the Holocaust story is communicated. Klein in particular raises the possibility, echoed by Avril Alba in her essay on the Sydney Jewish Museum, that a culture of memorialisation shaped by the 'third generation' might be rather more universal and less insistent on the Holocaust as *sui generis*.

The question of the uniqueness of the Holocaust is particularly important in the case of Australian memory and memorialisation. As John Docker highlights in his critical response to Patrick White's novel *Riders in the Chariot*, regarded as one of the landmarks of Australian Holocaust memory, memories of the Holocaust can (and from a twenty-first century perspective perhaps should) interact with memories of colonial crimes perpetrated against the indigenous Australian population. Yet as David Ritter's essay demonstrates the issue of aboriginal suffering is notable only by its absence from some aspects of Australian Holocaust memory. When interaction between Holocaust memory and the memory of colonial genocide does occur, however, it can, it seems, be both positive and negative. The moral challenges laid bare by active engagement with the Holocaust can be used, for example, to shed light on the historical sufferings of other communities that fell victim to state sponsored racisms. Witness the President of the Jewish Historical Society of Australia's 1998 declaration that Jews held personal affinity with aboriginal communities because of their shared understanding of suffering.[7] Yet greater awareness of the Holocaust does not necessarily promote greater enquiry into other victims of other state sponsored crimes – consider, for example, Ward Churchill's impassioned argument that the memory of the Holocaust in the USA has *prevented* and continues to prevent extended reflection on the historic and genocidal crimes perpetrated against native Americans.[8] Memory and forgetting have been closely intertwined in Australia too – as Dirk Moses has argued, the memory of Australia's war on the side of right between 1939 and 1945, and the memory of the tyranny against which that war (in a way) was fought, have combined to make it rather more difficult to acknowledge Australia's own genocidal past.[9]

The question of the future shape of Holocaust memory is therefore of contemporary importance in Australia – and is related explicitly to national historical memories and as such the building of the national, imagined or otherwise, community. It is, for example, often claimed that Australians became more and more aware of the Holocaust after governments became committed to a multicultural rather than 'White Australia'.[10] As it did in other Western nations, the Holocaust became the dark historical antithesis of the enlightened contemporary embrace of the 'other'.[11] But, again as can be seen throughout the West, Australia is now witness to the very specific limits of the multicultural present, limits for example highlighted by governmental response to refugees and asylum seekers. The memory of the Holocaust has been invoked to both condemn and validate policy towards such groups, policy which has famously included internment in detention centres.[12] That the *Shoah* is so politically flexible suggests that its future shape and texture is still to be determined, and the essays in this volume are to be read as a contribution to this discourse.

In more general terms the range of meanings attached to the Holocaust in contemporary Australia suggests that we might have to revise our understanding of the narrative significance of the development of Holocaust consciousness throughout the West. The argument is commonly proposed, for example, that the memory of the Holocaust became more widespread in public discourse with the emergence of the commitment to multiculturalism and especially the growth of identity politics – this model being as applicable to the United Kingdom and the USA as it is to Australia. However, that in Australian politics of memory the

Holocaust is, according to Judith Berman, being used to question the cultural openness of society suggests that in the future we will not simply be able to celebrate awareness of the Holocaust as another facet of our enlightened liberal democracies.

One of the other established features of the general narrative of the development of Holocaust awareness or consciousness is the idea that memories of the destruction of the European Jews were suppressed in its immediate aftermath. And the essays in this volume suggest that the Australian case can help us nuance orthodox interpretations here too.

Tony Judt argues that although 'there was never any mystery about what happened to Europe's Jews', the 'Final Solution' was little discussed as Europe rebuilt itself from the ravages of war.[13] In the former killing fields themselves, in the countries from which Jews had been deported, and in the countries where they sought refuge after, public conversation about the Nazi persecution of Jews was limited. In former Nazi occupied territories Jews were not welcomed back in part because they were uncomfortable reminders of the complicity and collaboration of local populations with the German occupiers, while stories of Jewish suffering were often seen to challenge the narratives of suffering and resistance which dominated popular memories of occupation from Belgium to the Ukraine. Jewish suffering at Nazi hands received no greater prominence in societies which had not experienced the ravages of Nazi occupation. For Britain and the USA, for example, war had been fought against humanity's universal enemy, and no racial particularities could be allowed to disrupt such a propagandistic narrative. Perhaps the archetypal example of this culture of neglect, and one which demonstrates its universality, is the International Military Tribunal at Nuremberg where crimes committed against Jews were subsumed within general narratives of Nazi criminality, as demonstrated by a charge sheet which included crimes against peace and humanity, but not the specific attack on Jews.[14]

Perhaps more striking even than the universal nature of the neglect of what we call the Holocaust in the immediate post-war years is the degree to which this narrative of memory is universally accepted within what one could call the historiography of the global memory and representation of the Holocaust. Scholars of its representation inside history, such as Dan Stone and Michael Marrus, argue for what Stone describes as, an 'aggressive silence' surrounding the *Shoah* after the war. Indeed more than that they point to the *absence* of the Holocaust from historical narratives.[15] In perhaps the most important, or at least the most commonly cited account of the popular memory of the Holocaust – Peter Novick's analysis of *The Holocaust in American Life* – the idea of a post-war silence around Jewish suffering figures prominently.[16] Other scholars of the Americanisation of the Holocaust also accept the silence model.[17] Historians of memory in the post-war Germanies have found, perhaps unsurprisingly, that the destruction of Europe's Jews did not feature particularly significantly in memorial narratives of suffering – displaced by memories of church persecution, the privations of the expellees and refugees from the Soviet east, and the trials of German communists and anti-Fascists respectively.[18] Accounts of Austrian, British, and Soviet Holocaust memory all, for example, concur.[19] More recently efforts to engage with the remarkable importance that memories of the Holocaust seem to have in the globalised twenty-first century have agreed that despite helping to shape post-war human rights thinking, memories of the Holocaust were either neglected or surrounded by 'relative silence' in the first decade or so after the end of the Second World War.[20] Even scholars outside Holocaust studies who attempt to critique the accepted narratives of the memories surrounding other epochal traumas quickly accept this orthodoxy surrounding the memory of the *Shoah*.[21]

This apparently universal silence resulted from a number of overlapping, and at times even competing influences. The liberalism of post-war Britain and America eschewed all racial distinction, even in the memories of racially inspired persecution and annihilation politics;[22] the Christian tendency to view all enemies in terms of an opposition to a Christian worldview ensured that Europe's Christians could remember only their own privations at Nazi hands;[23] the legal inspiration for the International Military Tribunal which attempted to tie all crimes into the conspiracy to wage aggressive war;[24] the tendency in all post-war societies to look towards the future and away from the past;[25] shame, often within Jewish communities, at the failure to provide succour for the victims;[26] all can account, in part, for this refusal to look back to what we call the Holocaust. In the Australian context Ruth Wajnryb, amongst others, has emphasised the individual psychological burdens that prevented reflection on the recent past in the aftermath of war – an idea which Suzanne Rutland explores further in her essay here.[27] Ultimately, though, it is the political culture of the Cold War that is most often cited as the root of the silence surrounding Jewish suffering – the capitalist West was unable to fit the murder of Jews into its totalitarian model which sought comparisons between the former, Nazi, enemy and the present Soviet foe.[28] The communist east had no place for accounts of Nazism which suggested the importance of a racial rather than class war.[29]

Of course this orthodoxy also has to account for the undoubted transformation of 'Holocaust consciousness', from silence to the contemporary prevalence of memory. The pressures which have been indicted as ensuring the growing prominence of Holocaust memory from the 1960s are again manifold. To highlight just two examples: threats to national survival inspired a new focus on the apocalyptic consequences of antisemitism in Israel and indeed throughout the Jewish diaspora;[30] Cold War culture, in the West at least, gave increasing prominence to individuals' struggle against totalitarianism and thus provided a hitherto absent audience for the survivors of the *Shoah*.[31]

The road of the Holocaust into public consciousness has a number of turning points about which, again, there is consensus. Various popular cultural renderings of the Holocaust have been highlighted as crucial, most notably the 1970s television mini-series *Holocaust* and more recently Steven Spielberg's *Schindler's List*.[32] But the most important single event, which for scholars of memory marks the beginning of the Holocaust's escape from its post-war shroud, in international terms, was the trial of Adolf Eichmann in Jerusalem. Eichmann's abduction, trial and then execution ensured that the Holocaust became 'news' at the beginning of the 1960s in a way that it had never been before.[33] The survivors called as witnesses for his prosecution encouraged others to tell their stories, and popular analyses of Eichmann's criminality such as Hannah Arendt's 'Banality of Evil' thesis provided a language with which Nazi perpetrators have been rendered ever since.[34]

At first glance the essays included here offer no dissension, fitting the Australian case study neatly into this silence model. David Ritter's analysis of the coverage of the Eichmann trial, for example, certainly sees it as transforming Australian public memory of the Holocaust, identifying it as a significant feature along what Alan Mintz has described, with reference to the USA, as the road from 'silence to salience'.[35] Suzanne Rutland's micro-history of Moriah College further contextualises that silence by demonstrating that even an educational institution which developed, explicitly, out of the 'shadow of the Holocaust' could not provide a platform for discussion of the events themselves. Both articles suggest a general disinterest in the Holocaust in a post-war Australia looking towards the future, despite the growing presence of survivors (both victims and perpetrators) of Nazi persecution.

However, Ritter's and Rutland's articles should perhaps also cause us to look more critically at the silence model not just in terms of its applicability to the Australian case, but universally. First, the very fact that Moriah College, the Sydney Jewish Day School whose relationship with the Holocaust Suzanne Rutland chronicles, developed out of the shadow of the *Shoah* must itself challenge at the very least the appropriateness of the term silence. It was specifically because of the Holocaust, the ruins of Jewish civilisation, that the Day School movement took hold in an Australian Jewry literally transformed by the *Shoah*. Jewish communities' numbers were swollen by refugees from Europe, but more than this, the mindset of Jewry was transformed from the assimilationist model of the Anglo-Jewish establishment to a community which wished to protect much more aggressively its Jewish identity – hence the growing desire for a specifically *Jewish* education. From the end of the Second World War onwards, then, Australian Jewry felt and experienced the *presence* of the Holocaust. Regardless of whether Auschwitz was discussed, Rutland demonstrates that it was, as it were, *there*.

Similarly David Ritter's article initially seems to confirm the applicability of the silence model to Australia. 'In 1960', he writes, 'the annihilation of the European Jewry simply did not hold the position in Australian intellectual, cultural and popular discourse that it would subsequently come to occupy.' Yet even though he finds the Eichmann trial and other events to be evidence of an upsurge in interest in the Holocaust at the beginning of the 1960s, Ritter, like Rutland, actually challenges the idea of the Eichmann trial as immediately, totally and irrevocably transformative – and with it the entire silence model. Ritter's evaluation of political, cultural and intellectual responses demonstrates how Eichmann's trial was discussed in Australia using the traditional discourses used to render Nazism meaningful there and indeed throughout the post-war West – chiefly of course the idea of its comparability with Soviet Communism as *totalitarianism*. That the trial of, until recently perhaps, the archetypal Holocaust perpetrator did not disrupt this comparative framework is telling. Eichmann's prosecutors wished, perhaps more than anything else, to demonstrate that Nazi antisemitism was *sui generis* and yet that prosecution was represented in anything but those terms. Far from transforming or disrupting Australian understandings of Nazism (and ergo the Holocaust) the Eichmann trial, and thus the history of the Holocaust that it represented, was domesticated within existing frameworks.

That is not to say that the trial was not a significant moment in the galvanisation of interest in the Holocaust, but rather that the oft-attributed seismic shift in popular recognition was neither as totally groundbreaking nor as lasting. Ritter argues that the trial marked an 'interpretative threshold' in respect of the Australian relationship to the Holocaust, and this, together with Rutland's observations, can be seen to challenge the very idea that frameworks such as traditional liberalism, or Cold War anti-Communism, were unable to deal with or ascribe meaning to the murder of Europe's Jews. If, faced with the relentless detail of Nazi anti-Jewish action presented in the Eichmann trial, the idea of totalitarianism and the essential comparability of the Nazi and Soviet dictatorships could endure, might we not have to accept that these narratives did not ignore the murder of Europe's Jews in the first place. Far from being silent about them, they were efforts (and honest ones at that) to ascribe meaning to what we call the Holocaust, but they are meanings that we struggle to recognise because these efforts had yet to cross the 'interpretative threshold'. That the articles here raise such problems suggests that the closed narrative of Holocaust memory, which accepts with certainty the idea of post-war silence, should at the very least be open to question.

One of the cultural sources cited by Ritter as an example of how the Nazi genocide began to enter the mainstream Australian public consciousness in the 1960s is the 1961 novel *Riders in the Chariot* by Patrick White. Whilst he discusses the contemporary significance of *Riders*, Ritter does not offer an extended literary criticism of the novel itself; John Docker's essay in contrast does precisely that.

Riders, the work of an internationally renowned author who would subsequently be awarded the Nobel Prize for Literature, is a story of assimilation and persecution, of insiders and outsiders, of prejudice and crucifixion, and was at the vanguard of Australian modernist writing as well as mainstream literary engagement with the Holocaust. Docker discusses both of these effects in a critique which offers a fresh appraisal and re-examination of White's representation of the Holocaust and Jewish identity, including a comparison of one of the protagonists, the Holocaust survivor Mordecai Himmelfarb, with James Joyce's Leopold Bloom.

Like Ritter, Docker acknowledges the significance of *Riders* in terms of Australia's changing relationship to the murder of the Jews of Europe, but while noting its merits in this respect, he also argues that 'certain aspects of the text are dubious, objectionable, and, sometimes, offensive'. Docker shows that from today's perspective *Riders* is a flawed novel that evidences not only the paucity of contemporary knowledge about the persecution of European Jewry, but also Australia's problematic relationship with its colonial past and multicultural present. When read alongside Ritter's evaluation of the novel's historical significance, Docker's literary critique demonstrates how the (cultural and historical) memory of the Holocaust in Australia has changed over time, altering not only our understanding of the Holocaust, but our relationship with those texts that seek to represent and remember it.

The final three articles in this collection are also concerned with this transmission of Holocaust memory, but each of these looks to the future as well as to the past, to consider how best to remember the Holocaust within and beyond the Australian Jewish community once the survivor generation has passed. The anxiety of memory surrounding this impending loss is at the heart of Sharon Kangisser Cohen's and Amelia Klein's articles on commemoration and transgenerational difference in which they investigate the role and interrelationship of survivors and their descendants in the shaping of Holocaust memory. Kangisser Cohen sketches the history of Jewish communal commemoration of the Holocaust in Sydney, charting its movement 'from the periphery to the centre of Australian Jewish consciousness'. This follows the conventional chronology outlined by Ritter, moving beyond the impact of Eichmann's trial, to the debates in the 1970s surrounding war crimes and Holocaust denial, and more generally by the Australian government's policy of multiculturalism. She shows how the rise in interest coincided with the increasingly public profile and voice of Holocaust survivors, arguing that this was prompted in part by the encouragement of the younger generation

Kangisser Cohen concludes that the Holocaust is today central to the public and private identity of the Sydney Jewish community, with survivors at the forefront of the commemorative activities. She also knows the value of the survivor to the transmission of stories of the past, but, she asks, what will happen when there are no survivors left alive? Based on evidence garnered from her own interviews, Kangisser Cohen examines the gap in knowledge and experience between the first and third generations, and the associated fears for a misremembered future, what she calls 'the conflict between generational memory'. 'How do survivors view the younger Jewish generation's knowledge of and commitment to the past?', she asks.

'Do survivors trust that this younger Jewish generation will be able to preserve the memory of the fate of those murdered and the stories of those who survived?'

One way already being used in the attempt to preserve the memory and experience of survivors is the digital and analogue recording of testimony to be found in places such as the Fortunoff Video Archive, Yale and the University of Southern California (USC), Shoah Foundation Institute Visual History Archive.[36] Amelia Klein continues Kangisser Cohen's discussion of the transgenerational relationship with a consideration of the specific example of video-testimonies held at the Jewish Holocaust Museum and Research Centre, Melbourne (JHMRC).

The use of recorded testimony is in part an obvious consequence of the shared anxieties as to the ability of the younger generations to remember the Holocaust. Survivors have long written and spoken of the necessity, 'an obligation', as Klein notes, 'to testify publicly as they promised those who did not survive that they would bear witness to the events of the Holocaust and remember all those who died'. Klein contends that because memory is integral to Jewish identity, this obligation to remember is transferred from generation to generation. She probes the attitudes of the third generation to this obligation, arguing that video testimony has an important role to play in enabling grandchildren to work through their relationship to Holocaust memory. To illustrate this, she interviews grandchildren before and after they view their grandparents' Holocaust video testimonies, documenting the variety of their responses and concluding therefore that Holocaust remembrance will continue to be shaped by the needs of successive generations.

These essays are, first and foremost, concerned with the response of the Jewish community, but if the Holocaust is indeed a global paradigm from which we are all meant to learn, then there must be wider implications and echoes of memory in wider society. One such place of commemorative confluence is the public museum and, indeed, Sharon Kangisser Cohen argues that '[p]erhaps the most significant development in Holocaust commemoration in Sydney was the establishment of the Sydney Jewish Museum (SJM)'. It is perhaps fitting therefore that the SJM is the focus of the final article. In this piece Avril Alba considers the future of Holocaust memory in Australia through a deconstruction of the SJM's Sanctum of Remembrance, a purpose-built space that 'is strategically located to allow the visitor space for contemplation after the confronting content of the Holocaust exhibit'.

Exploring 'the relationship between Holocaust memorials, the Jewish commemorative tradition and the sacralization of Holocaust memory in the Australian context', Alba, the Director of Education of the SJM, argues that the politics and purpose of the sanctum mark a significant departure from previous Jewish responses to destruction, and 'the building, design and function of the Sanctum reflects a deeply felt need within the Australian Jewish Survivor community to develop alternative commemorative forms as a response to perceived "inadequate" theology'.

Alba's contribution is, therefore, interested in the lack of systematic liturgical response to the Holocaust that has implications of theodicy on both personal and communal, even covenantal levels. These candid discussions question the place of religion in the largely secular commemoration of Holocaust and the search for a form of remembrance/commemoration that goes beyond the individual and inscribes the Holocaust into Jewish traditional ritual. As Sharon Kangisser Cohen writes of the survivors she interviewed: 'There was a clear sentiment amongst all the groups that one of the only ways the memory of the Holocaust can survive is by being cast as a religious act, duty and obligation, to be codified in the Jewish religious calendar. … They want the Shoah to fit into a day whose "form" inevitably recurs.'

But this is not an issue for the Jewish community alone because the location and purpose of the Sanctum has implications for the universal, too:

> [T]he public nature of the Sanctum has the dual effect of transforming the Jewish commemorative tradition from within and conveying that tradition to a largely non-Jewish public, explicitly linking Jewish tragedy to broader public concerns. In this progression, a sacred Holocaust memory is created that is at once particular and universal, providing Australian Holocaust memorials with unprecedented opportunities for empathy and identification with other victims of genocide.

And so this in conclusion returns once again to the global nature of Holocaust memory in the twenty-first century, as well as the particular demands of the Australian case, as the remembrance of the Holocaust, the particular commemoration within the Jewish community and the acknowledgment beyond of Australia as both 'perpetrator *and* resistor of genocidal acts'. It may be that this is the future of Holocaust memory in Australia.

NOTES

1. Robert Manne, 'The Strange Case of Helen Demidenko', *Australian Humanities Review*, Vol.1 (1998), available at www.lib.latrobe.edu.au/AHR/archive.html (accessed 24 July 2007).
2. See *Australian Style Magazine*, March 2000. See also Deborah Lipstadt, *History on Trial: My Day in Court with David Irving* (London: Harper Perennial, 2006), pp.124–5, 228–9.
3. *Sydney Morning Herald* and *Melbourne Age*, 28 February 2000.
4. The idea of the global memory of the Holocaust is explored through three case studies, USA, Israel and Germany in Daniel Levy and Natan Sznaider, *The Holocaust and Memory in the Global Age* (Philadelphia, PA: Temple University Press, 2006).
5. Norman Finkelstein, *The Holocaust Industry: Reflections on the Exploitation of Jewish Suffering* (New York: Verso, 2000).
6. This is especially the case if you accept that the Holocaust has emerged as the ultimate atrocity in part because historical memories of the Nazi enemy filled the vacuum left by the disappearance of the Soviet foe at the end of the Cold War. See R.J. Evans, 'What is History?', in David Cannadine (ed.), *What is History Now?* (London: Palgrave, 2004), p.12.
7. Judith Berman, *Holocaust Agendas, Conspiracies and Industries? Issues and Debates in Holocaust Memorialisation* (London: Vallentine Mitchell, 2006), p.96.

8. Ward Churchill, *A Little Matter of Genocide: Holocaust and Denial in the Americas 1492 to the Present* (New York: City Lights Books, 1998).
9. A. Dirk Moses, 'Genocide and Holocaust Consciousness in Australia', *History Compass*, Vol.1 (2003), pp.1–11.
10. Berman, *Holocaust Agendas*, p.6.
11. Donald Bloxham, 'Britain's Holocaust Memorial Days: Reshaping the Past in the Service of the Present', in Sue Vice (ed.), *Representing the Holocaust* (London: Vallentine Mitchell, 2003), pp.41–63.
12. Berman, *Holocaust Agendas*, pp.101–3.
13. Tony Judt, *Postwar: A History of Europe since 1945* (London: Pimlico, 2007), pp.804, 808.
14. Donald Bloxham, *Genocide on Trial: War Crimes Trials and the Formation of Holocaust History and Memory* (Oxford: Oxford University Press, 2001).
15. Dan Stone, *Constructing the Holocaust* (London: Vallentine Mitchell, 2003), p.87; Michael Marrus, *The Holocaust in History* (London: Penguin, 1993), p.4.
16. Peter Novick, *The Holocaust in American Life* (Boston and New York: Houghton Mifflin Co., 1999), pp.63–126.
17. See for example Alan Mintz, *Popular Culture and the Shaping of Holocaust Memory in America* (Seattle: University of Washington Press, 2001), pp.3–35.
18. See for example Robert Moeller, *War Stories: The Search for a Usable Past in the Federal Republic of Germany* (Berkeley: University of California Press, 2001).
19. On Austria see Herbert Hirsch, *Genocide and the Politics of Memory* (Chapel Hill: University of North Carolina Press, 1995), p.28; on Britain see Tony Kushner, *The Holocaust and the Liberal Imagination* (Oxford: Blackwells, 1994), pp.205–70; Zvi Gitelman, 'History, Memory and Politics – The Holocaust in the Soviet Union', *Holocaust and Genocide Studies*, Vol.5, No.1 (1990).
20. Levy and Sznaider, *The Holocaust and Memory*, p.90.
21. Jay Winter, for example, suggests that the Holocaust required a new language, in his effort to place the Great War into European Cultural History, see *Sites of Memory, Sites of Mourning* (Cambridge: Cambridge University Press, 1995), p.228.
22. Kushner, *The Holocaust and the Liberal Imagination*, pp.205–47
23. Tom Lawson, *The Church of England: Christianity, Memory and Nazism* (Woodbridge: Boydell, 2006), *passim*.
24. Bloxham, *Genocide on Trial*, pp.101–28, 185–220.
25. For example within the nascent state of Israel. On this see Tom Segev, *The Seventh Million: The Israelis and the Holocaust* (New York: Hill and Wang, 1993), p.185.
26. For a discussion of the idea of guilt conditioning Anglo-Jewish memories of the Holocaust see Dan Stone, 'The Domestication of Violence: Forging a Collective Memory of the Holocaust in Britain, 1945–46', *Patterns of Prejudice*, Vol.33, No.2 (1999), p.15.
27. Ruth Wajnryb, *The Silence: How Tragedy Shapes Talk* (Sydney: Allen & Unwin, 2001).
28. This argument can be found in virtually all histories of the representation/memory of the Holocaust, but for a particularly explicit statement see Robert Cherry, 'Holocaust Historiography: The Role of the Cold War', *Science and Society*, Vol.63, No.4 (1999), pp.459–77.
29. Jeffrey Herf, *Divided Memory: The Nazi Past in the Two Germanies* (Cambridge, MA: Harvard University Press, 1997), pp.106–200
30. Levy and Sznaider, *The Holocaust and Memory*, p.99.
31. Mintz, *Popular Culture*, p.22.
32. Tim Cole, *Images of the Holocaust: The Myth of the Shoah Business* (London: Duckworth, 1999), p.90.
33. James Young, *Writing and Rewriting the Holocaust: Narrative and the Consequences of Interpretation* (Bloomington: Indiana University Press, 1998), p.88.
34. Hannah Arendt, *Eichmann in Jerusalem: A Report on the Banality of Evil* (London: Penguin, 1977); for a critique of Arendt's vision of Eichmann see Michael Thad Allen, 'Grey Collar Worker: Organisation Theory in Holocaust Studies', *Holocaust Studies: A Journal of Culture and History*, Vol.11, No.1 (2005), pp.27–54.
35. Mintz, *Popular Culture*, p.3.
36. The first Australian repository of the Shoah Foundation Visual History Archive was officially launched at Monash University on Thursday 17 May 2007.

'I boxed my way through life!': The Incredible Story of Bully Salem Schott

KONRAD KWIET

When I came to Australia in 1976 I met Gerda and Bully Schott, two witnesses to the horrors of the Holocaust. Born in Poland, Bully grew up in the environs of Berlin's *Scheunenviertel*, the proletarian quarter of Eastern Jews. He survived the 'Final Solution' in Sachsenhausen and Auschwitz and then, following his escape in 1944 from the epicentre of the Holocaust, in the Berlin underground. In 1937 he had met and fallen in love with Gerda Lewinnek, a courageous young woman, born in Berlin. She was subjected to forced labour during the war, but devoted herself to saving Bully's life – including providing support after his escape. After the end of the war they married, as so many survivors did, and rebuilt their shattered lives. In 1950 they arrived in Australia, at the 'Edge of the Diaspora', together with their one-year-old son Martin.

In the company of family and friends flung together in Australia, Bully always spoke German, interlaced with smatterings of English and Yiddish. His Berlin accent, acquired in the working-class eastern districts of Berlin, was easily discernible. He attached little importance to reading and writing, preferring to rely on his *hellen Kopf* (clear-headedness) and his *geschickte Hände* (dexterous hands), particularly his left hand which was dominant. From childhood onwards he had been a handyman par excellence, a *Bastler* (do-it-yourselfer) and *Tüftler* (tinkerer). He was an avid card player. But Bully also loved to light the *Shabbat* candles and he never forgot to say *Kaddish* on the *Jahrzeiten* (anniversaries) of his parents' deaths. Bully felt totally at home in the world of boxing and – like his brothers – in the wrestling fraternity and later at the race track. After surviving Auschwitz and emigrating to Australia he became accustomed to completing the betting forms with the numbers which were tattooed on the underside of his left arm: his Auschwitz prisoner number 70212.

Bully was 1.63m tall, squat but with a strong build. His blue eyes, light brown hair and 'nose of a boxer' were at odds with the 'typical racial features' that the Nazi had imposed upon the Jews. He was also quick-witted, which manifested itself in both language and gestures and in his talent for boxing. At age 16 and as a member of the Jewish sports association *Makkabi* Bully began to devote himself to competitive boxing. He reached the pinnacle of his sporting career when he won the title of Brandenburg State Champion in the bantamweight division. His stature and bearing earned him the nickname Bully at an early age and he adopted it as a second name and went on to use it on all official documents without ever changing his name officially. In all the conversations I had with Bully, he kept coming back to the phrase: '*Ich habe mich durchs Leben geboxt!*' ('I boxed my way through life!').

Bully belonged to the *kleine Leute* or ordinary people whose lives have received scant attention at the hands of scholars exploring German-Jewish history, the Holocaust and the period of exile. Indeed, Bully and Gerda had little time for intellectualising. They did not, for example, see any need to join the debate, re-ignited by Gershom Scholem in the early 1960s, as to whether there had been ever a German–Jewish 'dialogue' or *Lebensgemeinschaft* (co-existence). They also felt no need in their final years of life to engage in the discussions on Holocaust memory and trauma. They preferred to leave this to the iconic figures of Elie Wiesel and Primo Levi or to the growing number of academics now preoccupied with a booming 'memory culture'. Yet Gerda and Bully Schott had incredible stories which they started to tell in 1981. And it is these stories, and stories like them, that make up the history of the Holocaust, the history of millions of shattered lives. In charting Bully's journey from Poland to Australia, through Sachsenhausen and Auschwitz, we can also see that it is through these stories that the history of the Holocaust is intrinsic to the Australian past too.

Bully's childhood and youth were spent in the simple, impoverished circumstances of an eastern Jewish home. His family was pious and typically large. His father was a strict disciplinarian and his mother devoted herself to the household and eight children. For generations Bully's family had resided in Chrzanow, a Galician township situated only a few kilometres from Oswiecim. Work could be found there in the Jewish workshops and businesses. Most of the men in the extended family were tradesmen: metalworkers and mechanics, tailors and furriers. Bully was born as the sixth child on 24 February 1914. In 1919, after the First World War and a resurgence of Polish antisemitism, the family moved to Berlin. Like many Eastern Jews they moved into one of the rundown tenement houses around Alexanderplatz, in Prenzlauer Berg and in Friedrichshain. At first they occupied the small, dark and uninviting cellars; later they took up residence in somewhat larger and lighter apartments. Once he had completed primary school Bully, like his siblings, was compelled to take up an apprenticeship and to pay for his food and board at home. He was trained as a metalworker and electrician in the workshop of Leo Friedmann. It was with a certain pride that Bully recalled that even as a young boy he not only repaired bicycles and motor scooters but also rented them out, earning himself his first pocket money in the process.

His childhood memories also include the beatings that he received at the hand of his father, who would not tolerate any form of disobedience. The punishment was swift, even on *Shabbat* when Bully was caught distributing and consuming lollies. Canings were also part and parcel of his Jewish religious education. In time-honoured tradition Bully was repeatedly beaten by the orthodox rabbi in the small *Cheder* (religious school) in Grenadierstrasse for disruptive behaviour and poor performance. As a member of the *Makkabi* boxing team he quickly earned himself the reputation of being a 'wiry', 'tough' and 'battle-tried' boxer. He took part in matches both at home and abroad but more than anywhere else he liked to box in the Berlin *Sportpalast.* His talents were rewarded with rapturous applause, certificates, medallions, trophies, pins and a gold watch. Bully had contested over 50 boxing titles when his career was cut short by the National Socialist racial laws. Bully, however, managed to maintain many of his sporting contacts and friendships. He was later able to find German boxers on whom he could rely, among them the renowned boxing champion Paul Noack. They were prepared to risk their lives when called upon to hide their Jewish comrade after his escape from Auschwitz.

The National Socialist seizure of power did not initially catapult Bully from his profession. After completing his apprenticeship in 1933, he continued to work as an electrician in Friedmann's work plant. In the first years of Nazi rule he was even able to acquire certain assets as a result of his diligence and working overtime. On weekends he paddled in his boat on the lakes and waterways of Berlin. He had no trouble attaching an outboard motor which increased his speed on the water considerably. Bully was especially proud of his motorbike, which he tinkered with incessantly. When Friedmann's *Judenbetrieb* (Jewish business) was liquidated in 1937 in the wake of *Arisierung* ('Aryanisation') Bully received a small payment, which he invested in the purchase of a complete motorcycle outfit. Later the leather boots, trousers and jacket would help buy contact with Gerda from a helper who originated from the Hamburg underworld and had risen in the Sachsenhausen concentration camp to the position of *Lagerältester* (camp elder).

Bully had met Gerda in the summer of 1937 when, aged 23, she had been a young, 'beautiful' and 'self-assured' woman. From then on, to use Bully's words, 'she went with me through thick and thin'.[1] Gerda came from a simple, working-class background, spoke with a strong Berlin accent and after primary school completed an apprenticeship – in her case with a tailor and in a trade school. What for the handyman and tinkerer Bully was the motorbike and later the automobile, was for Gerda, a highly talented and fashion conscious seamstress, the sewing machine. Her treasured Singer machine ensured her a livelihood even though Nazi racial doctrines and regulations classified Gerda Lewinnek as a *Geltungsjude*, a *Halbjüdin* or *Mischling* – to be treated as a Jew.[2]

Gerda's parents lived in a *Mischehe* (mixed marriage), classified as 'non-privileged'. Her father was a Jewish butcher well known not only in abattoirs and butcher shops but also in riding stables and in particular on the Berlin trotting track in Mariendorf.[3] In Summer 1941 this popular *Vieh-Jude* (cattle Jew) and *Pferde-Jude* (horse Jew) was arrested by the Gestapo, denounced for *Schiebereien* (black market dealings) and *Schwarzschlachtungen* (illegal killing of cattle), interrogated and tortured over several weeks and then taken to the Jewish Hospital in Iranische Strasse. Martin Lewinnek died in October 1941, a broken man who no longer possessed even the strength to commit suicide.[4] His body was buried in the Jewish cemetery at Weissensee.

Gerda's mother was a Christian who had remained true to her Lutheran faith. Emma Lewinnek had, however, raised no objections when her daughter and son Norbert were accepted into the Jewish community and raised as Jews. From childhood onwards Gerda was no stranger to taunts of '*olle Judengöre*' (dirty Jew kid) on the street or at school. She had learnt to defend herself against antisemitic insults and attacks. In Jewish youth and sport associations she found refuge and, as fortune would have it, in Bully a friend and partner from whom she would become inseparable. At the same time as Bully's acceptance into the 'half-Jewish' Lewinnek family and circle of friends, the Schott family structure started to dissolve.[5] Bully's older siblings escaped Nazi persecution by emigrating to Palestine and Shanghai, South Africa and the USA. His two younger sisters stayed behind in Berlin to care for their parents. One, Sabine, was deported to Auschwitz and murdered there. The other, Fanny, went into hiding in Berlin when the deportations started but was denounced in December 1944, imprisoned and sent first to Ravensbrueck concentration camp and from there to Bergen-Belsen. In November 1945 she returned home.[6] Bully's father had already died, on the eve of the mass deportations, and was buried in Weissensee, where he had once worked as a tradesman. In November 1943 his mother was forced to leave her apartment in Landsberger Strasse designated as '*Judenhaus*' (Jew House) and was deported first to Theresienstadt and from there to Auschwitz.[7] When she was murdered in Birkenau, Bully was fighting for his survival in Auschwitz-Monowitz, only a few kilometres away.

After the outbreak of the Second World War Bully had toyed with the idea of emigrating to Palestine. It was an idea that he never realized. In the course of the *Polenaktion* he was deported in October 1938 to the land of his birth. A few months later he reappeared in Berlin in order, with Gerda's help, to expedite the emigration process. But, on 8 September 1939, a week after the German invasion of Poland, the *SS-Reichssicherheitshauptamt* (RSHA) issued an order that all Polish and stateless Jews were to be taken as *Geiseln* (hostages).[8] Several thousand *Ostjuden* were arrested, amongst them many that had previously had Polish citizenship. On 13 September Bully presented himself voluntarily at the police headquarters at Alexanderplatz. He assumed that he would be sent back to Poland. Instead, three days later he arrived at Sachsenhausen.

The rituals surrounding his arrival in a concentration camp left an indelible mark on his memory. The *Neuzugänge* (new arrivals) were beaten '*grün und blau*' (green and blue) or were beaten to death with punches and kicks, whips and hammers or with other objects.[9] But Bully quickly adjusted to camp life, grew accustomed to the rampant brutalisation and even the dead bodies. In 1940 the number of inmates in the overcrowded *Judenbaracken* (Jewish barracks) reached 3,892. In the registry office 601 deaths were recorded. Bully noticed that the SS camp guards and *Kapos* routinely chose 'particular types of inmates to lay into',[10] specifically Jewish intellectuals and academics, those who wore glasses or were conspicuous because of their height. He concluded that body size helped determine the targets of mistreatment. As he explained it, the guards had to 'look up at' the taller inmates; they could 'look down on' the smaller prisoners and need not resort to beating those over whom they could easily exert their authority. But Bully too was repeatedly beaten. He proved capable of tolerating the blows without defending himself with his fists. As we shall see, he took his revenge later when his counterattack would not have life-threatening consequences for him.

Bully found it easier than other inmates to cope with the back-breaking forced labour intended to result in total physical exhaustion and a broken spirit. When sent to help in the construction of the infamous *Klinkerwerk* he even survived the rigours of the cement and earth moving works as well as lugging sacks of sand and clay for hours at a time. It was not long before his professional skills were in demand. With his ability to install plumbing and electrical appliances he was soon elevated to the ranks of the privileged *Funktionshäftlinge* (functional prisoner). Since his arrival at the camp Bully had known what it was like to go hungry. He knew that he had to find sources of nourishment if he was to stay alive. Whenever the opportunity presented itself on the long treks to and from his places of work or at the worksites themselves he scavenged for and found anything edible or other useful objects. He vividly recalls the *Kämpfe* (fights) that broke out over a piece of bread. Looking back, he explained: 'Sachsenhausen was much worse than Auschwitz. In Sachsenhausen I didn't know whether I was still human. I had no feelings left – I was just hungry all the time'.[11]

Bully also spent a few '*gute Stunden*' (good hours) in Sachsenhausen. The good times that he referred to were spent not only playing cards but also attending lively musical evenings or cabarets which formed part of the organisational grey zones of the camp operations and were offered within the framework of a *Kulturprogramm* (cultural programme).[12] Participation in such events, whether in Sachsenhausen or other camps, was generally a privilege reserved for the SS and prominent inmates. They represented a welcome diversion from the monotony of camp life. For those prisoners who performed or who were allowed to attend, such occasions offered rare moments in which it was possible to suppress the feelings of isolation and demoralisation and to regain the will to survive. Sporting competitions, held as a rule on weekends or holidays, played an important role within the cultural programme. Boxing matches were particularly popular and Bully was an absolute stand-out in the ring. His prowess was rewarded with enthusiastic applause and *Essenszulagen* (supplementary food).

On his striped prison garb Bully wore a six pointed Star of David which comprised a yellow and a red triangle and as such distinguished him as a political *Schutzhäftling* (prisoner in protective custody) of Jewish origin. Despite this, Bully saw no reason to identify with the *Politische* (political prisoners), the red triangle wearers, who had come largely from the ranks of the organised workers' movement, most specifically the Communists. He was and remained an *Einzelgänger* (loner) who rejected all ties with particular ideologies and groups. But this did not mean that Bully shunned all contact; amongst his friends were Jewish prisoners from Eastern Europe who had grown up with him in Berlin. He also found a friend among the green triangle wearers, the *Gewohnheits-* or *Berufsverbrecher* (habitual or professional criminals). This man had fought his way to the top of the prisoner hierarchy. As *Lagerältester* the tall Fiete Granopol (phonetic spelling, hereafter referred to as Kranepuhl) placed a '*schützende Hand*' (protective hand) over the '*kleiner Jude*' (little Jew) and his *jüdisches Arbeitskommando* (Jewish work detail). Kranepuhl continued to do this when he was discharged from custody and assigned by the SS camp leadership the role of *ziviler Arbeitsführer* (civil work leader). The relationship paid off for Bully: Kranepuhl offered his services in establishing contact with Gerda in Berlin.[13]

In 1940 Gerda had been recruited for forced labour. As a member of a Jewish *Arbeitskommando* she worked in one of the factories belonging to the IG Farben concern where she operated a machine which spun silk for parachutes. For the long and strenuous day or night shifts she received the weekly sum of 15 Reichsmark. Of this amount 3 Reichsmark were needed for the long trips to and from work. Before her recruitment Gerda underwent the customary gynaecological examination (to establish pregnancy) which resulted in severe pains and month long bleeding. In one interview she recalls: 'I've never forgotten it my whole life. I could have killed that bastard!'[14] In the short work breaks the conversations centred on love and marriage, pregnancy and abortion. They reflected the despair and hopelessness felt by the Jewish women workers about their current lives and their anxiety about the future. As Marion Kaplan has shown, some Jewish women rejected the idea of marriage.[15] A few even took the decision to terminate their pregnancy. Doctors and others who carried out abortions faced harsh sanctions. There is also some evidence to suggest that newborn Jewish babies were wrapped up and placed in baskets which were then left in front of the doors or on the stairs of Catholic families or institutions. Gerda remembers the words of one rabbi at the time of the deportations: 'The Germans don't know how many children of Jewish parents are still living in Germany today.'[16]

Fiete Kranepuhl won the trust of Gerda. Together they made plans to contact Bully and to smuggle food into the camp. Having first removed the yellow Star of David from her clothing Gerda repeatedly undertook the trip to Oranienburg to scour the open areas of Sachsenhausen in the hope of once glimpsing Bully. As remarkable as it may seem, Fiete Kranepuhl succeeded in arranging a secret meeting with Gerda. The short reunion took place in a workshop beyond the confines of the camp. The *Judenfreund* (Jew friend) expected to be paid for his services. Bully's payment was in the form of the leather motorbike outfit that he had left with Gerda for safekeeping.

In autumn 1942 Bully's contact with the outside world came to an abrupt end. On 5 October 1942 Heinrich Himmler issued the order that, in the course of the 'Final Solution', all Jewish prisoners would be deported from concentration camps and prisons in the *Reichsgebiet* to camps in the east.[17] Bully was not one of the 18 young camp inmates who, on 22 October 1942, refused the order in Sachsenhausen to step up for roll call. To loud shouts of: 'We won't let ourselves be slaughtered! We want to die fighting! Go on, shoot, you dogs!' they stormed through the camp. They were quickly caught and made to see reason. This mutiny, a spontaneous act of despair, entered the annals of the history of Sachsenhausen and the history of German Jewish anti-fascism as an act of resistance without parallel. It passed without consequences.[18]

Bully was among the 459 Jewish prisoners who were deported to Auschwitz the next morning. One episode during that journey left an indelible mark on Bully's memory. It demonstrates clearly the limited solidarity amongst camp inmates and the extent to which they had been brutalised. In the overcrowded, sealed carriage of the cattle train some prisoners became agitated about the persistent groaning of one in their midst. Bully reported in an interview that they grabbed hold of the offender and forcibly removed the windpipe from his throat. He died as a result of their actions.[19]

On 25 October the transport arrived in Auschwitz. Of the 454 *Neuzugänge* registered barely 10 per cent survived.[20] On the *Appellplatz* of Auschwitz 1 – the main camp – the young, strong and healthy Bully was selected for forced labour, sent to the showers, tattooed, registered and, together with other *Sachsenhausener* deemed fit for work, taken to Auschwitz III to help in the construction of IG Farben's *Bunawerk*.

The three years that Bully had spent in Sachsenhausen made it easier for him to adjust quickly to the camp routine in Auschwitz-Monowitz. He fully understood and mastered the *Lager-Jargon*, the special German terms of command and compliance, which punctuated daily camp life, a skill essential to survival. His expertise as a skilled tradesman was once again in demand, as were his special abilities in *Organisieren* (a wheeler and dealer) and his public appearances as a boxer. As he had in Sachsenhausen, Bully made use of his routes to and from work, the work sites as well as work equipment to forage for food or any other objects which he would hide or distribute as he saw fit. Bread and potatoes were precious trading commodities. Bully developed the special technique of *schmoren* (braising) pieces of potato and potato skins on hot water pipes. The finished product made an excellent bartering tool. Bully recalled in meticulous detail the *blühenden Handel* (flourishing trade) which developed in the Auschwitz underground, despite the draconian punishment if caught. The goods came from four sources: there were the gift parcels sent by the Red Cross to British prisoners of war which their recipients might choose to barter. In addition there were those Red Cross parcels whose intended recipients were *unbekannt* (unknown) or *unauffindbar* (untraceable) because they had already been murdered. There were also the items that came from the *Kleiderkammer* (clothing room), *Schuhkammer* (shoe room) and other depots which were confiscated from the prisoners upon arrival in the camp and sorted through by Jewish work commands in the *Kanada* barracks or were found by Jewish *Sonderkommandos* in the course of the industrial *Leichenfledderei* (gutting of corpses) following gassing. Added to this assortment of goods were the items smuggled into the camp from the surrounding Polish villages.[21]

Bully's contacts and privileges helped him to survive and to plan his escape. The private company Käufer & Söhne, based in Mainz, which had been given the contract to install and maintain the heating system, requested an electrician and metalworker from the SS. They were given the Jewish *Schutzhäftling* Bully Schott. Armed with a *Sondergenehmigung* (special permit) and with a cart at his disposal on which he transported a welding machine as well as other tools and materials, Bully was now able to move freely around the expansive camp complex. Again, as he had in Sachsenhausen, Bully also found a civilian German worker in Auschwitz who proved to be a *Judenfreund.* Richard Sommerlad (phonetic spelling), an employee of the Mainz company, offered to establish contact with Gerda and to prepare with her Bully's escape from Auschwitz.[22]

This undertaking, however, had to be financed. To this end, Bully achieved the seemingly impossible by coming up with several new shoes, a considerable amount of cash – both German and American currency – as well as several rings. The escape was carefully planned. Gerda travelled to Auschwitz and handed over to Richard Sommerlad civilian clothing and tickets, which were then hidden in the workshop of an outside work detail of the Bunawerk. On 16 August 1944, a Saturday, Bully had himself locked inside the workshop. When it became dark Bully changed his clothes, cut through the wire fence and made his way to the station. He got off the crowded night train to Berlin in Fuerstenwalde where he hid in a country house belonging to the Sommerlads. On 17 August his escape from Auschwitz was discovered. A memo was circulated to all Gestapo posts to hunt down the escaped Jewish prisoner *Salem Schott (70212).*[23] The search proved unsuccessful. Bully Schott is one of only 76 Jews who succeeded in escaping from Auschwitz. In total 667 escapes were recorded; 270 escapees were caught and immediately executed.[24]

Bully waited several weeks before he continued his journey to the Berlin underground. He was assisted by friends, former fellow sportsmen from the world of boxing and acquaintances from the milieu of German–Jewish 'mixed marriages'. These *stille Helden* (quiet heroes) provided him with false papers, ration cards and *sichere Adressen* (safe addresses), accommodation which he changed constantly. Air raids and denunciations destroyed hiding places and networks of helpers. In autumn 1944 in Berlin there were an estimated 2,000 Jews who had managed to escape deportation. A year earlier there were more than 5,000.[25] Gerda, Norbert and Emma Lewinnek too can be counted among the *stille Helden* who distinguished themselves in their efforts to save Jewish and non-Jewish fugitives. They 'organised' food, cooked meals and distributed ration cards and other goods that were essential for survival underground.[26] Bully avoided the Lewinnek apartment, however. Instead he chose other 'safe' locations for short visits.

On his flight routes through the Berlin underground Bully crossed paths with *Greifer*, the Jewish Gestapo agents grouped around Stella Kuebler-Goldschlag who excelled in hunting down Jews who had gone underground.[27] He acquired a revolver on the black market which he used on one occasion only: when he was discovered in an apartment he shot at the Jews who had betrayed him and escaped. As it happened, they were wounded but not killed. In the underground world in which Bully lived there were still employers willing to take on illegal workers, provide papers and pay wages. Paul Noack, the renowned boxing champion, owned a coal business and it was here that Bully found temporary shelter and spent his days stacking and delivering briquettes and wood. His last place of employment was a metal workshop that belonged to the OT (Organisation Todt) and which, in the face of the catastrophic shortage of workers, employed forced labourers and refugees. Bully operated metal-plating machines for the German war industry. In his *Freizeit* (free time) he even went on walks and bike rides, passing columns of starving people, soldiers and SS patrols in the process. Once again, he was confronted on his excursions through a Berlin under bombardment with scenes that had become all too familiar to him in the concentration and death camps – dead bodies, victims of allied air raids or of National Socialist fury because, in the dying days of the war, they had committed *Fahnenflucht* (desertion) or *Defätismus* (defeatism). On one trip through the city he discovered a bombed out butcher shop. In the smoking chamber he found three sides of ham. Bully took them with him and distributed them amongst his Jewish friends in hiding.

After liberation Bully, like all survivors of the Holocaust, undertook the search for missing family members. He also set about discovering the whereabouts of German murderers of Jews as well as Jewish informants who had gone into hiding – enacting revenge for the suffering he had endured. He was accompanied in his search by officers of the NKVD, the Soviet Secret Service. Walter Dobberke was the first '*grosser Fisch*' (big catch) made with

Bully's help.[28] As head of the collection and transit camp in Schulstrasse, Dobberke had not only been in charge of the Jewish *Greifer*, he had also incarcerated and mistreated the Jewish victims, amongst them Gerda. At the end of December 1944 Gerda and her brother Norbert had been arrested, charged with *Judenbegünstigung und Hilfe für KZ-Leute* (aiding and abetting Jews and providing assistance to concentration camp inmates).[29] During the interrogations Gerda was beaten repeatedly and pressured to reveal the whereabouts of the escaped Auschwitz prisoner. Her answer to their constant question, 'Where is your fiancé?' was always the same: that she had separated from him in 1939 and that he had probably found refuge with the *Berufsverbrecher* in the Berlin underworld.[30]

On 20 April 1945 Dobberke disbanded the *Sammellager* and disappeared underground, together with scores of other perpetrators. Gerda lost no time in locating Bully amongst the ruins and devastation of Berlin. Together they then captured Dobberke. On 13 August 1945 Gerda gave a statement from which the following was recorded: 'A week after the war ended, together with my fiancé, a concentration camp survivor, I detained *SS-Hauptsturmführer* Dobberke as well as four Jewish informants who had worked for the Gestapo.'[31] At the Jewish hospital in Iranische Strasse Dr. Walter Lustig,[32] the last head physician and *Vertrauensmann* (confidante) of the *Reichsvereinigung der Juden* (Reich Association of Jews), who had the reputation of having worked closely with the Gestapo, was also called to account. Bully accused the doctor of being responsible for the deportation and murder of his mother. After a long and heated exchange of words he knocked Lustig to the ground in the presence of high-ranking Russian officers. 'At that moment', he explained later, 'I was only intent on revenge.'[33] It is believed that Dobberke later died in a Soviet work camp; Lustig was in all probability gunned down in Berlin.

The Soviet Secret Service assisted Bully in building a new life. They immediately provided him with a licence to trade in old wares and valuables. Bully brought with him considerable experience to this new business venture. In no time at all he had familiarised himself with the flourishing black markets, where coveted goods could be bought and sold with ease in post-war Berlin. He opened two used goods shops. 'We buy everything!' was the catchphrase employed on his shop signs and business cards.[34] The goods Bully sold ranged from jewellery and paintings through watches and cameras to fur coats and Persian rugs. Bully was aware that some of his merchandise came from *Judennachlässen* (confiscated Jewish bequests), from which so many Germans had filled their coffers. When asked how he had gone so quickly from being a concentration camp inmate to a businessman and from a tradesman to an antique dealer Bully always gave the same response, 'You can teach an elephant to dance. I was taught how to deal in antiques.'[35] It proved a lucrative business. After a few days he was able to exchange his bicycle for a motorbike and, before too long, replace this by a car. His improved economic and social circumstances were also apparent in his clothing and household furnishings. When the question of *Wiedergutmachung* (restitution payments) became acute in 1952 Bully sent his application and documents to the relevant Restitution Office in Berlin. In a sworn statement he wrote: 'When emigrating to Sydney, Australia in September 1950 … I was forced to give up my apartment filled with antique furniture, genuine Persian rugs and porcelain, silver and valuable pictures'.[36]

Like many survivors of the Holocaust who were on their own, Gerda and Bully married immediately following liberation. Love and a will to live, the shared memories of the fates of family members and the long struggle for survival proved to be strong binding factors. The civil ceremony took place on 16 June 1945 in the registry office in Pankow, despite the lack of official identification papers. *Vorläufige* (provisional) documentation was sufficient to identify both parties. A small celebration in the company of fellow survivors followed the ceremony. Bully even succeeded in finding kosher wine for the blessing: he attached importance to certain Jewish traditions. Bully and Gerda were among the first members of the newly established Berlin Jewish community and in 1947 Gerda undertook an orthodox conversion. A year later, shortly before the birth of their first and only child, the couple finally married under the *Chuppa* (wedding canopy). The ceremony was conducted by Martin Riesenburger, the spiritual leader of the remnants of Berlin Jewry in the underground.[37] This rabbi, protected by his non-Jewish wife, had performed the last Jewish wedding in Germany in June 1943. The bridegroom was aged 40, the bride aged 37. A few days later the couple was deported to the east. Riesenburger had also continued to bury the dead at Weissensee until liberation. He even compiled a calendar with the dates of the Jewish festivals. A special rescue operation secured the survival of an extensive collection of cultural and religious objects, among them 560 Torah scrolls and almost 800 rare books including parts of the Babylonian Talmud. With little delay Riesenbuger was installed as the first rabbi of a post-war German community. One of his first duties was to perform weddings for those who had resurfaced from underground or had survived deportation to the east and the death marches back to Germany.

Martin Schott was born on 19 January 1950. In naming their son Martin Gerda and Bully were upholding the Jewish law of keeping the memory of deceased loved ones alive. Many survivors gave their children the names of murdered relatives. The name Martin helped to keep alive the memory of Gerda's father. Martin Schott grew up with parents who, having experienced the horrors of the Holocaust and a brief *Neubeginn* (new beginning) in post-war Berlin, had made the decision to seek a new home in Australia.

The outbreak of the Cold War, the division of Berlin, the resurgence of antisemitism and the lifting of rigid entry quotas were all factors that led the

Schotts to join the throng of Jewish 'displaced persons' seeking to turn their backs on Europe. In 1948 they briefly toyed with emigrating to Israel but rejected the idea, just as they had done in the years immediately preceding the war. The reason for this had most probably to do with a proposal made to Bully by the Soviet Secret Service. Bully later testified under oath that when the NKVD learnt of his emigration plans, he was put under pressure to act as a spy in Israel. He then opted for migration to Australia, to avoid any obligation and '*meine persönliche Sicherheit nicht weiter zu gefährden*' (not to put my personal security at any further risk).[38]

Through Lewinnek family contacts a sponsor in Sydney was found who organised landing permits and visas. As Holocaust survivors the Schotts fulfilled all the conditions required to be accepted into the Migration Programme of the United Nation's International Refugee Organisation (IRO) and the Support Programme of JOINT, the American Jewish Distribution Committee.[39] However, it took weeks before the bureaucratic process, which involved a plethora of applications, letters, certificates and travel documents, was finally completed. Medical examinations were required to confirm the good health of the applicants and their 'good character' had to be attested to by lengthy police reports. The Schotts dissolved their home and business interests, sold their goods, furniture and car, gave away their two dogs and said farewell to family, friends, including those buried at Weissensee.

On 29 September 1950 they commenced their long journey, first by plane to Munich and then by train via the Brenner-Pass to Genoa. The *Cyrenia*, a ship filled with migrants, left the Italian port city on 4 October. The Schotts were able to pay their fares from the money made from the sale of their property. The total cost was equivalent to the average yearly income of an Australian worker. When Gerda and Bully disembarked in Melbourne on 6 November they had to note the purpose and duration of their stay in one column of their Passenger Cards.[40] With the help of a translator they wrote 'Forever' and 'For Work'. From Melbourne they flew on to Sydney. The train services had been brought to a standstill by striking workers.

In Bully and Gerda's case, not surprisingly, the integration and acculturation process was to take years.[41] Like almost all immigrants the Schotts found it difficult to adjust to conditions in their strange, new country of refuge and to feel at home there. The first social contacts were with German-Jewish refugees who had been driven out of Germany before the war and with Holocaust survivors who had come largely from Eastern Europe. More than 30,000 Jewish refugees from Europe found a new home in Australia. With this number Australia accepted more Holocaust survivors per capita than any other country except Israel. The waves of immigrants had a decisive impact on the demographic and religious structures of Australian Jewry, which today numbers about 100,000.[42] In time, the integration and acculturation of the Holocaust victims were successfully completed and evoked a strong feeling of loyalty to and identification with their adopted home. Essential to this process was not only the strong drive of the refugees to succeed but also the prevailing conditions of Australian society: the much acclaimed openness and fair-mindedness of a society which allowed the integration and acculturation and which, in the wake of the massive waves of migration after the war, abandoned its 'White Australia' policy and developed and implemented the model of a multicultural society. Within this model the small German-Jewish Diaspora community dissolved. Almost all former German-Jewish refugees see themselves today as Australians and as Jews and feel no need to wrestle further with the old issues of German-Jewish identity. For Bully, such intellectual or philosophical debates had never existed anyway. He had always identified as a Jew and, if he had ever felt a further identification, then it was as a Berlin Jew. Unlike Gershom Scholem, who sought to destroy the 'Myth of the German Jewish dialogue',[43] Bully clung to his belief even after the Holocaust that, for him at least, there had been such a thing as a German-Jewish *Lebensgemeinschaft.*

After their arrival in Sydney, Gerda and Bully moved with their son to the eastern suburbs, a smart residential district not far from the city and hugging the Pacific coastline. It was here that almost half of Sydney's Jews lived. The Schotts joined the Orthodox Synagogue community based in Maroubra and bought a house. Bully had brought with him to Australia a considerable sum of money which was enough for a deposit. The bank notes had been brought into the country illegally, hidden in the frame of a baby's pram. After their arrival in Melbourne, Bully discovered to his horror that the pram and other pieces of luggage were missing. They resurfaced later with customs in Sydney and were handed over to the owners without undergoing an inspection. Bully made a loss when he exchanged currencies. Although it was something he had to accept, he could never quite forgive himself for changing his cash in Berlin into American dollars and not into English pounds.

The first years were marked by hard work. Economic success was hampered by linguistic barriers and the lack of professional training documentation. Gerda spent years earning money by sewing at home on her old Singer machine, her first customers all coming from migrant circles. Bully too was offered some initial help from Jewish immigrants. For a short time he found employment as a tradesman and security officer in a hotel bar, located in Kings Cross, Sydney's red light district. A camera shop that he opened with a business partner was soon declared bankrupt. Bully's employment on a chicken farm, delivering goods to customers in a minivan, was equally short-lived. He then moved on to delivering goods for a courier service. Before too long Bully made the decision to strike out on his own. By now he was familiar with the complex network of roads and suburbs that made up the Sydney metropolis. With the money that he had earned Bully bought himself a taxi licence and a car, an Australian-made Holden, which he was to drive, look after and repair over many years. Bully was often asked about the blue tattoo on the underside of his left arm. Amongst his passengers there were Germans and Austrians who, once they heard the word Auschwitz, abruptly broke off the conversation.

After eight years the required waiting time for naturalisation had elapsed. In 1958 the Schotts lodged their application for Australian citizenship.[44] They were able to submit outstanding character references from Australian neighbours as well as reports from the police and security services confirming his crime-free past. On 1 June 1959 Gerda and Bully swore allegiance to Queen Elizabeth II as the sovereign Head of State of Australia in a ceremony in Randwick Town Hall. They accepted their certificates of Australian citizenship with gratitude and joy.

Two years later Bully sustained severe injuries in a work accident. While repairing his taxi one day the jack gave way and his legs and hip were wedged under the vehicle. Several operations and years of rehabilitation followed, culminating in a forced premature retirement from professional life. House and taxi had to be sold, but the new apartment on Coogee Beach at least afforded a view of the sea. After the move Gerda's health quickly deteriorated and she was finally relieved of her long suffering in 1993. Bully never really overcame her loss.

Bully returned to the landscape of his past. His visits to Berlin took him through familiar streets, to past places of training and work, to the *Sportpalast* and to the *Judenbaracken* in Sachsenhausen and the cemetery in Weissensee. At the beginning of 1995 he was invited by the *Stiftung Brandenburger Gedenkstätten* to take part in a ceremony commemorating the 50th anniversary of the liberation of the Sachsenhausen concentration camp. I helped him compose a letter to the premier of the state of Brandenburg. In this letter, dated 10 February 1995, he communicated his arrival date and the fact that he would be accompanied by his son and granddaughter.[45] But Bully became ill and the visit to Sachsenhausen never eventuated. He withdrew to the Montefiore Old Age Home, in which numerous survivors of the Holocaust spent the last years of their life. Whenever there was ever something to be installed or repaired at this idyllic Jewish aged care facility Bully offered his services. If he woke at night to intense hunger pangs for something sweet he groped his way slowly along in the dark to places where he knew he would find cake, biscuits and sweets.

Bully later entrusted memorabilia to two museums. Today these artefacts and photographic images can be found in the *Judenbaracke* of the memorial site at Sachsenhausen and in the Sydney Jewish Museum, symbolically at either end of Bully's long journey from Sachsenhausen to Sydney. Bully died on 21 December 2000 at the age of 86. He was buried next to Gerda in the Jewish section of Sydney's Rookwood cemetery. On each *Jahrzeit* of his death Martin follows the tradition of his father and ancestors by saying *Kaddish*, the mourners' prayer. This prayer underlines the continuity of Jewish life.

Neither Bully nor Gerda had ever really felt the need to engage in ongoing discussions about Holocaust memory. As *kleine* and *einfache* (simple) survivors their recollections remained unadulterated, expressed in straightforward language. Bully and Gerda Schott's memories resurfaced in treasured photos, in letters and other correspondence and oral communications with relatives and friends, in conversations laced with typical Berlin and Yiddish expressions and accents. They do not appear to have been distorted by literary ambition and as such cannot be read as being subjected to imposed layers of philosophical or intellectual speculation. They are the surviving fragments of a lost past and yet were, in some senses, a part of their post-war lives too. With the passage of time survivor stories like Bully's and Gerda's have become the inheritance of scholars who feel the need to fit them into conceptual frameworks which often have little to do with Holocaust history but clearly fall into the burgeoning field of what Christopher Browning has termed 'aftermath' studies.[46] This has resulted in a welter of memory approaches, definitions and representations. This 'memory industry' emerging in recent years seems now to have given way to 'memory work' that no longer requires the voices of survivors.[47] But it is individual stories like Bully's which constitute the history of the Holocaust, and it is through the journeys that survivors made to the 'edge of the Diaspora' that the Holocaust can be seen to be an immanent part of the recent Australian past too.

ACKNOWLEDGEMENTS

This article was first published in the *Festschrift* in honour of Monika Richarz, entitled *Jüdische Welten. Juden in Deutschland vom 18. Jahrhundert bis in die Gegenwart* and edited by Marion Kaplan and Beate Meyer (Göttingen: Wallstein Verlag, 2005), pp.231–47. The article was revised and extended for this collection and then translated into English by my wife Jane Sydenham-Kwiet. I would like to thank her for that.

My reconstruction of Bully Schott's life story is based on the recollections and testimonies of Bully and Gerda Schott as well as on historical records kept in public archives and private family collections. Over many years I have had countless conversations with Bully and Gerda as well as with their son Martin. In 1981 Sophie Caplan, then my research assistant at the German Department of the University of New South Wales, interviewed Bully and Gerda Schott as part of our oral history project 'Testimonies of Migrants'. The conversations were recorded and later transcribed. Bully's testimony is found on cassettes C 28, Gerda's on cassettes C 45. They form part of the *Caplan Collection* which includes more than 100 interviews and constitutes the first major oral history project conducted in Australia with survivors of the Holocaust. The original testimonies remain in the possession of Sophie Caplan. However, in the meantime they have been transferred to DVD and entrusted to the Sydney Jewish Museum and the US Holocaust Memorial Museum in Washington DC where they are accessible for ongoing research projects. It is Sophie Caplan's intention to write a biography of Bully Schott and she has already completed an unpublished MS manuscript entitled 'A Unique Case of Survival during the Holocaust'. Shortly before his death Bully told the story of his survival in front of a video camera. It is recorded on two video cassettes which now form part of the Spielberg Foundation collection. I would like to sincerely thank Martin Schott for allowing me access to documents, photos and other material from the personal family records to assist in my research.

NOTES

1. Caplan Collection, Cassette 45 (henceforth CC, C).
2. For the history of Jewish and 'mixed families' under Nazi rule see the ground-breaking studies of Beate Meyer, *'Jüdische Mischlinge'. Rassenpolitik und Verfolgungserfahrung 1933–1945* (Hamburg: Doelling und

Galitz, 1999); Marion A. Kaplan, *Between Dignity and Despair. Jewish Life in Nazi Germany* (New York and Oxford: Oxford University Press, 1998), esp. pp.74–118; Saul Friedländer, *Nazi Germany and the Jews. Vol. 1: The Years of Persecution, 1933–1939* (New York: HarperCollins, 1997).
3. CC, C 45.
4. Ibid.
5. A brief description of the Lewinnek family and their network of friends can be found in the gripping book by Knut Elstermann, *Gerdas Schweigen. Die Geschichte einer Überlebenden* (Berlin: be.bra Verlag, 2005).
6. Archiv Centrum Judaicum (CJA), Questionnaire of the Berlin Jewish Community, Fanny Schott, 22 November 1945.
7. Zentralinstitut für sozialwissenschaftliche Forschung der FU Berlin (ed.), *Gedenkbuch der jüdischen Opfer des Nationalsozialismus* (Berlin: Edition Hentrich, 2000), p.1157.
8. See Kathrin Kühlow, 'Jüdische Haeftlinge im KZ-Sachsenhausen 1939 bis 1942', in Günter Morsch and Suzanne zur Nieden (eds.), *Jüdische Haeftlinge im Konzentrationslager Sachsenhausen 1936 bis 1945* (Berlin: Edition Hentrich, 2004), p.180; Yfaat Weiss, *Deutsche und polnische Juden vor dem Holocaust. Jüdische Identität zwischen Staatsbürgerschaft und Ethnizität 1933–1940* (München: Oldenbourg, 2000), pp.211f.
9. CC, C 28.
10. Ibid.
11. Ibid.
12. See Wolfgang Sofsky, *Die Ordnung des Terrors: Das Konzentrationslager* (Frankfurt a.M.: S. Fischer, 1993), p.175.
13. CC, C 45.
14. Ibid.
15. Kaplan, *Between Dignity and Despair*, p. 82.
16. CC, C 45.
17. Kühlow, 'Jüdische Haeftlinge', p.197.
18. See Konrad Kwiet and Helmut Eschwege, *Selbstbehauptung und Widerstand. Deutsche Juden im Kampf um Existenz und Würde 1933–1945* (Hamburg: Christians Verlag, 1984), p.285.
19. CC, C 28.
20. Auschwitz Kalendarium, in *Hefte von Auschwitz* Vol.3 (1960), p.98; see also Danuta Czech, *Auschwitz Chronicle* (New York: Owl Books, 1990), p.258
21. On the corruption emerging in Auschwitz see Laurence Rees, *Auschwitz. A New History* (New York: Public Affairs, 2005), pp.173ff.
22.. CC, C 45.
23. Czech, *Auschwitz Chronicle*, p.258.
24. T. Iwasko, 'Häftlingsfluchten aus dem Lager', *Hefte von Auschwitz*, Vol.7 (1964), pp.3–57.
25. See Beate Kosmala and Claudia Schoppmann (eds.), *Solidarität und Hilfe für Juden während der NS-Zeit*, Vol.5. *Überleben im Untergrund. Hilfe für Juden in Deutschland 1941–1945* (Berlin: Metropol Verlag, 2002).
26. Elstermann, *Gerdas Überleben*, p.62
27. See Peter Wyden, *Stella* (New York: Doubleday, 1992); also Christian Dirks, '"Greifer". Der Fahndungsdienst der Berliner Gestapo', in Beate Meyer and Hermann Simon (eds.), *Juden in Berlin 1938–1945* (Berlin: Philo Verlagsgesellschaft, 2000), pp.233–57; and Doris Tausendfreund, *Erzwungener Verrat. Jüdische Greifer im Dienst der Gestapo 1943–1945* (Berlin Metropol Verlag, 2006).
28. Wyden, *Stella*, pp.219–22.
29. CJA, Questionnaire of the Berlin Jewish Community, Gerda Schott, 6 August 1945 and Norbert Lewinnek, 13 August 1945.
30. CC, C 45.
31. CJA, Questionnaire Gerda Schott, handwritten file note.
32. On Lustig see the report written by Bruno Blau, published in Monika Richarz (ed.), *Jüdisches Leben in Deutschland*, Vol.3 (Stuttgart: Deutsche Verlags-Anstalt, 1982), pp.459–75; and Beate Meyer, 'Gratwanderung zwischen Verantwortung und Verstrickung – Die Reichsvertretung der Juden in Deutschland und die Jüdische Gemeinde zu Berlin 1938–1945', in Meyer and Simon (eds.), *Juden in Berlin*, pp.291–337.
33. CC, C 28.
34. Ibid.
35. Ibid.
36. Restitution Office Berlin, Reg. No. 77 456. File Bully Salem Schott. Copies are in my possession.
37. See Martin Riesenburger, *Das Licht verlöschte nicht* (Berlin, 1960), new edition edited by Hermann Simon with contributions from Andreas Nachama and Hermann Simon (Berlin, 2003).

38. Restitution Office Berlin, File Schott, handwritten CV, 10 August 1952 and affidavit, August 1953.
39. Australian National Archives, Sydney, SP 1122/1 N 58/62980, Certificate of IRO Eligibility. The Record folder also contains the official documents on emigration and naturalisation.
40. Ibid., Passenger Card, 6 November 1950.
41. See Konrad Kwiet, 'The Second Time Around: Re-acculturation of German-Jewish Refugees in Australia', *The Journal of Holocaust Education*, Vol.10 (2001), pp.34–49.
42. Standard works on the History of Australia Jewry are the studies of Suzanne Rutland, *Edge of the Diaspora: Two Centuries of Jewish Settlement in Australia* (Sydney: Brandl & Schlesinger, 2001), and *The Jews in Australia* (Cambridge and Melbourne: Cambridge University Press, 2005).
43. Gershom Scholem. 'Wider dem Mythos vom deutsch-jüdischen Gespräch', *Bulletin of the Leo Baeck Institute*, Vol.27 (1964), pp.278–81.
44. Australian National Archives, Sydney, SP 1122/1 N58/62980.
45. Copies of the correspondence are in my possession.
46. Christopher R. Browning, 'Future Directions in Holocaust Studies', *Yearbook of the Leo Baeck Institute*, Vol.XLV (2000), p.220.
47. See the brilliant article by Kerwin Lee Klein, 'On the Emergence of Memory in Historical Discourse', *Representations*, No.69, Special Issue: Grounds for Remembering (Winter 2000), pp.127–50.

In the Shadow of the Holocaust: The Development of Moriah College, Sydney

SUZANNE RUTLAND

The major transformative period in Australian Jewish history occurred with the refugee flight from Nazism in the late 1930s and the survivor emigration in the aftermath of the Second World War. In 1933 Australian Jewry was a small, isolated community, consisting of only 23,000 members. Between 1938 and 1961 the community almost trebled to 61,000. The Jewish victims of Nazism who found refuge in Australia completely changed the nature of Australian Jewry in terms of its religious, educational and cultural life, its representational structures and the nature of its Jewish identification. One of the major features of this transformation was the growth of the Jewish day school movement. As a result of the arrival of pre-war Jewish refugees and Holocaust survivors, as well as the impact of the Holocaust itself on the established community, the desire to nurture and protect the community's Jewish identity became imperative. The prevailing, conservative Anglo-Jewish approach that had fostered non-distinctiveness and complete acculturation was discarded in favour of religious and cultural pluralism to ensure group survival.[1]

The first twentieth century Jewish school to be established in Australia was the North Bondi Jewish School and Kindergarten, founded in Sydney in 1942 at the height of the Holocaust by East European Jewish migrants who had arrived before and after the First World War, together with refugees from Nazi Germany. Initially, the school developed very slowly because the established Anglo-Jewish community opposed the idea of separate Jewish schools, fearing they would hinder integration and create antisemitism. After the war, the main supporters of the College were survivors of the Holocaust, many of whom settled in the beachside suburb of Bondi, where Moriah's first campus was situated. From the 1920s, Bondi developed as the first area of settlement for European Jewish immigrants, who were attracted by the proximity of the beach and the availability of inexpensive accommodation in blocks of flats. As the survivors moved up the socio-economic ladder they relocated to the nearby middle class suburb of Bellevue Hill, where the main school campus was opened in the early 1950s with the new name Moriah War Memorial College. Whilst these survivors retained a strong sense of Jewish identification and ensured that their children received a

Jewish education in a community environment, most remained silent about their wartime trauma and the topic of the Holocaust was not taught in a systematic manner at Moriah College in the 1950s and 1960s.

In the 1970s, with the second generation, a further transformation occurred. This included a growing awareness of the need to teach and learn about the Holocaust in order to secure and strengthen Jewish identity. By the mid-1970s members of the second generation, the 'baby boomers', began to graduate from university as teachers. Moriah's principal, at the time British-born Harold Nagley, preferred to employ Jewish teachers for secular subjects, as he believed that they would reinforce the school's Jewish ethos. A number of these teachers were children of Holocaust survivors who were employed for different subject areas and continued to teach in the school over a long period of time.[2]

Holocaust awareness emerged largely as a phenomenon of the second generation, who wished to come to terms with their parents' experiences. For example, Australian Holocaust historian and author Mark Baker explained that as a child he dealt with the legacy of his parents by imagining himself escaping though sewers from the ghetto to find food; by asking himself how he would have reacted to the situation; and even by trying to take on the role of the perpetrators by one year 'dressing up as my parents' Haman, the other H villain' on Purim.[3] However, he mainly 'sublimated these desires to dream my parents' dreams by reading voraciously, any book with a Holocaust theme, and then still later, teaching Holocaust studies at the University of Melbourne. I was there without being there'.[4] This second-generation experience, whether of pre-war refugees or of Holocaust survivors, was the motivating force for learning about the Holocaust and introducing its teaching at Moriah.[5]

This article will analyse these two phases in the transformation of Australian Jewry, using Moriah College as a case study of this educational and cultural phenomenon. Amelia Klein's article in this volume explores further the experiences of the third generation. Whilst there is a growing literature on Jewish refugees and Holocaust survivors in Australia, its impact on the development of Australian Jewish schools is still largely unexplored, apart from my work, together with that of Sophie Caplan and Judith Berman.[6] This article seeks to fill this gap.

The Community in the 1930s: The Anglo-Jewish Identity in Australia

In 1933 Australian Jewry was a small, isolated and highly acculturated community, distanced from its Jewish heritage. This manifested itself in a high rate of intermarriage and Jews being lost to the community. Elazar and Medding have described the Jewish community, which developed in the Australian colonies in the nineteenth century, as a community emerging within a frontier society.[7] Louis Hartz in his seminal book, *The Founding of New Societies*, argued:

> Fragments that were broken off, as it were, from European civilisation, and had to implant themselves in new soil, pursuing lines of development that reflected their European heritage but were, nevertheless, substantially different because of the transplantation. These fragments began their separate development from the point at which they were separated from European civilisation as a whole, maintaining patterns common to the civilisation they left behind in forms that remained more or less frozen or took radically different directions from those of their original civilisations, which continue to undergo adaptations of their own.[8]

This pattern of development was evident in the case of Australian Jewry. The various Jewish settlements in Australia began as fragments of Anglo-Jewry. As a result of the small numbers and lack of Jewish learning, the early Australian Jews were fearful of any change and their pattern of religious life remained frozen in the Anglo-Jewish mould. Efforts to establish Reform Judaism at the end of the nineteenth century failed, as did attempts to create a more Orthodox Jewish lifestyle in the European model, whilst Conservative Judaism was not even considered. Thus, the plurality that emerged in post-emancipation Judaism, initially on the European continent and later in North America, was not reflected in Australian Jewry. The different waves of non-British European Jewish migrants, which arrived in Australia from the 1850s until the 1930s, were too few in number and too dispersed geographically to radically change this fossilisation of Jewish life.[9] In addition, the Jewish community tended to emulate their non-Jewish neighbours and as a result of their English backgrounds they were very acculturated. Australian Jews regarded themselves as more 'British than the British',[10] almost in the same manner as German Jews in the so-called 'Golden Age' of their German-Jewish symbiosis.[11] This was reflected in the early 'cathedral' synagogues established in Sydney and Melbourne, which maintained a 'high church atmosphere'.[12] Similarly, as in Germany, the 'splendour of the new synagogues reflected the growing wealth and self-satisfaction of the Jewish upper and middle classes'.[13]

Until the 1930s Australian Jewry made every effort to minimise outward differences from the majority population, creating an ideology of non-distinctiveness. Most Australian Jews considered themselves Australians of the Jewish religion. Distinctive religious practices such as the observance of the Jewish dietary laws, the wearing of a skullcap and the practice of ritual baths (*mikvah*) were poorly maintained. The denominational Jewish schools established in Melbourne and Sydney in the second half of the nineteenth century were closed after 1880 with the introduction of free, compulsory secular education through Public Instructions Acts. The community became dependent on part-time educational systems, which offered minimal hours and produced Jews who were largely Jewishly illiterate. The focus of the community was on success in the outside world, rather than on strong Jewish knowledge and identity. Thus, in many ways Australian Jewry was a spiritual desert, a place where it was difficult to remain a fully orthodox Jew. This applied more to Sydney than to Melbourne because in the nineteenth century Melbourne attracted more European Jews as a result of the gold rushes of the 1850s, so that it developed a more ethnically diverse community with both German and East European Jews. In addition, Melbourne's colder climate tended to foster a culture which was more religious and less hedonistic, so that church attendance was higher in Melbourne than in Sydney, and this also impacted on the Jewish community.[14] The other communities were even smaller and weaker in terms of their Jewish practice. Everywhere the rate of intermarriage increased. The growth of the Australian Jewish community remained static in the 1920s even though there was immigration, largely from Eastern Europe. This situation only began to change with the arrival of the refugees from Nazism in the late 1930s.

The First Transformation: The Establishment of Moriah College

In the period before 1939, 7–8,000 Jewish refugees found sanctuary in Australia, with the majority arriving in 1939 so that they became known as the 'thirty-niners'. Most of the pre-war refugees settled in Sydney and Melbourne where they felt alienated from the established Anglo-Jewish community. They created their own institutions, influencing every aspect of Jewish life. In the immediate post-war period a further 17,000 Holocaust survivors arrived, largely sponsored by family members who had arrived before the war. They reinforced the changes initiated by the pre-war refugees, bringing about a transformation of Australian Jewish life and gradually took over communal leadership positions, ending their initial sense of alienation. One of the key developments was the re-introduction and development of Jewish kindergartens and day schools.

In March 1942, at the time when Hitler's 'Final Solution' was being implemented in Europe and casting its long shadow across the Jewish world, a small group of dedicated men, including East European migrants and pre-war refugees who were dissatisfied with the state of Jewish education in Sydney, met in the schoolroom of the old Central Synagogue in Bondi Junction to discuss the establishment of a *Talmud Torah* (traditional Jewish school).[15] This meeting was to be the progenitor of Moriah College. Within a few months of the meeting, Abraham Rabinovitch, inspired by a German Jewish refugee, Rabbi Hans Elchanan Blumenthal, purchased a property in Glenayr Avenue in Bondi to accommodate the planned kindergarten and school.

Blumenthal had arrived in Australia in September 1940 on the *Dunera*, which berthed in Sydney Harbour with 2,542 passengers on board. Most were male German and Austrian Jewish refugees who, at the outbreak of war, had been classified as 'enemy aliens' in England and placed in internment camps. After Dunkirk, the British government became concerned that these refugees would prove to be a fifth column and decided to deport them to Commonwealth countries. Canada and Australia both agreed to accept some of these internees. Some '*Dunera* Boys' experienced the journey as a hellish voyage. They suffered privations, and many were robbed of their property or were subjected to brutality and physical abuse at the hands of their British guards. Others – the younger ones – called the '*Dunera*' an experience of a lifetime, but Blumenthal remembered the voyage as a nightmare. Upon arrival, they joined other 'enemy aliens' who had been rounded up in Australia and sent to the internment camp in Hay, New South Wales. They were later transferred to Tatura in Victoria.[16]

Blumenthal was a member of the small group of Orthodox Jews who arrived on the *Dunera* and were classified by the Australian authorities as 'strictly kosher Jews'.[17] A young German-born rabbi, he was a very lively person: energetic, intelligent, highly educated and extremely charismatic.[18] He had studied at the University of Frankfurt am Main, the Yeshivot of Telz and Kelm, and the Russian Mir Yeshiva; he was ordained both in Telz and Mir. He had served for a short time as rabbi in Oradea-Mare in Transylvania before escaping to England where he continued his studies at London University from 1938 until 1940, majoring in Hebrew and Psychology.[19] Coming from his strictly orthodox background, he was confronted by a very different style of religious observance and life in Australia, one that he found unacceptable.

After his reclassification as a 'friendly alien' and release from internment, Blumenthal travelled to Sydney where he met Felix Freeman, the president of Central Synagogue, the second largest congregation. Freeman offered him a position as rabbi at the synagogue but Blumenthal soon realised that the community 'was not especially outstanding in its religious way of life and his [Freeman's] own links with Judaism were not strong'.[20] When Freeman told Blumenthal to shave off his beard, he resigned from his post. Furthermore, he also lamented that the synagogue had a mixed choir.

Shortly after this, Blumenthal met Abraham Rabinovitch, a local businessman who had migrated to Australia from Eastern Europe before the First World War. In his memoirs, Blumenthal recalled Rabinovitch's remarkable words of welcome: Rabinovitch spoke of a dream that Blumenthal had come 'to save Australian Jewry from spiritual annihilation'.[21] Rabinovitch was disturbed that Sydney had neither a *Mikvah* (ritual bath) nor a *Talmud Torah*, and he stated: 'I have a great deal of money and no children. Together we can change the nature of the community.'[22] Blumenthal persuaded Rabinovitch to concentrate first on a kindergarten, then a *Talmud Torah* and finally a Jewish day school,[23] as he believed that it was best to work through the children. In this way Rabinovitch and Blumenthal became the 'mother and father' of the emerging vision for a Jewish day school in Sydney.

However, the idea of a separate Jewish day school met with opposition. One of the leading rabbis in Melbourne and a key representative of Anglo-Australian Jewry, Jacob Danglow, even telephoned Blumenthal to express his disquiet that the concept of separate Jewish day schools would prevent integration and thus engender antisemitism. In the 1940s and 1950s such fears were prevalent throughout the English speaking Diaspora. Many believed that 'day schools oppose the democratic idea … by segregating children because of religion'.[24] However, Danglow changed his mind when he heard that Rabbi Dr Joseph Herman Hertz, the chief rabbi of the British Empire, supported the concept. Orthodox leaders recognised that Judaism requires intensive knowledge and that 'for those who want to remain Jewish, day schools are the only solution'.[25]

Despite strong opposition from Sydney's Anglo-Jewish community, Blumenthal persevered. He had the quality of 'single-mindedness': Jewish leaders at the time saw him as 'a dreamer – he had a certain immaturity – he was impulsive, not tactful, but when he embraced an idea he was capable of going it alone'.[26] In May 1942 Rabinovitch joined the *Talmud Torah*'s committee as honorary treasurer, by which time Blumenthal was already employed, teaching six children in a private home.[27] In July 1942 Rabinovitch purchased a cottage in Bondi to house a kindergarten, and in August 1942 the first kindergarten teacher was engaged and a publicity campaign for the school followed. Advertisements appeared in the Jewish press noting the acquisition of the property and inviting enrolments for the Hebrew School and Kindergarten where 'highly qualified staff is available'.[28] In an article by 'Elisheva', the importance of kindergarten education was explained. The development of preschool education at this time was still in its infancy and 'Elisheva' set out and then responded to the common objections to such preschool educational programmes. The article then went on to evoke the positive aspects of a Jewish kindergarten:

> I have painted the picture of a good kindergarten, in our case this picture will be fitted in a Jewish frame. Of course kindergarten children are much too young to be taught the concepts of Judaism. Our aim in the kindergarten will merely be to create the right attitude towards Jewish things. The very fact that the children will be together with other Jewish children and Jewish teachers is very important. It will, we hope, lay the foundations for a love of the Jewish people, which we find so sadly lacking in many Jews.[29]

On 3 September 1942 Nathan Haneman, a Board member, wrote an article explaining the importance of the establishment of the Hebrew School and Kindergarten, as well as stressing the role of the *Talmud Torah* which was already operating. Haneman referred to the tragedy of European Jewry: whilst the details of the Jewish catastrophe unfolding in Nazi-controlled Europe were not known, he was aware that Jews were persecuted and that thousands of Jews had been murdered. He argued that the German Jewish assimilation had failed and that the events in Europe showed that 'the dream of assimilation is only a fading mirage'.[30] He stressed that only a good Jewish education would help 'our youngsters … should the occasion arise, to successfully survive similar periods of reaction, and carry on the torch of Judaism',[31] and concluded his article with the moving appeal for the community to take advantage of 'the bitter lessons taught by the history we are living through, for the benefit of the oncoming generation'.[32]

At the start of the new school year in February 1943 the new kindergarten and school was officially launched by communal stalwart Sir Samuel Cohen, president of the New South Wales Kindergarten Union. He was presumably invited to do so as an attempt by the East European Jews on the Kindergarten Board to involve a representative of the Anglo-establishment.[33] Sir Samuel expressed his pleasure at being asked to perform the ceremony and hoped that the North Bondi Hebrew School and Kindergarten would be 'the forerunner of many more such educational aids to the progress of the ideals of Jewry'.[34] Blumenthal gave a most moving address, and his speech was reported in the press as follows:

> The reason why in this solemn moment of consecrating the new school, he [Blumenthal] recalled to mind and also wished to recall to mind of those present, the saddest reality of the present time, the unspeakable agonies of European Jewry. Let us sadly remember them, all those who over there on the other side are experiencing the full brunt of mysterious Jewish suffering and all centres of Jewish learning are lying in ruins. A young pupil wrote recently from a distant country: 'At the moment when so many Jewish centres had to close down, you have to open a new one at that end of the globe' ... Whilst not as assuming as to believe that we are already striving for that goal, but we must feel that we are 'on the way' and that we must do our share.[35]

For Blumenthal, the opening of the kindergarten was only the first step towards 'our unshakeable aim'[36] to foster Jewish education in Sydney. He believed that Jewish learning must rank as the 'foremost in value when, our very national existence, is impugned through the greatest physical disaster that ever in our history had befallen us'.[37] Thus, in early 1943, Blumenthal understood that the foundations of European Jewry would be destroyed. He responded to the 'Jewish catastrophe' with this plea to set up the Jewish day school system in Sydney in order to strengthen and to secure the continuity of the existence of Jewish life in Australia. In this way he sought to introduce the two key elements of Modern Orthodoxy as developed by Rabbi Samson Raphael Hirsch in Germany in the nineteenth century: the traditional knowledge of Judaism combined with the secular studies of a day school – known as *Torah im Derech Eretz* (religious and secular studies).[38]

In May 1943 Abraham Rabinovitch was elected president of the school, a position he retained until his death in 1964.[39] In the ensuing months Blumenthal negotiated with the Department of Education to expand the kindergarten into a day school and in September 1943 the decision was made to commence an infants' school for years K to 3. During this period another *Dunera* internee, Dr Siegfried Cohn, joined the school's team. Dr Cohn had a teacher's diploma from the Hildesheimer Seminary in Berlin and had taught in England before his internment.[40] The kindergarten and infants school was 'a happy place for the young pupils, a school remembered with affection'.[41]

When Rabinovitch assumed the presidency, he built around himself a likeminded team of Orthodox Jews, largely from East European backgrounds,[42] and attempts to broaden the base of this leadership were strongly resisted over the ensuing years. In contrast, Blumenthal sought to reach out to the broader Anglo-Jewish community so that he clashed with Rabinovitch and their partnership did not last long. In December 1943 Blumenthal decided to resign, stating: 'I feel that I have really exhausted the scope of my abilities in Sydney being unable to develop things further under the prevailing conditions.'[43] Even though he offered to teach for a further term, until a replacement head was found, the Board immediately accepted his resignation. Reflecting later on his resignation, he wrote:

> Whereas I strove to achieve a scope which would include the entire community for each group of Sydney Jews, Rabinovitch was thinking of a separate parochial institution limited to people of his persuasion. Since he purchased the building out of his own pocket and also paid for most of its activities, his opinion overcame my own.[44]

In February 1944 Rabbi Blumenthal left Sydney for Melbourne, serving for a short period first as minister and then high school teacher, before leaving for South Africa and later settling in Israel.[45]

Blumenthal's departure left the school without educational leadership, creating what was to become a problematic and ongoing story for the next 20 years of its history. In July 1944, an educational sub-committee, chaired by Rabinovitch, was established 'to regulate teachers and report on progress of the pupils',[46] and at the same time the president was to contact educational authorities in Palestine. Further school board resolutions left the appointment of a headmaster to the 'absolute discretion' of the president,[47] so that Rabinovitch continued to totally dominate the school, which had to await his death in 1964 to start to develop into an enterprise supported by the entire Jewish community.

'The code of silence': Children of Survivors

In the period from 1947 to 1954, Sydney Jewry greatly expanded in size with the arrival of Holocaust survivors. These Displaced Persons (DPs), especially those who came from Eastern Europe, arrived with a greater sense of Jewish identification and an understanding of the importance of day school education than the local Australian-born Jews. Before the war Jews in Eastern Europe enjoyed a high level of educational and cultural autonomy with a high proportion – over 80 per cent in Latvia and Lithuania – attending Jewish schools.[48] Some of the newcomers were committed to their children receiving a good education, including a Jewish education. While the established and more acculturated local Jews were reluctant to send their children to what became Moriah War Memorial College in 1953, it was the survivors who formed the backbone of Moriah's parent body in the immediate post-war era. Survivors also formed part of its lay executive and teaching staff.

Since most of the pupils were children of Holocaust survivors who had arrived from Poland, Hungary and Romania with nothing, both parents worked long, hard hours, often in the *shmatte* (clothing) business, to establish themselves in their new country and to afford to send their children to a private Jewish day school. For those with transportation problems, the school organised for a hire car to pick the children up in the morning and return them in the afternoon. Since both parents often worked, and it was rare for grandparents to survive, many of the children were 'latchkey kids'.[49] Despite this, they grew up being very protected by their European parents.[50]

Another major feature of the children of survivors has been their academic success. The stress on scholarship reflected the traditional attitudes to study in Judaism, as well as being a vehicle to rise up the social ladder. In addition, a generation of Jewish parents who were denied a normal childhood and schooling during the Holocaust were determined that their children should enjoy the highest standards of education. Strong pressure was exerted in the home for academic success, with the well-known phrase being 'for this I survived Auschwitz' if their children were not sufficiently serious about their studies.

Oral testimony indicates that for the students at the school, their years at Moriah in the 1950s were happy ones. The school was small, with a supportive family atmosphere, and close friendships were made that tended to last well past their school years. With the combination of classes at the school followed by afternoon classes for the boys at the Yeshiva, the boys felt that they received a good knowledge of *Yiddishkeit* (Jewish life) and developed a love of Judaism. Whilst the teaching facilities were very basic, consisting of desks, chairs and a blackboard, they did not feel as if they were lacking in anything. They thought they had 'everything, even though we were in the dark ages compared to the situation today'.[51] The general sense was that this was a happy, carefree period providing the happiest of memories.[52]

However, these early years were also marked by the code of silence. Most survivors did not talk of their traumatic experiences of suffering and survival. Many believed that the best way to keep their story alive was by having children to replace those who had died.[53] They wished to shelter their children from the horrors that they had experienced. In her book *The Silence: How Tragedy Shapes Talk* Ruth Wajnryb described as follows her experience of growing up in suburban Sydney, distant from the Jewish centre in the eastern suburbs:

> It was as if we'd arrived from another planet, with no records or recollections, no memory. We lived in the present and for the future. We were busy. We had plans. We had ambitions. We had this space in time that was now. And we

> were working hard toward what we could imagine ahead of us. But there was no past. The past was cordoned off, sealed out. There was a complete severance with what went before.[54]

She went on to describe the reluctance of her parents to talk about their experiences:

> The temptation to seal off the past so as not to allow its horrors to intrude into the present must have been overwhelming. I don't know if they made a pact not to talk about where they came from, what they'd seen and experienced, what they'd lost. But it was as if they had. I am aware now of the enormous energy invested daily, yearly and across decades, in keeping the past to the past, preventing it from engulfing us.[55]

This sense of disconnection with the past is also highlighted in Mark Baker's historical novel *The Fiftieth Gate* (1997), which traces his parents' story during the Holocaust, contrasting this with his experiences of growing up in Melbourne as a child of survivors and attending Mount Scopus College, the largest Jewish day school there. Whilst he was not permitted to speak about the Holocaust at home, his father's regular nightmares were a constant reminder of a secret but threatening past.[56] Reflecting on his childhood in 2005, Baker wrote: 'looking back over those days now, I am more aware of how Auschwitz cast its shadow on day-to-day life. Who can dissect why this one was depressed, or how deep was the lament that ran through a thousand sighs.'[57] He referred to the way his mother fed him as though this was 'the last morsel', became worried that a common cold would prove to be tuberculosis, and 'in the way they dreamed through you and devoured the dividends of every achievement'.[58] These same family dynamics of surviving Auschwitz also cast a continuous shadow on most of the students of Moriah College. As with Dr Baker's parents, most did not talk; but those who did were obsessed with their story.

In analysing Wajnryb's book, Gelski and Wajsenberg discuss three main factors that account for survivors' inability to discuss their trauma with their children: the linguistic problem, as they did not have sufficient English skills to explain their trauma; the internal psychological problems, which include 'a complex amalgam of internal and external factors that inhibit the survivors' ability to communicate their personal versions of hell – the pain, deprivation, abuse, humiliation, loss, and guilt of having survived – to someone who encounters it indirectly, the outsider, the one who was not there';[59] and the external factors, because many members of the outside community were not interested in listening to survivors tell their stories.[60] This reluctance of survivors to speak of their experiences to outsiders in general and often to their children in particular, was by no means unique to Australia. Many found it difficult to find the language to 'express a trauma of such magnitude'.[61] Thus it is not surprising, as David Ritter comments in his article on the Eichmann Trial in this volume, that in 1960 'such references as are made to the extermination of Europe's Jewry (by Baume, for instance) are made in passing, sometimes in language that seems lacking in gravity and solemnity' (p.60).

The code of silence about the Holocaust was also seen at Moriah, where the school curriculum contained nothing about the Holocaust, which focused on traditional Jewish Studies. Indeed, Jewish history ended with the destruction of the Second Temple and almost nothing was taught about post-Second Temple history, which spanned almost two millennia. In addition, the annual community commemoration held each year in the 1950s marked the Warsaw Ghetto Uprising, and was known as such. This emphasis on Jewish heroism during the war mirrored what was happening in other parts of the Jewish world in the 1950s: when Yad Vashem opened its main memorial in 1964, its major sculptural piece marked the heroes of the Warsaw Ghetto. The awakening of a realisation of the need to speak and talk about the Holocaust only emerged later at Moriah, in the 1970s.

The Claims Conferences

With the gradual increase in the school population in the 1950s, more classroom facilities were required. However, since the parent body largely consisted of survivors who were working hard to rebuild their lives and were often not in a position to pay the full school fees, let alone finance building developments, other sources of funding had to be found. With time, the Conference of Jewish Material Claims against Germany (COJMCAG, known as Claims Conference) came to play an important role in funding the expansion of Moriah College.

The Claims Conference was established in 1951 to represent Diaspora Jewry in negotiations with the Federal Republic of Germany. In September 1952 the Federal Republic of Germany, the government of Israel and world Jewry signed the restitution agreement, with claims funds to be paid both as individual restitution and as compensation to communities.[62] Most of the money was to be allocated to assist survivors, but about 10 per cent was to be used each year for Jewish educational, religious and cultural institutions on condition that the money was to assist survivors of Nazism.[63] Dr Nahum Goldmann, president of the World Jewish Congress, strongly advocated support for educational and cultural institutions. In 1953, he stated in his opening address to the World Jewish Congress Assembly:

> We have lost our great centers of Jewish learning and culture … everything must be done to strengthen Jewish life in all parts of the diaspora. Education of Jewish youth, strengthening of Jewish communal life, hebraisation of the diaspora, deepening of the knowledge of Jewish history, are today much more essential for the survival of our people than they were centuries before.[64]

It was Goldmann's belief in the need to rebuild Jewish cultural life that played an important part in the cultural and educational reconstruction of the Jewish world.

In all, the Claims Conference assisted 150 Jewish schools in 18 countries. In Australia 21 schools, mainly afternoon and Sunday School Centres, were assisted in the period from 1952 to 1964.[65] Due to representations of Melbourne leader Maurice Ashkanasy the school that received the most substantial grant was Mount Scopus College of Melbourne, which in 1955 was allocated a total of £36,000 to be distributed over three years. In 1957 it was mooted that, from 1958, the Conference would cease funding elementary and secondary education outside continental Europe. Mark Uveeler, representing the Claims Conference, was distressed about this decision, writing to Herbert Katzki from the American Joint distribution Committee that:

> You know better than I how much Australian Jewry contributed for the victims of Nazi persecution and you are aware of their helpful attitude towards the Hungarian refugees. It is, therefore, quite difficult to decline support for cultural activities in Australia, while we have similar programs in the United Kingdom, or in Argentina.[66]

On the basis of these arguments, the Australian Jewish schools continued to be funded by the Claims Conferences and this decision was to prove vital for Moriah College.

In June 1952 Rabinovitch purchased the home of Mark Foy, built in the 1890s and located in Bellevue Hill. The old home was remodelled and the school opened on its new site in January 1953.[67] In 1959 it was decided to build classrooms for a high school, to be opened in 1960. Following effective representation by Executive Council president Sydney Einfeld, who argued that the majority of Moriah's student population consisted of children of Holocaust survivors, the school received a grant in 1958 of £5,000 on condition that it raised a further £10,000. This was achieved and the first extension to the original building was opened in 1960. In 1962 the College received a further grant from the Claims Conference for building work and the Board decided to demolish the Mark Foy home and build a modern classroom complex. The demolition started in December 1964 and the building project was completed in early 1966.

When Moriah College applied to the Claims Conference for financial support, Rabinovitch argued the College's case on the basis of the fact that the majority of the pupils were children of Holocaust survivors.[68] The funds received from the Claims Conferences from 1958 to 1964 totalled £26,000 and assisted significantly in the College's building projects of 1960 and 1964 to 1966.[69] The allocation of these funds was clear recognition of the important contributions that survivors made to the growth of the school in the Rabinovitch era.

It is interesting to note that in his applications to the Claims Conferences Rabinovitch did not seem to be aware of the irony that on the one hand he was appealing on behalf of the large survivor population at Moriah, while on the other hand there was no specific educational programme dealing with the history of the terror that they had survived. This dichotomy is understandable given the fact that most survivors wanted to put their past behind them and were reluctant to speak about their experiences. In addition, for Rabinovitch Jewish Studies meant the traditional areas of Torah, *Tenach* (Biblical Studies) and Talmud (the oral law) with maybe some medieval works such as the sixteenth century work by Joseph Caro, the *Shulchan Aruch* (Prepared Table). This situation at Moriah reflected what was happening in Jewish education in other parts of the Jewish world.

Thus, Moriah College was established in the shadow of the destruction of European Jewry, and in the early years of its history from 1942 until the early 1970s the Holocaust was the motor for change in Sydney Jewry, and contributed significantly to the development of the day school movement. However, the memory of the trauma was suppressed and the students at the school graduated without learning about the events or the historical context of the Holocaust that had so devastated most of their parents' lives. This had to wait for the next phase in the College's development, which started after Rabinovitch's death in 1964 and the appointment of a new principal, British-born Harold Nagley, in 1965.

The 1970s: Second Transformative Phase – A Generational Change

Holocaust Teaching and Remembrance

In the 1970s major changes were instituted in the school in terms of teaching and remembering the Holocaust. In 1973 experiential camps for an intensive one-week Jewish experience, known as the 'Counterpoint Seminars', were introduced for Years 10 and 11 and they devoted a session to the Holocaust, but this was outside the structure of formal classroom learning. In the early 1970s this pattern of only sporadic teaching of the Holocaust was common across all the Jewish day schools in Melbourne, Perth and Sydney, despite the fact that Melbourne had the largest number of Holocaust survivors on a pro rata population basis of any place outside Israel.[70] This reticence in confronting the Holocaust was also seen in Israeli high schools, again apart from the annual *Yom HaShoah*. It was only in 1979 that the Israeli Ministry of Education introduced into Israeli high schools a compulsory 34-hour subject dealing with the Holocaust.[71]

As Judith Berman notes, 'the birth of Holocaust studies in each school is a unique story'.[72] Moriah was the first school to introduce such an initiative when, in 1976, its High School Director of Jewish Studies, Max Wahlhaus, introduced a new Years 7–10 syllabus dealing with post-biblical history from the destruction of the Second Temple to the present day. Born in Germany in 1930, Wahlhaus and his family escaped in 1936, arriving in South Africa on the *Stuttgard*, the last group of German Jewish refugees to be permitted into South Africa. He entered the field of Jewish education in South Africa and migrated to Australia in 1970, serving first at Mount Scopus College in Melbourne before joining Moriah College in 1973.[73] With the new Jewish history syllabus, for the first time in the College's history subject matter dealing with the Holocaust was introduced in Year 10. The school year was divided into three terms and at least one full term was devoted to teaching the history of the Weimar Republic, the Nazi assumption and development of power in the 1930s and the destruction of European Jewry during the Holocaust. Each student chose one European country, studied the implementation of the destruction process in that country and presented their findings to the class. The diverse experiences of communities from Greece to Denmark were discussed and analysed. Thus the original Year 10 Holocaust syllabus was devised within the framework of Jewish history as chronological development, with its focus on 'flourishing life and culture of the Jewish communities of Europe prior to the Holocaust'.[74] The aim of the course was for students to base their understanding of the Holocaust on a whole range of Jewish experience. This chronological approach to teaching the Holocaust within the broader framework of Jewish History and with its focus on thorough knowledge of events rather than universal lessons or post-Holocaust issues has remained at the core of Holocaust teaching at Moriah until the present day, and it also followed the pattern at other Australian Jewish day schools.[75]

In addition, a major essay competition dealing with the students' family history was made a compulsory part of the course. Sophie Caplan, who survived the Holocaust as a child in France, introduced this competition. It was called the 'Dr Hans Kimmel Memorial Essay Competition' in memory of a Viennese Jewish refugee lawyer, Hans Kimmel, who arrived in Sydney in 1939 and became actively involved in the community. Recently, Caplan described the beginnings of the competition:

> In 1975, I had a son in Year 9 at Moriah College, and another son in Year 8. The history of the Jewish people they were learning ended with the fall of the Second Temple in 70 C.E. There was no mention or learning about the *Shoah* (Holocaust), or about modern Zionism and the establishment of the Jewish State. I knew that, as a parent, even a former high school History teacher, I could not approach my sons' teachers and ask them to teach these events. But I knew the then Principal, Mr. Harold Nagley … So I went to see Harold Nagley and suggested an essay competition, open to the students of the whole high school, for which I would provide several prizes, and which I was happy to help assess. I also told Mr. Nagley that I thought the Moriah high school should teach modern Jewish history.[76]

Nagley approved this suggestion in April 1975 and Caplan devised five questions, one of which dealt with family experiences during the Holocaust and another with family immigration experiences. The first group submitted their entries in January 1976. When the Modern Jewish history course was introduced in the College in 1976, this competition was made a compulsory part of Year 10 Jewish history assessments and has remained so until the present day.

In 1976 many of the students' parents had survived the Holocaust, but in most cases this was the first time they had spoken about their experiences to their children. In her study of Holocaust remembrance in Australia, Judith Berman described the initial reactions as follows: 'during the initial years of the competition students did not know how to cope with so difficult a topic: they were both "attracted and revolted" by the task of inquiring into Holocaust suffering'.[77] When Moriah Year 10 students first began to talk to their parents about their Holocaust experiences in the late 1970s, it was a difficult and painful process. With time, the Year 10 essay competition gradually gained a momentum of its own, making 'the difficult task of interviewing survivors more acceptable to the students'.[78] Students from those early years, who initially objected so strongly to interviewing their parents about the Holocaust, are now grateful that they did. As one of the prize winners of 1977 commented, if she had not questioned her elderly father about his previous life for the essay competition she would never have known about his first wife and her own baby half-brother who perished in Hungary during the Holocaust, and about whom her father had never spoken. As her father died only two or three years later, it was good that she questioned him when she did.[79] This was a common experience of many of the Year 10 students whose parents, and often even more so grandparents with the third generation, spoke of their Holocaust experiences for the very first time for the essay competition.

From the 1980s, Holocaust memory has continued as an important part of the College's curriculum. Each year *Yom Hashoah* is commemorated in a meaningful way. The Year 10 Jewish History programme has continued to incorporate a substantial section on the Holocaust and the essay competition has continued to include many moving Holocaust memoirs. Since 1982, the prize winners have read their entries at a special meeting of the Australian Jewish Historical Society convened at Moriah College. Over time the number of lessons devoted to teaching the Holocaust at Moriah has increased so that about half of the Year 10 Jewish history syllabus is dedicated to this topic. Other Jewish day schools across Australia have also increased the amount of time dedicated to Year 10 and in some cases to Year 11 to the teaching of the Holocaust.

There are a number of reasons for this expansion of Holocaust teaching at Moriah College, and indeed across the entire Australian Jewish school system. Berman has argued that it is the result of a fusion of three interrelated developments. First, she argues that there has been a major investment of finance and resources in Jewish education since the late 1970s. Teacher education programmes were introduced at the University of Sydney and Monash University; national Jewish Education conferences were convened, the first held in 1988, discussing issues relating to the teaching of the Holocaust; and the formation of the Principals' Association in 1989. These developments, together with migration from South Africa that strengthened the Jewish Studies teaching staff, have allowed for a more systematic teaching approach to Jewish history and the

Holocaust. Second, this development must be seen as part of a worldwide trend of increasing awareness of the importance of transmission of Holocaust memory, which in Australia started with the 1985 gathering of Holocaust survivors held in Sydney, and the development of Holocaust museums in the 1980s and early 1990s in Melbourne, Sydney and Perth. Finally, there has been a growth of specialist teachers as a result of the opening of the Winter Institute for Educators from Abroad at Yad Vashem in 1987, specifically for Australian teachers. This resulted from the urging of Professor Colin Tatz, who continued to lead groups until 1997. Local experts such as Mark Baker have also emerged.[80] In addition, concerns over Holocaust denial, which began in the 1970s, encouraged survivors to talk about their experiences. As one leading Holocaust survivor put it, it is important for survivors to talk, particularly in the face of Holocaust denial, for they can say 'I was there; I know'.[81] The Australian war crimes debate also attracted significant media attention between 1986 and 1992, adding to the awareness of the need to teach about the Holocaust.

There is no doubt that the strengthening of Moriah's programme in Holocaust Studies is a result of these factors. It has also been fostered through the official leadership of the New South Wales Jewish Board of Deputies, which has continually expanded its Holocaust awareness programmes during Holocaust Remembrance week, and which, since the opening of the new Moriah campus in 1994, holds its annual commemoration ceremony at the Moriah auditorium.[82]

Moriah College's Jewish history teachers do not share 'the concerns of some Jewish educationalists in the United States about the dangers of the possible development of a skewed or negative Jewish identity in the shadow of the Holocaust'.[83] From the programme's initiation, there has been a belief that teaching the Holocaust as part of the broad span of Jewish history, with all its diversity, prevents this from happening. Not everyone in Australia supports this chronological approach as part of a Jewish history programme. For example, Professor Tatz has:

> decried the teaching of the Holocaust and its lessons within 'Jewish Studies', which he claims causes students to 'perceive Jewish life as somehow extra-curricular'! He argues that Holocaust education should be included in mainstream disciplinary teaching as 'there can be no monopoly of ownership of an event that confronts humankind'.[84]

Also, whilst Australian Jewry is largely a strongly Zionist community, most Jewish history teachers do not support making too close a connection between the Holocaust and the creation of the modern state of Israel, arguing that the Jewish state was created by a variety of different factors, with the events of the Holocaust being only one of these.[85]

Survivors and their Financial Support

The development of Moriah during this second stage cannot be understood without a discussion of the financial contribution of the refugees and survivors. In the late 1970s, the College experienced rapid growth and needed to expand its facilities. The College Board managed to lease the site of a discarded government hospital and in 1985 and 1992 held two major capital appeals to finance a new purpose-built primary and high school. The majority of donors to these two appeals were refugees and survivors from Europe and Shanghai who had brought with them initiative and new industrial skills. Most had reacted to the challenges of a new land with hard work, drive and enterprise, so that by the late 1970s they had become financially secure, with some achieving significant financial success. They were deeply concerned with maintaining Jewish culture and tradition, and believed that the only way to achieve this was through Jewish education at school level. They had witnessed not only the loss of their families during the Holocaust but also the destruction of the rich Jewish culture in Europe, and wanted to support its rebirth in Sydney, Australia. Contributing to a magnificent new Jewish primary and high school seemed a most appropriate memorial to the decimation of the Jewish centres of scholarship in Europe, as well as to lost families.[86]

This financial contribution demonstrated that, despite the horrors of the Holocaust, most refugees and survivors wanted to ensure Jewish continuity through Jewish education. Indeed, the awareness of remembrance of the Holocaust, as discussed by Sharon Kangisser Cohen and Avril Alba in this volume, corresponds with the rapid development of Moriah College during this second phase. It is not coincidental that the new Moriah College was completed in 1994, the same year that the Sanctum of Remembrance was opened at the Sydney Jewish Museum. Unlike the Rosetrees, described by John Docker in his discussion of Patrick White's *Riders of the Chariots* in this volume, most refugees and survivors were committed to Jewish survival and wished to preserve their heritage and memory in their newly found Australian homeland.

Conclusions

From its beginnings, most of the parents who supported Moriah College were refugees from Nazism and Holocaust. They were only too conscious that Hitler and his followers had tried to obliterate the Jews of Europe. This destructive process also meant that: 'Ancient centres of Jewish culture and learning in Poland and Russia were wiped out, sages, Torah scholars and Jewish intellectuals were sacrificed to the monstrous ideology of a *Judenrein* world'.[87] The newcomers rejected Hitler's desire to destroy the Jewish world and they worked hard to create a renaissance of Jewish life in Australia through an effective system of Jewish schooling. This renaissance was facilitated by distributions from German restitution payments to Moriah College for its building programme. At the same time, the survivors suppressed their memories of the past, and their children grew up with the 'code of silence', which was also reflected in the school's curriculum, which excluded the topic of the Holocaust.

A second transformation occurred when the children of refugees and survivors, the second generation, began to enter adulthood and some became high school teachers at Moriah. From the mid-1970s Holocaust education has become part of the school's curriculum, with Moriah College being a pioneer in Australia in this endeavour. When undertaking their major Year 10 family roots project, students were faced with an initial reluctance of their parents to talk about their experiences, but both external and internal factors gradually changed this situation. Many survivors began to share their experiences with their children and grandchildren, as well as with the wider community at Holocaust commemorations and at talks in museums. Thus, the Holocaust has had an ongoing impact on the school both in terms of its student population, their family background and its educational programme. In the 1940s, surviving Auschwitz was a motivating factor for the founders of the school; their children and grandchildren continue to have their Jewish identity moulded by the shadows of this catastrophe.

Thus, the silence of Jewish survivors in Australia in the 1950s and 1960s, and the breaking of that silence beginning in the late 1970s as discussed in this case study indicate that this phenomenon was largely due to coping with the personal trauma and generational shifts as the second generation sought to understand their parents' stories. This produces a different picture to that presented by American Jewish historian, Peter Novick, who argued that 'political concerns shape talk' in his 1999 book on American and the Holocaust.[88] In a critique of Novick's book, Maurice Kriegel stressed that:

> In the quarter century following on the Second World War, a series of elements seem to come together in a similar fashion in the three countries in question [Israel, the United States and France], to create a sentiment of relative amnesia: these are, first, the attitude of the Jews themselves, for whom the direct experience of the Holocaust was rapidly cast within rather rigid matrices of interpretation that were more or less incapable of keeping this felt experience alive; second, the fact that post-War states were more inclined to a sort of general national celebration than to maintaining a sense of the specificity of the Jewish genocide; and third, the spectre of anti-Semitisms both present and past.[89]

As the story of Moriah College in Sydney, and indeed the Australian Jewish experience has demonstrated, there is a fourth factor which needs to be brought into the academic debate: that is the impact of dealing with trauma over successive generations, starting with the code of silence from the first generation which led to the need to unpack that experience in the second generation, a need which was further strengthened with the third generation as grandparents opened up to their grandchildren. It is no coincidence that Kathy Grinblat entitled her collection of reflections of second-generation descendants in Australia 'Children of the Shadows',[90] as dealing with the shadows of Auschwitz has had a significant impact on the post-war evolution of Australian Jewry.

ACKNOWLEDGEMENTS

I would like to thank Professor Konrad Kwiet, Roth Lecturer in Holocaust Studies at the University of Sydney, for reading this article and making valuable comments.

NOTES

1. See P.Y. Medding, *From Assimilation to Group Survival: A Political and Sociological Study of an Australian Jewish Community* (Melbourne: Cheshire, 1968).
2. They included Kathy Grinblat (English), Sophie Gelski (History), Anne Joshua and Evie Satmari later Appfelbaum (both Mathematics), with the latter two still teaching at the school in 2006.
3. Mark Baker, 'As If: Born Under the Sign of the Shoah', in Michael Fagenblat, Melanie Landau and Nathan Wolski (eds.), *New Under the Sun: Jewish Australians on Religion, Politics and Culture* (Melbourne: Black Inc, 2006), p.250.
4. Ibid.
5. Ibid., p.254.
6. See Suzanne D. Rutland and Sophie Caplan, *With One Voice: the History of the NSW Jewish Board of Deputies* (Darlington, Sydney: Australian Jewish Historical Society, 1998); Judith E. Berman, *Holocaust Remembrance in Australian Jewish Communities, 1945–2000* (Crawley: University of Western Australia Press, 2001); and Suzanne D. Rutland, *If You Will It, It Is No Dream: The Moriah Story 1943–2003* (Sydney: Playright Publishing, 2003).
7. Daniel J. Elazar with Peter Medding, *Jewish Communities in Frontier Societies: Argentina, Australia and South Africa*, (New York: Holmes & Meier, 1983).
8. As quoted in ibid, p.10.
9. Suzanne D. Rutland, *The Jews in Australia* (Cambridge and Melbourne: Cambridge University Press, 2005), pp.34–35.
10. In 1903 the Reverend J.H. Landau, minister at the Great Synagogue, Sydney, commented that 'it happens that the community as a whole is more English than the Jews of England', see *Hebrew Standard of Australasia* (*HSA*), 6 November 1908.
11. Amos Elon, *The Pity of it All: A Portrait of the German-Jewish Epoch, 1743–1933* (New York, Picador, 2002), p.260.
12. Elazar with Medding, *Jewish Communities in Frontier Societies*, p.10.
13. Elon, *The Pity of it All*, p.261.
14. Rutland, *The Jews in Australia*, pp.153–4.
15. This meeting was held on 16 March 1942 and was chaired by Leon Waxman, with Rabbis Levi and Bernard Frampton, Simon Gilovitz, Jacob and Maurice Allen, Chaim Scher (later Sher), Myer Wise and Roseman present. Apologies were noted from Davis, Ellitt and Baffsky and Messrs Simons and Sobel were noted as absent. Abraham Rabinovitch was not present at this first meeting. Minute Book of the Talmud Torah of Sydney. At the second meeting held on 5 April 1942 Dr Isaac N. Steinberg and M. Davis were noted as being present as visitors by invitation.
16. See Benzion Patkin, *The Dunera Internees* (New South Wales: Cassell Australia, 1979); and Cyril Pearl, *The Dunera Scandal* (Sydney: Angus and Robertson, 1983).
17. Konrad Kwiet, '"Be Patient and Reasonable!" The Internment of German-Jewish Refugees in Australia', in Konrad Kwiet and John A. Moses (eds.), 'On Being a German-Jewish Refugee in Australia', Special Edition of *The Australian Journal of Politics and History*, Vol.XXXI, No.1 (1985), pp.61–77.
18. Blumenthal was born on 16 May 1915 at Fulda, Germany. See Sophie Caplan, 'The Jewish Day School Movement in New South Wales', M.Ed. (Hons) thesis, University of Sydney, 1974, p.81.
19. See Elchanan Blumenthal, *Trials and Challenges* (Jerusalem: Jerusalem Academy Publishing, 1994), p.56; and Caplan, 'The Jewish Day School Movement', pp.32–6.

20. Blumenthal, *Trials and Challenges*, pp.73–4.
21. Ibid., p.74.
22. Ibid.
23. This refers to primary and high school, as compared with afternoon classes in Jewish education.
24. See Herman Wouk, *This is My God: The Jewish Way of Life* (New York: Pocket Books, 1976), p.292. Wouk argues that whilst this question can be debated, it was clear that one cannot impart Jewish knowledge in a couple of hours of part-time Jewish education a week.
25. Ibid.
26. Interview with Rabbi Dr Israel Porush, 26 January 1970, based on written questions and notes.
27. *HSA*, 31 May 1942. At this meeting it was moved that Abraham Rabinovitch and Simon Burns, an English solicitor who had migrated to Australia, be co-opted onto the committee.
28. *HSA*, 20 August 1942.
29. *HSA*, 27 August 1942. Rabbi H.E. Blumenthal told Sophie Caplan that he had not written this article.
30. *HSA*, 3 September 1942.
31. Ibid.
32. Ibid.
33. Caplan, 'The Jewish Day School Movement', p.66.
34. *HSA*, 25 February 1943.
35. Ibid.
36. Ibid.
37. Ibid.
38. M. Breuer, *Modernity within Tradition: The Social History of Orthodox Jewry in Imperial Germany* (New York: Columbia University Press 1992).
39. Minutes of the Annual General Meeting, Sunday 30 May 1943.
40. *HSA*, 1 April 1943.
41. Caplan, 'The Jewish Day School Movement', p.103.
42. For a detailed discussion of these men see ibid., Chapter VI: 'Rabinovitch and the Board of the NBJDS&K', pp.377–423.
43. Ibid., p.111.
44. Blumenthal, *Trials and Challenges*, p.81.
45. Caplan, 'The Jewish Day School Movement', p.111.
46. Minutes of the North Bondi Jewish Day School and Kindergarten, 15 July 1944.
47. Minutes, 9 January 1945.
48. Ronald W. Zweig, *German Reparations and the Jewish World: A History of the Claims Conference* (London: Frank Cass, 2001).
49. Kathy Grinblat (ed.), 'Introduction', *Children of the Shadows: Voices of the Second Generation* (Crawley, Western Australia and Montrose, Victoria: University of Western Australia Press with Benchmark Publications, 2002), p.1.
50. Focus Group Interview, September 2001.
51. Ibid.
52. Ibid.
53. Rutland and Caplan, *With One Voice*, p.318.
54. Ruth Wajnry, *The Silence: How Tragedy Shapes Talk* (Sydney: Allen & Unwin, 2001), p.6.
55. Ibid., p.13.
56. Mark Raphael Baker, *A Journey Through Memory: The Fiftieth Gate* (Sydney: HarperCollins, 1997).
57. Mark Baker, 'As If: Born Under the Sign of the Shoah', p.250.
58. Ibid.
59. Sophie Gelski and Jenny Wajsenberg, 'Teaching the Holocaust Today', in Konrad Kwiet and Juergen Matthaus (eds.), *Contemporary Responses to the Holocaust* (Westport, CT and London: Praeger, 2005), p.225.
60. Ibid.
61. Ibid., p.224.
62. The first allocations to Australian Jewry from the Conference for Jewish Material Claims against Germany were made in 1954. See Suzanne D. Rutland, *Edge of the Diaspora: Two Centuries of Jewish Settlement in Australia* (Sydney: Brandl & Schlesinger, 2001), pp.338–9 Appendix III, pp.411–12.
63. Zweig, *German Reparations*, p.107.
64. 'Official Communiqué No 1, 4 August 1953, Third Plenary Assembly, World Jewish Congress, Geneva, p.18, in 'World Jewish Congress – Speeches, Press Releases, Newspaper Cuttings, 1953, Z6/751, Central Zionist Archives, Jerusalem.
65. Zweig, *German Reparations*, p.179.

66. Mark Uveeler to Herbert Katzki, 1 August 1957, Geneva II, Box No 304B, File No 5, American Joint Distribution Committee Archives, Ramat Gan, Jerusalem.
67. The school remained in this location until April 1994.
68. See Claims Conference Files, Boxes C1–C9, Archive of Australian Judaica, Fisher Library, University of Sydney.
69. See Appendix III, Rutland, *Edge of the Diaspora*, p.412. On 16 February 1965 the 1961 Claims Conference grant of £A2500 was transferred to the ECAJ to pay Moriah College, 'Australia: Sydney, Perth and Bondi', Geneva 1, Box No 44A, File No, 35, JDC Archives, Givat Ram, Jerusalem.
70. Berman *Holocaust Remembrance*, p.79.
71. Ibid., p.80.
72. Ibid., p.82.
73. Interview with Max Wahlhaus, Sydney, 13 March 2002.
74. Berman, *Holocaust Remembrance*, p.93.
75. Ibid., pp.94–6.
76. 'The Origins of the Hans Kimmel Awards', Australian Jewish Historical Society (AJHS) Newsletter, 69, September 2005.
77. Berman, *Holocaust Remembrance*, p.83.
78. Ibid.
79. 'The origins of the Hans Kimmel Awards', AJHS Newsletter, 69, September 2005.
80. Berman, *Holocaust Remembrance*, pp.87–8.
81. Interview with Marika Weinberger, past president of the Australian Association of Jewish Holocaust Survivors in Sydney (1990 to 2004), Sydney 1998.
82. Rutland and Caplan, *With One Voice*, Chapter 12, pp.317–43.
83. Berman, *Holocaust Remembrance*, p.93.
84. Ibid.
85. Ibid., pp.96–7.
86. *Australian Jewish Times* (*AJT*), 26 April 1984.
87. Ibid.
88. Peter Novick, *The Holocaust in American Life* (Boston: Houghton Mifflin, 1999).
89. Maurice Kriegel, 'The Holocaust and Collective Memory: Three Pathways', EHESS, Paris, www.celat.ulaval.ca/histoire.memoire/histoire/cape2/kriegel.htm (accessed 2 July 2006).
90. See Grinblat, *Children of the Shadows*.

Distant Reverberations: Australian Responses to the Trial of Adolf Eichmann

DAVID RITTER

In early January 1960, swastikas and antisemitic slogans were daubed by night on a variety of Jewish buildings in Melbourne, Sydney and Canberra, following a pattern of similar vandalism in Europe and North America.[1] The defacement was shocking and prompted a number of demonstrations, as well as considerable public comment. Writing in the Australian journal *The Observer* in late January 1960, broadcaster and newspaper editor Eric Baume commented that '[s]o much' had been written about antisemitism in recent weeks, that it was time for him as 'a Jew to discuss the matter impersonally'.[2] Baume went on to 'debunk' antisemitism, but did so with some reservations, emphasising his own family's effective assimilation and suggesting that it was best left to 'Australian ex-servicemen of the Jewish religion; men who have the right to speak for their country'.[3] Baume seemed to implicitly accept that enough force remained in antisemitic discourse to make it necessary for him to have to stress Jewish loyalty to the Australian nation. Baume's article was the first in a sequence of items dealing with antisemitism but evincing some degree of ambivalence that punctuated *The Observer* in the course of 1960. For instance, an article by Hugo Wolfsohn, a Jewish political scientist who had fled the Nazis, condemned antisemitism in unequivocal terms, but the magazine then gave a number of writers from the fringe right a very considerable right of reply.[4] The magazine also published a letter from émigré Czech novelist V.L. Borin containing reference to 'intense Jewish propaganda against Hitlerism' as if there were two sides to an argument, both of which were equally capable of excessive views.[5] The sense that emerges from contents of *The Observer* is that in 1960, opposing antisemitism remained in some sense a matter of live debate, rather than a given of civic and intellectual discourse.

What is so arresting about the antisemitism debates in *The Observer* in 1960 is what is missing. The mass-murder of European Jewry was mentioned on multiple occasions, with one lonely correspondent even writing that '[n]o man, after the world's greatest massacre, could possibly accept in silence any antisemitic outburst, however small or insignificant it may appear',[6] but what is absent is 'the Holocaust', understood as a distinct phenomenon going by that single name, of extraordinary moral, political and philosophical gravity and bearing of no discursive abbreviation or interdiction. Instead, such references as are made to the extermination of Europe's Jewry (by Baume, for instance) are made in passing and some times in language that seems lacking in gravity or solemnity.[7]

What the commentary in *The Observer* strongly illustrates is that in 1960 'the Holocaust' did not yet exist in Australia. Indeed, prior to the 1960s, few articles of any kind had been published on the terrible fate of Europe's Jews and there was virtually no creative prose or poetry on the subject.[8] Tellingly, in the first volume of Sir Paul Hasluck's official history, *Australia in the War of 1939–45: The Government and the People 1939–41* which was published in 1952, not once in 644 pages was the antisemitic character of the Nazi regime mentioned.[9] Not a single 'survivor' autobiography or biography had been published since the ending of the Second World War.[10] Even within a publication like the *Australian Jewish Historical Society Journal and Proceedings*, the extermination of the Jews of Europe was barely a subject of notice. In 1960 the annihilation of European Jewry simply did not hold the position in Australian intellectual, cultural and popular discourse that it would subsequently come to occupy.[11]

The apparent Australian disinterest in the murder of Europe's Jews[12] may be explained by reference to a number of broad forces at work of which the persistence of sectarianism and some largely genteel antisemitism was only one factor.[13] The war with Japan (and the friendly 'invasion' by American forces) figured more prominently in Australia, in both popular and elite understandings, acting to obscure the far-off conflict with the Nazis. Australian troops had after all played a comparatively small part in fighting the European War and when they had actually engaged with their German counterparts, most lengthily in the North African campaign, the Axis soldiers behaved more or less according to the rules of warfare, particularly when compared to the experience of fighting the Japanese.[14] Perhaps, too, the Australian experience of the conflict was not conducive to feelings of easy superiority to Nazi racism. The Pacific War had at times been explicitly racialised, both as a matter of national political rhetoric as well as within the minds of many individual soldiers.[15] The bitter clash with Japan was understood in part as a struggle to preserve 'White Australia'. Finally, by 1960 the end of the war with Germany was 15 years in the distant past – one Liberal parliamentarian called it 'ancient history'[16] – and for the anticommunist mainstream there were new 'totalitarians' to worry about, in the form of the communist regimes in Russia and China. In any event, the ethic of the 1950s was to 'look forward' and 'move on', living with Cold War anxieties while making the most of rising prosperity under stable conservative government.[17]

In May 1960 the lack of any particular ongoing interest in the facts of the murder of Europe's Jews was challenged by reports of the sensational capturing of Adolf Eichmann by Mossad agents in Argentina. Brought to Israel, Eichmann was tried before the District Court of Israel in Jerusalem in proceedings which ran from 10 April to 14 August 1961, with judgment then reserved until December, at which time the accused was found guilty and sentenced to death. An appeal and a petition for clemency were both unsuccessful and Eichmann was hanged on 31 May 1962. In Australia, the saga was reported extensively in the media, including multiple front page stories in the quality papers and various related feature articles. A significant percentage of Australian households already owned televisions by 1961 and the Eichmann trial was one of the top news stories of the year.[18] The televising of the proceedings almost certainly marked the 'first time that the Holocaust received prominent, extended television coverage in the form of news reports, public affairs programs, documentaries, and dramas aired over a period of months'.[19] All three Melbourne TV stations for example, planned comprehensive news coverage 'including film highlights shot inside the courtroom'.[20] Such a popular source as *Australian TV: The First 25 Years* noted the proceedings in Jerusalem as one of the prominent news features for 1961.[21] The ubiquity of the Eichmann trial as a media event is also indicated by *The Bulletin* attributing two quotes of the year to the accused.[22]

If the pre-existing cultural mood towards the extermination of Europe's Jews in Australia was one of disengagement, what were the cultural consequences of the confrontation with the Holocaust precipitated by the Eichmann trial? This article describes the way in which the Eichmann trial was viewed and understood in Australia through analysis of reports in the newspapers and having regard to the public reactions of intellectuals and parliamentarians. The point of the analysis is not simply to describe 'representations' of Eichmann, but rather to test the hypothesis that the trial constituted a watershed in 'the making of the Holocaust' in Australia. American historian Peter Novick has explained that the Eichmann trial was a pivotal event in the US context, because coverage of the case 'effectively broke fifteen years of near silence' in public life on the extermination of the Jews, after which there emerged 'a distinct *thing* called 'the Holocaust' – an event in its own right, not simply a subdivision of Nazi barbarism'.[23] This article seeks in part to test the trans-national applicability of Novick's analysis by considering the impact of the Eichmann trial in developing Australian cultural understandings of the Holocaust.

Reporting the Trial

Although the trial of Eichmann was widely covered in the Australian media, the vast majority of newspaper reports were the product of syndicated news services.[24] Typically for any long running story, exposure peaked with particular milestones in the proceedings but dwindled to nothing in the interim.[25] By the middle of May 1961 the trial had disappeared from the news, suddenly re-emerging when there were dramatic developments, or perhaps when other news was particularly 'slow'. Australian television also participated in a more general public narration of relevant events by scheduling other features which took advantage of the topicality of the Nazis. One commercial station, for example, screened the 1944 American film *The Hitler Gang* (dir. John Farrow, USA, 1944) to coincide with the beginning of the trial.[26]

Among the print media, the *Sydney Morning Herald*'s coverage of the Eichmann hearing was distinguished by a series of articles written by professor of law at Sydney University, Julius Stone.[27] In 1960 Stone's public stature (and notoriety) was well established as a new kind of public intellectual, transcending the boundaries of the academy, with regular appearances as a pundit on radio and television.[28] Stone was appointed as an observer of the Eichmann trial by the International Commission of Jurists and he attended some weeks of the proceedings, which provided the basis for his pieces in the *Sydney Morning Herald* as well as a subsequent more formal report.[29] Stone's commentaries were by far the most extensive contemporary response to the Eichmann affair of any Australian intellectual, albeit one whose 'Australianness' was deeply ambiguous, complicated not only by his Jewishness and Zionism, but more general 'Europeanness' (Stone had Lithuanian émigré parents and his first serious academic work had dealt with the 'minorities question' in Eastern Europe),[30] a stint in New Zealand and a manifest distaste towards certain ordinarily valorised cultural institutions and traditions of the 'mother country', England.[31] Stone was acutely aware that the reliability of his account might be attacked on the basis that he was Jewish and therefore more prone to being 'emotionally *engagé* with the prosecution'.[32] Stone also self-consciously watched the trial 'as a lawyer' which, intellectual breadth and commitment to legal realism notwithstanding, inevitably attenuated his perceptions to some extent.[33]

Eichmann's physical appearance and personal behaviour was the subject of much reportage in the Australian media, including by Stone. Numerous pictures were printed in the broadsheets, particularly early on in the trial, including one sensationalist bare upper-body shot of Eichmann undergoing a medical examination in gaol.[34] Editors no doubt were interested in the face (and torso) of the monster, but the impression is of there being frustratingly little to report because of the soon to become infamous physical ordinariness of the accused.[35] One newspaper report described Eichmann as merely 'sallow-faced and clerk-like' while Stone thought the charged man resembled 'a minor public servant hearing grievances from the citizenry'.[36] The absence of a dramatic physical spectacle seemed to drive observers to the most banal of observations. As the trial progressed, so the newspapers reported the physical impact on Eichmann, who had 'aged visibly' and was seen to 'occasionally [screw] up his eyes behind horn-rimmed spectacles' with 'an expression of drawn concern' that had not been 'seen on his face before'.[37] According to Stone, when the evidence was at its most appalling, Eichmann might 'patiently reclasp his hands' but there was 'no other sign or movement either of face or body'; however he saw no evidence to vindicate the rumour 'that during some of the most terrible testimony' the accused was to be seen 'picking his nose'.[38]

The Political Response

On 12 April 1961 Senator Victor Vincent asked whether, '[i]n view of the very high degree of international importance' attached to the Eichmann hearing, Australia was 'represented by an accredited observer', to which Senator and later Prime Minister of Australia, John Gorton, replied that Australia's 'accredited representative in Israel' was a certain Mr McMillan and that Australian diplomats would be 'afforded opportunities to be present at the trial'.[39] In general, though, the hearing in Jerusalem was not something that particularly interested the Federal Parliament.[40] However, other events in 1961 did give cause for the Australian government to articulate a position in relation to Second World War criminals more generally, which sheds light on how the Eichmann trial was viewed and understood. In March 1961 Sir Garfield Barwick, then Acting Minister for External Affairs, addressed the House of Representatives to outline the government's response to the USSR's request for the extradition of one Ervin Viks, a migrant naturalised as an Australian citizen, whom the Soviets wished to try for alleged serious war crimes committed in Estonia during the Second World War.[41] Barwick, a brilliant lawyer who would later go on to be appointed Chief Justice of the High Court of Australia, concluded that as Australia had no extradition agreement with the Soviet Union there was no legal obligation to either extradite or prosecute Viks. However, Barwick elaborated in Parliament, 'all questions of legal obligation apart', the time had come 'to close the chapter' and to desist from any further pursuit of Second World War criminals, because while an 'utter abhorrence' was 'felt by Australians for those offences against humanity', there was a greater countervailing imperative:

> the right of this nation, by receiving people into this country, to enable men to turn their backs on past bitternesses and to make a new life for themselves and for their families in a happier community. This has formed a precious part of the heritage of the West, in which Australia has an honourable share.[42]

Although he did not mention Eichmann by name, Barwick explicitly distinguished 'the case in Israel' and stressed that he did not wish 'for one moment' to 'be thought to be critical of any nation' which felt a 'duty' to exercise the 'right' to make 'a different decision in any particular instance' and continue to legally pursue war criminals.[43]

The proposition advanced by Barwick that immigrants – including alleged war criminals – should 'turn their backs' on the past and lead 'new lives' was an expression of the prevailing philosophy of assimilationism, which envisaged that non-British migrants would abandon pre-existing cultural identities and adopt 'Australian' socio-cultural norms.[44] Policy makers attempted to attract immigrants who would, they thought, be the most easily assimilable and some social scientists set about trying to develop scales of 'Australianness' against which assimilation could be measured.[45] Assimilation remained the dominant policy paradigm in relation to immigration until the turn to 'multiculturalism' in the 1970s. Within assimilationist discourse, considerable emphasis was placed on the preservation of Australia's peaceable political traditions, which meant that the partisan allegiances of old world politics must be abandoned by individual migrants.[46] In declaring that had the law been different and 'a choice had been necessary to resolve the matter' then Australia's 'right of asylum must have prevailed' and those who had been 'allowed to make their homes here must be able to live, in security, new lives under the rule of law', Barwick was putting a lawyer's turn on the established ideology of assimilation.[47]

Apart from wanting all migrants to become peaceable New Australians, there was also another reason to 'close the chapter'. The Australian government was never inclined to surrender a former Estonian accused of war crimes to the Soviet Union – the putative enemy in the midst of the Cold War – particularly given the controversy associated with the annexation of the Baltic States and the general pall which hung over the justice system in communist states. In extolling the Commonwealth's right to extend asylum to former wrongdoers, Barwick contrasted Australia with nations that knew 'nothing of the rule of law which protects the liberty of the people', most obviously implying the regimes of the Eastern Bloc.[48] Anticommunist (or ultra-nationalist or fascist) post-war refugees from Eastern Europe had also in some instances developed strong links with the Liberal Party and right-wing émigré 'Balts' might well be considered as political allies in the face of attacks and demands from the Soviet Union.

Eichmann and the Cold War of the Australian Intellectuals

While Australians did not experience civic and cultural repression of the severity that occurred in America during the Cold War, the prevailing political conditions of the period nevertheless did have a 'chilling' effect on the standard and content of much intellectual debate. As literary historian John McLaren has summarised, on both right and left, rhetoric was used that 'demonised' political opponents and 'excluded the possibility of a reasoned debate', locking the protagonists 'into positions of mutual incomprehension while providing an ideological cloak for the intellectual paralysis of government and public life'.[49] Communist and anticommunist intellectuals and other commentators offered radically different accounts of society embedded in the different ideological systems, which admitted of little compromise or civil dialogue between them. Accordingly, the overwhelming tendency was for major public events, like the Eichmann trial, to be interpreted *a priori* according to the precepts of communism and anticommunism. The overall effect was one of de-contextualisation and flattening of analysis on both sides, as the exposition of theory was given priority over both inconvenient evidence and situational particularity.

Among anticommunists, one analytical product of the Cold War was the emergence of theory which suggested that fascism and communism were actually expressions of a single underlying political system known as 'totalitarianism', characterised by all the institutions and individuals within a society having been totally subverted to one-party state interest. The thesis of totalitarianism offered the dominant non-communist interpretation of Nazism in 1960–61 and provided a ready intellectual framework within which to understand the Eichmann trial. Stone, for example, though hardly a vulgar Cold War thinker,[50] implicitly accepted that totalitarianism produced a 'dehumanisation of human relations'[51] in characterising Eichmann as a new kind of man who felt 'no relation of common humanity as they kill other men, pursuant to a coldly calculated plan'.[52] Being a lawyer, in the absence of specific evidence Stone did not feel able to speculate about Eichmann's personal motivations, but in accepting the totalising claims of the Nazi state at face value, what Stone thought most significant was the dehumanisation of the accused. In an 'age of totalitarian ideologies',[53] Stone believed that Eichmann wore 'the face that man shall have' if 'Cain and Abel cease to know each other as brothers even in homicidal strife'.[54] 'Totalitarian man' lacked faith, compassion, empathy, doubt or ambiguity of motive.

Eichmann had served the Nazi state, but that regime had been utterly destroyed in 1945, leaving the most powerful remaining 'totalitarian' government as the USSR. Understood not as a 'German' or a 'Nazi', but as a 'totalitarian', Eichmann could be implicitly compared to the regime communists of the early 1960s, with the result that the nauseating events narrated in Jerusalem became a warning about the frightening potential of the Soviet Union. *The Bulletin* argued explicitly that the Eichmann trial was in effect more about the Soviet Union than Nazi Germany because 'far more than a matter of punishing old "crimes"', the proceedings could establish a 'precedent for dealing with the new type of totalitarian murderers'.[55] Eichmann was a product of the 'totalitarian' Nazi state, so his trial could be interpreted as relating to the dangers of 'totalitarianism' generally, making the proceedings an obvious source for reflecting anticommunist sentiment.[56]

While anticommunists relied upon totalitarian analysis to render the Eichmann trial as a demonstration of the evils of communism, their opponents in the miniscule Australian hard left argued that the proceedings in Jerusalem could only be correctly understood through an appreciation of 'the facts of class struggle'.[57] Writing in *The Observer* in May 1960, Stalinist novelist Judah Waten argued that the 'whole course of modern history' demonstrated 'that there is a certain species of anti-Communism which slides irresistibly into antisemitism'.[58] A year later the communist and noted jazz aficionado Harry Stein asserted that the crimes of Eichmann were above all a 'creation' of 'anti-communism'.[59] Although approving of the trial of Eichmann (and in Stein's case explicitly noting the contrast with Barwick's failure to act in relation to Viks),[60] Australian communists claimed that the very nature of the hearing was superficial, in that it failed to account for the structural role of private enterprise in supporting fascism. What was clear, maintained Queensland trade unionist Kath Thomas, was that while Eichmann had been dealt with as he deserved, 'the big monopolies' which had put the Nazis in power remained unpunished and still constituted the 'the main threat to world peace'.[61] Stein discerned hypocrisy in the trial because the same big capitalism which had put Hitler in power and produced Eichmann, now found political expression in a 'neo-Nazi West German Government staffed by war criminals in high places', supported not only by 'the US and other Western imperialists', but by the 'puppet' state of Israel.[62]

The Cold War intellectual divide also had fundamental consequences in terms of explaining the origins and significance of antisemitism. Among anticommunists, the Nazi's campaign against Jews was likely to be interpreted as a product of totalitarianism, meaning that the abiding contemporary concern should not be tracking down Second World War criminals, but heightened sensitivities about persecution in the Soviet Union.[63] At the height of the Eichmann trial, *The Melbourne Age* reported the unlikely comment of 'Rabbi Richard Hertz, of Detroit', that 'Jews behind the iron curtain were in greater danger' than they had been from Nazism, because they were facing 'spiritual genocide'.[64] On the other hand, Australian communists specifically repudiated the idea that antisemitism was about race rather than class, seeing the fate of the Jews as bound up with the reactionary tactics of radicalised capitalism. Communist educationalist W.E. Gollan argued that antisemitism was principally strategic in nature, providing a useful 'tactic for launching an attack on the whole labour movement'.[65] Linking the 1930s in Germany to the vandalism in Australia at the beginning of 1960, Gollan claimed that Jews were 'the stalking horse' behind which an attack was 'being prepared on the trade unions, the parties of the working class, and the apparatus of popular rule'.[66] Another communist writer, Vin Bourke, asserted that 'while one would expect complete unity among the Jewish people in the struggle against Nazism', the very fact that the head of the World Jewish Congress had recently announced that his principal current concern was antisemitism in the Soviet Union demonstrated that 'representatives of the reactionary ruling class' among Jews were prepared to act against the interests of workers, even of their own kind.[67]

The Silence of the New Australians

Although Australia had not been occupied by the Nazis, the massive post-war immigration programme ensured that among the national population by 1961 there were large numbers of people who had direct experience of fascist rule in Europe.[68] However, while the migrant population included many who had been in the camps, or experienced other horrific events at the hands of the Nazis, the memories of 'New Australians' rarely featured in the public response to the

Eichmann trial. A rare exception was provided by an exposé in the *Sun-Herald* in June 1961, which featured two 'tough, strong and mentally robust ex-concentration camp victims' who 'came to Australia to get a second start': one, former Polish pilot Richard Markowski, had become 'one of Sydney's best cooks' and the other, who was not identified by name or ethnicity, was 'working round the clock, building a successful carpet cleaning business'.[69] Though neither fine cuisine nor working too hard may have been considered as quintessentially 'Australian' in 1961 (if Nino Culotta was any guide), the clear implication is that both the men described were successfully 'assimilating'.[70] The article was highly critical of the West German government for hold-ups in getting compensation to those who had been in the camps and noted how important the payments were to Markowski in particular in making a new start on life. 'Jewish authorities', referred to in the article, expressed their concern that delays would prevent 'many sufferers from launching out into business on their own, [or] finding new happiness in life in a new profession or trade', or would lead to actual destitution with 'the saddest cases of all' being 'the old people'.[71] Significantly, the entire discussion of compensation was couched in instrumental terms: money should be paid so people could get on with new lives, not for reasons of symbolic recognition. The prevailing ideology of assimilation would have soundly discouraged public reflection on the pre-immigration life experiences of migrants, but celebrated those who had most successfully blended in to Australian society. Those who could not 'move on' were to be pitied; valorisation was saved for individuals who had put victimhood behind them and 'started again'. Survivor status was not seen as a matter particularly worthy of either commendation or commemoration.

A short article in *The Bulletin* by Ludwik Kruszelnicki published in 1961, is anomalous as a first person survivor account of a 'New Australian' which was published in direct reflection on the Eichmann trial.[72] The author, a Polish gentile, had been captured by the Nazis in 1941 after serving in the underground and spent the remainder of the war in Sachsenhausen concentration camp. After the war he married a Jewish survivor of Auschwitz with whom he ended up migrating to Australia in 1950, becoming a prolific writer and journalist (though usually in Polish) including as a correspondent for Radio Free Europe.[73] Kruszelnicki argued that, while the Eichmann trial focused attention on the number of people who had been killed, too little attention was given to the many former inmates of Nazi concentration camps who were still deeply psychologically troubled by their experiences. Kruszelnicki concluded that '[t]he survivors are still victims'.[74] Yet although he based the piece around some of his own recollections from incarceration, Kruszelnicki did not express a personal sense of victimhood. The article ambiguously referred to survivors being commonly found in 'sanatoriums and mental hospitals throughout Europe',[75] a geographically confined reference not only consistent with the ideology of assimilation in Australia (and the associated reluctance to admit that migrants might be unwilling or unable to wholly put aside their past lives) but which obscured the obvious inference that Kruszelnicki, too, was likely to be experiencing the ongoing effects of extreme trauma from his own horrific experiences. Kruszelnicki's son Karl, who became a well-known Australian scientist and public intellectual, later remembered his father as 'basically an optimist', but who periodically suffered from deep depression and 'black moods', a fluctuation that perhaps explained a partition of experience capable of producing an autobiographical account that featured ghastly incidents recalled at first hand, but referred to ongoing psychological disturbance in the third person.[76]

Conspicuously, neither Markowski nor Kruszelnicki were Jews and none of the anecdotes recounted by the latter involved any Jewish victims. Indeed, in general there is an absence of Jewish voices and personal experiences from the Australian literature associated with the Eichmann trial, a striking omission which requires explanation. The silence of 'newly Australian' Jewish survivors can no doubt in part be attributed to wider pressures to blend in and move on, though the combination of the Cold War with the ideology of assimilation also had a more specific impact on the Jewish community in particular. While a gentile 'Balt' (for example) could be deeply and actively anti-Soviet, yet remain in keeping with majority political feeling in Australia, which was profoundly anticommunist, migrant Jews remembering Nazism would have been fighting the wrong war; a conflict that was over, where the former enemy (at least in national terms) was now a crucial ally. Thus, anticommunism might conceivably be read as a sign of accepting 'Australian values', while agitating for the further pursuit of Nazis could in contrast be interpreted as a failure to assimilate, particularly in light of Barwick's 'closed chapter' dictum.[77] Feelings of vulnerability among Jews, heightened by the vandalism of early 1960, also no doubt precipitated anxiety about the potential for the old and deadly antisemitic equation of Judaism with Bolshevism to resurface[78]

Fears of being marked apart as aided by totalitarian theorising led to the explicit universalising of the Eichmann trial by Jews in America,[79] and the same dynamic may have featured in Australia. Stone, for example, argued that the 'final significance' of the proceedings 'concerned not Jews or Israel, or Germans, or even Nazis as such, but rather every man, woman and child of every people in the world'[80] and 'might renew among all peoples … certain elementary teachings about human life'.[81] Among non-Jewish pundits and again as a consequence of either or both of the Cold War and assimilationism, there was also a certain tendency to universalise what had occurred. Commentators sometimes did not mention the Jewishness of the victims, or referred expressly to national rather than the ethnic or religious designations, or emphasised the multinational dimension to the Nazis' murderous programmes. Kruszelnicki, for example, did not mention Jews or Jewishness at all in his short memoir, but rather 'fifty-thousand prisoners representing 14 European nations',[82] while Dymphna Cusack (who is discussed further below) evoked a women's concentration camp in polyglot terms as containing 'anti-Nazi German women,

Jehovah's witnesses, Resistance fighters from every country, a French Ballerina, Belgian nuns, Russian nurses, pilots, officers, doctors'.[83]

In addition to the external forces militating against Jewish public reflection on the crimes of the Nazis, there was also the absence of a significant internal 'push factor' among Australian Jewry. Historian Judith Berman has argued that although the trial of Eichmann led to a brief flurry of interest, it was not until the 1970s that 'the Holocaust began to move from the periphery of Australian Jewish consciousness'.[84] More broadly, it is crucial to recognise that identity-based political formations associated with campaigns for greater rights and recognition did not emerge until later in the 1960s. At the time of the Eichmann trial, ethnic or religious particularism was not thought to be a matter of celebration and was certainly not seen as offering a path to empowerment. Perhaps most fundamentally of all though, given that 'the Holocaust' did not yet exist as a distinct and separate phenomenon, the now iconic trope of the 'Holocaust survivor', capable of relaying 'the lessons' of his or her experiences, was simply not yet in existence in 1961. Although Primo Levi's *If this is a Man*, newly translated into English, received an early review in *The Observer* in 1960, it then disappeared into obscurity for another 20 years.[85] In later decades, whenever the Holocaust was in the news there would be no shortage of survivor reminiscences to draw upon, but in 1961 such recollections collectively did not exist as a recognised genre and were absent from the public domain.

However, if for all these reasons Jews and others who had been in the camps and later migrated to Australia largely remained publicly silent, it did not mean that there was an absence of ongoing psychological suffering and the Eichmann trial played a significant and specific role in unearthing personal matters which had been deeply buried.[86] Summarising almost a decade of clinical evidence in 1969, Australian psychologist Alan Stoller referred to a range of findings to the effect that the Eichmann trial in particular had 'helped reactivate' certain psychological disturbances produced by extreme trauma experienced during the Second World War, particularly among concentration camp survivors. Stoller described 'high rates of psychiatric disorder' which included not only 'the ordinary stress of assimilation', but 'psychopathological reactions of guilt and depression through having survived when those emotionally close to them had perished, diffuse anxiety to symbolically significant stimuli, impaired memory, insomnia with nightmares, low stress-threshold with resultant panic and confusion', a 'general distrustful and paranoid attitude' and '[e]motional outbursts' which 'could quickly progress to the point of attempted self-destruction'. The spectacle of the Eichmann proceedings did not prompt a flurry of public recollection by survivors, but the psychological research of the period suggests that the trial did indeed precipitate some intense personal reactions that were expressed in private.[87]

'What do you mean by "going in"?' Australian Holocaust Literature in 1961

Among the demonstrators protesting in response to the antisemitic graffiti in Sydney in January 1960 was Patrick White, who made an immediate personal effort to promote awareness of the dangers of neo-Nazism by purchasing numerous copies of Lord Russell of Liverpool's *Scourge of the Swastika* and sending one to each of Sydney's municipal libraries.[88] At the time, White was completing *Riders in the Chariot*, a novel in which one of the four principal characters was Mordecai Himmelfarb, a Jew who, the reader learns, escaped from a concentration camp in remarkable circumstances and circuitously made his way to Australia. About 90,000 words of the first draft of *Riders* had been written by December 1960, but the final manuscript was not ready until January 1961, so while White is likely to have been cognisant of the clamour surrounding Eichmann's arrest in the latter stages of writing, the work was completed before the trial had commenced. Given both the timing and the massive significance of White's overall impact on Australian intellectual life,[89] the publication of *Riders* should be understood as a threshold event in itself, which occurred more or less contemporaneously with the Eichmann trial, rather than the former being a response to the latter.

Riders was the first serious work of Australian prose literature to deal with the murder of the Jews as its central subject matter and can properly be regarded as Australia's inaugural 'Holocaust novel'.[90] The significance of *Riders*, though, does not lie simply in thematic primogeniture. What is so striking about White's treatment of the subject matter is his complete disregard for the existing paradigms for understanding the extermination of the Jews, offering an account that was not rooted in Cold War theorising of either the right or the left but which owed more to metaphysics, cultural history and social psychology.[91] In *Riders*, the Jewishness of the victims is seen to be of central significance, with the slaughter unambiguously recognised as a campaign directed against the Jews *per se*, not as surrogates for the working class and not simply to be explained because the Nazis were 'totalitarians'. White also narrated the experience of Himmelfarb on arrival to Australia in a manner which was radically inconsistent with the cosy mythology of assimilation. Himmelfarb's inability to assimilate was not only attributed to the impossibility of the hapless Jew to escape 'the dark of history, ageless, ageless, interminable', but to Australian prejudice and antisemitism, offering suggestions of uncomfortable continuities with the Old World.[92] Himmelfarb ends up being subjected to a mock crucifixion at the hands of co-workers as a vicious Easter prank in which he is injured, leading ultimately to his death, a turn in the narrative which disconcertingly linked what had happened in Europe with what might be possible in Australia.[93] As the poet Chris Wallace-Crabbe noted in his review of *Riders* for *The Bulletin*, White offered the unsettling suggestion that 'evil flowers as blackly in the brick veneers of Sarsaparilla and Barranugli as in Hitler's Germany'.[94]

White clearly intended the inference that Australia be considered part of the broader civilization that had produced the death camps, a historical and moral conclusion underlined by the fate of Himmelfarb.[95]

White's evocation of Himmelfarb's arrival at a death camp, including the moment where the doomed Jew asks what is meant by 'going in' (to the gas chambers), is hideously revelatory in tone.[96] The Jews on Himmelfarb's train are in a mixture of denial and ignorance of their doom until the last. However, given the Australian cultural ignorance of the extermination of the Jews which so offended White in January 1960, it is reasonable to infer that the account of the extermination process given in *Riders* might have had at least some didactic purpose. Though the novel is not a work of vulgar instruction, it does seem likely that at one level White was simply trying to teach the readers about what had happened to the Jews in Europe. The initial critical reactions arguably served to bear out the author's apprehensions of Australian ignorance: reviewers simply did not notice the singularity of White's portrayal of the fate of Europe's Jews, with one pundit even going so far as to dismiss the narrative as 'derivative' of 'any number of books about Nazi Germany'.[97]

Dymphna Cusack's *Heatwave in Berlin* was another Australian novel published in 1961 which gave prominent treatment to the Holocaust. Cusack was more obviously influenced by contemporary events in Jerusalem than White, demonstrated by a gratuitous reference in the text to the role of 'the SS mass-murderer Eichmann' in implementing the extermination.[98] Cusack was on the cultural far left in Australia and her novels were strongly influenced by socialist realism and tended to focus on specific social or political problems. In *Heatwave*, Cusack was preoccupied with what she saw as a general failure to apprehend the threat posed by the emergence of neo-Nazism in post-war Germany. Cusack had been personally disconcerted by contact with a reunion of nostalgic Nazis when travelling through Germany in the late 1950s and the composition of *Heatwave* was strongly influenced by that experience.[99] The central character in the novel was an Australian woman named Joy, married to a naturalised German migrant with an anglicised name (so presumably quite respectably 'assimilated')[100] who joins her husband in visiting his estranged family, almost all of whom turn out to be unrepentant Nazis. Joy is shattered to find the extent of support for Hitler that remains in Germany and the number of war criminals who are still at large.

Like White, though with far greater obviousness and much less artistic sophistication, Cusack's novel used revelatory narrative to educative purpose. In *Heatwave* Cusack gave a blunt warning about the dangers of neo-Nazism and what she saw as the blind complicity of the liberal democracies in re-arming an unrepentant Germany. Joy's fictionalised abhorrence at pervasive cultural 'amnesia' about Nazi crimes reflected Cusack's own assessment of the actual state of affairs.[101] The novel is a story of appalling discovery which occurs in dramatic stages, leading to a climactic and almost pornographic account of atrocities at

Auschwitz; but it also functions as a didactic tract, intended to educate the reader about the nauseating reality of Nazi crimes and the lack of consequences for the perpetrators. As Joy makes her discoveries, so the reader becomes informed. At one point in the narrative an elderly survivor tells Joy that she must go back to Australia and tell her country 'the truth' about Nazi crimes which, of course, was Cusack's own public purpose in writing *Heatwave*.[102]

Cusack's novel is clearly embedded within the intellectual structures imposed by the Cold War, in which her own position was firmly on the left. In *Heatwave*, the success of Nazism (and resurgence of the neo-Nazis) is explicitly attributed to the failure of bourgeois liberalism to provide effective resistance, while forgetfulness about war crimes is in part attributed to pathological anticommunism. According to one character in the book referring to Germany (but with implications for the Menzies government in Australia), everything opposed to government policy whether 'against military conscription … atomic weapons, or former Nazis in high places' was 'branded Communist' to silence debate.[103] Cusack, though, did not entirely forsake culture for class analysis in explaining fascism, retaining a certain radical nationalist fondness for the idea that the Holocaust could not have happened in Australia. Joy, embodying the essence of imagined Australian egalitarianism, is out of place in the Old World and portrayed in contrast with her elitist and fascist aristocratic in-laws, with whom she clashes over the pay and treatment of their servants.[104] One former Nazi exposed by Joy is not only nasty to one of the latter's daughters, but goes so far as to treat the child's soft toy, conspicuously called 'Kanga', with some roughness.[105]

There were two poems by Australian poets that responded directly to Eichmann. The first, written by a young David Malouf and called 'Epitaph for a Monster of our Times', ran to six short verses and addressed, in ironic tone, the junction between the admirableness of bureaucratic 'precision' with the despicable nature of the resultant consequences, which were manifest in Eichmann, 'who at his desk, a slave / to files and paper-clips, / while children died and cities / burned at his finger-tips'.[106] The second was from writer, reviewer and future priest John Hanrahan, who in his 1962 poem 'To Adolf Eichmann' responded to the condemned man's banal and bizarre last words 'I have always believed in God' by highlighting the absurdity of a Nazi appealing to a Jewish deity.[107] Far more notable was Peter Porter's extraordinary 'Annotations of Auschwitz', published in 1961.[108] Here, though, the contemporaneousness is misleading. At the time of the Eichmann trial, Porter had already been in residence in England for some years and the poem's origins date back to the early 1950s, inspired by Alan Resnais' documentary film about Auschwitz entitled *Nuit et Bruillard*.[109] 'Annotations of Auschwitz', though published at the time of Eichmann's trial and perhaps the most famous 'Holocaust poem' written by an Australian, 'was quite uninfluenced by Eichmann's trial and execution'.[110]

The 'Making of the Holocaust' in Australia[111]

The Eichmann hearing created an interpretive threshold after which, for the first time in Australia, the extermination of the Jews began to be understood as a phenomenon apart, known as 'the Holocaust'. In April 1961 *The Age* actually explained directly that 'holocaust" meant 'the Nazi attempt to exterminate European Jewry'.[112] Later in the year, the *Sydney Morning Herald* interpolated the remarks of Chief Justice Moshe Landau from the Israeli District Court to the effect that 'it was not the first time the "holocaust" had been brought up in Courts of Law, but it was the first time it had stood at the centre of a trial'.[113] Against a background of ignorance and disinterest, the principal didactic significance of the Eichmann trial was often seen as simply teaching 'the facts' of what had happened. As Stone recognised, the Eichmann trial forced a pedagogic confrontation with 'what actually went on in the death camps', creating an 'obligation towards the victims' and 'a duty at least to be willing to learn about their sufferings'.[114]

Yet if the Eichmann trial marked an important phase of the 'making of the Holocaust' in Australia, there were persistent ambiguities like the ambivalence as to whether what had gone on in the death camps should be understood as an especially 'Jewish' experience. The reporting of affairs in Jerusalem also did not bring an instant end to the use of anti-Jewish stereotypes in Australia. While the Australian reports largely eschewed overt antisemitism, allusions to the cultural trope of the 'vengeful Jew' seem clearly evident in a number of press accounts. *The Age*, for example, reported a 'deluge' of offers from concentration camp survivors prepared to be Eichmann's hangman if he were found guilty.[115] Overtones of antisemitic caricature also plainly informed an editorial in *The West Australian* which argued that Eichmann's execution 'so long after the war, adding one more death to the slaughter' did not add 'anything significant to the human story outside of the satisfaction the Jews may get from exacting personal retribution'.[116] In similar vein, the *Sun-Herald* had earlier reported that a 'blood thirsty lynch mood' was 'sweeping Israel',[117] while Hanrahan's verse about Eichmann's death made reference to 'that sweet blood the Jewish lawyers won', lines that must have contemplated *The Merchant of Venice*.[118]

Neither did the Eichmann trial suddenly end racialised thinking in Australia, a process which was long, slow and uncertain. In the middle of Eichmann's trial the *Sydney Morning Herald* ran a syndicated feature under the banner:

> With the world focused on Eichmann, accused of betraying thousands of his kin to the Nazis, the question again arises: ARE THE JEWS A RACE APART? Who are the Jews? Where did they come from? Are they a racial group with distinct characteristics, as Hitler sought to prove?[119]

The article carried with it four photographs of faces with the caption: 'Which of these are Jews? In fact, all of them, in spite of their varied physiognomy [*sic*]'.[120]

It seems that racial 'science' which, as much as any other discourse, might be suggested as encapsulating the 'spirit of Eichmann', had not been entirely discredited. Certainly in the early 1960s debates about race in relation to Aboriginal people continued in Australian 'scholarly' life, the consequences of 'miscegenation' remained a matter of live concern and physical anthropologists carried on with their 'scientific' work. The 'Report of the Committee on Physical Anthropology' at the inaugural 1961 Aboriginal Studies Research Conference, for example, declared an urgent need for psychological, biochemical, biometrical and descriptive work to be completed, in part in order to 'assess both the results of interbreeding and the rate of progress towards physical Europeanization'.[121]

There was also no real sense in which the Eichmann trial prompted any immediate introspection about Australia's own record in relation to the Holocaust. Like many other liberal democracies in the 1930s, Australia had taken only strictly limited numbers of Jewish refugees and even after the Second World War had actually imposed immigration quotas. In the meanwhile, the *Dunera* incident had resulted in the harsh treatment and arbitrary confinement of a boatload of fleeing Jews by Commonwealth authorities.[122] Although not a major military power, by implication Australia too had 'stood by' and been party to the Allied cause that had 'failed to bomb the train tracks'. While in subsequent years Australian thinking about the Holocaust would become embroiled with controversies associated with the country's record as a 'bystander nation' that retained racially restrictive immigration policies, those connections were seldom made in 1961.[123]

In later decades the relationship between the Holocaust and the dispossession of the Indigenous peoples of Australia would also come to be a matter of specific debate, flaring into political, legal and historiographical controversy at the very centre of national political and scholarly life.[124] However, in 1961 Patrick White was atypical in linking the extermination of the Jews with contemporary treatment of Australia's Indigenous people, through his connecting of the doomed Himmelfarb with another of the 'riders', the Aboriginal artist Alf Dubbo. *Riders* can be read in part as a critique of the ethic of assimilationism which, at the time of the Eichmann trial, was the prevailing Australian policy paradigm towards Aboriginal people, just as it was toward migrants. Although there were ambiguities associated with the term,[125] according to one government definition from 1965 the thrust was 'that all aborigines and part aborigines' were 'expected to eventually attain the same manner of living as other Australians and to live as members of a single Australian community enjoying the same rights and privileges, accepting the same responsibilities, observing the same customs and influenced by the same beliefs, hopes and loyalties as other Australians'.[126] Outside official channels, the emerging Indigenous rights campaigns in the early 1960s were nonetheless more concerned with gaining access to the mainstream of society rather than with advancing a particularist agenda.[127] Modern Aboriginal historiography, preoccupied with investigating the dispossession and experience of colonisation of the original inhabitants only really began with a series of influential broadcast lectures by anthropologist W.E.H. Stanner in 1968.[128] The intellectual and political climate was simply not conducive to the Eichmann proceedings being reflected onto Australia's colonial past.[129]

Although later debates would sometimes conflate cultural with biological absorption as part of a single genocidal enterprise that was said to have marked Australian history, in the early 1960s there was no sense that the government's policy of assimilating Australia's Indigenous peoples had anything at all to do with Nazism.[130] Unusually, in a paper read on 26 September 1961 (so in the midst of the Eichmann trial) Australian historian Russell Ward made protracted reference to the 'systematic and cold-blooded murder of some 7,000,000 men, women and children for the crime of not having been born into the "Master Race"'.[131] Ward's reference to the Holocaust, included within a critical reflection on racism and racial thinking in Australia, is an anomaly within the Australian historiography of the time. Yet, as Ward disclosed in a national history published a few years later, he saw the 'movement in Australia toward assimilation of its aboriginal noncitizens' not as evidence that the horror of the genocide had gone unnoticed, but as an indication of the 'effectiveness of the lesson' taught by Hitler, because 'the Nazis demonstrated to everyone the logical end of racist delusions'.[132] A young Colin Tatz, having emigrated from South Africa only half a dozen years earlier, was another who believed at the time that assimilation was essentially emancipative in character: it was, he wrote, 'essentially a policy of equality'.[133]

The Eichmann trial marked a threshold in awareness and understanding of the Holocaust in Australia, but the dynamic was not one of an immediate transformation. The extensive media coverage of the Eichmann trial certainly ensured that the proceedings were part of the lived experience of many Australians in 1960–61 and prompted a considerable public and intellectual reaction, but the interpretation of events in Jerusalem was heavily conditioned by the crucial context of the chilling and polarising rigidity of the Cold War in combination with the muffling effect of assimilationism and the associated ethic of 'moving on'. The Eichmann trial did not singly 'make' the Holocaust in Australia, but did give significant impetus to a shift in awareness and understandings.

NOTES

1. This is described in David Marr, *Patrick White: A Life* (Sydney: Random House, 1991), p.367; see also William D. Rubinstein, *The Jews in Australia. A Thematic History Volume Two* (Port Melbourne: Heinemann, 1991), pp.424–5.
2. E. Baume, 'Eric Baume Debunks Antisemitism', *The Observer*, Vol.3, No.2, 23 January 1960, pp.12–13, at p.12.
3. Ibid., p.13.
4. The exchange included a rejoinder and counter-rejoinder and so on, before the editor finally closed the exchange on the subject in the last issue of December 1960.

5. V.L. Borin, 'The Uprooted Survive', *The Observer*, Vol.3, No.4 (20 February 1960), pp.28–9, p.29. Borin was responding to R. Fischer, 'Voice of New Australia?', *The Observer*, Vol.3, No.2, 23 January 1960, p.27. Borin's novel, which was deeply anticommunist and somewhat apologetic for the Nazis, was Vladimir L. Borin, *The Uprooted Survive: A Tale of Two Continents* (Melbourne: Heinemann, 1959). In early 1961 Borin wrote another short article, discounting the domestic threat of Nazism in Australia: V.L. Borin, 'That Nazi Spectre', *The Observer*, Vol.4, No.4, 18 February 1961, p.7.
6. G. More, 'Antisemitism', *The Observer*, Vol.3, No.3, 6 February 1960, p.39
7. For example, Baume made the following references: 'the German people eagerly accepted Hitler's doctrine that the Jews should be exterminated. His assistant, Himmler, saw to it pretty well in the gassing of millions' and later, that '[t]he daughters of the wealthy married cavalry officers in the guards regiment. They had their salons until Himmler changed those to gas chambers at Auschwitz': Baume, 'Baume Debunks Antisemitism', p.13.
8. The few exceptions or partial exceptions include: Simon Hochberger, *Warsaw Ghetto-Tale of Valor* (Melbourne: Ofboy Publishing, 1946); J. Lindsay, 'Peace is our Answer', *Meanjin*, Vol.10 (Winter 1951), pp.117–23; and Walter Kaufmann, *Voices in the Storm* (Melbourne: Australasian Book Society, 1953).
9. Paul Hasluck, *Australia in the War of 1939–45: The Government and the People 1939–41* (Canberra: Australian War Memorial, 1952). In terms of abiding influence, according to historian Joan Beaumont, the explanations for Australia's participation in the war in Europe provided by Hasluck 'still remain widely accepted': Joan Beaumont, 'Australia's War: Europe and the Middle East', in Joan Beaumont (ed.), *Australia's War 1939–45* (St Leonards, NSW: Allen & Unwin, 1996), p.2.
10. Perhaps the closest thing is the 'bystander' hybrid novel-memoir of Hungarian refugee Cecile Kunrathy, *Impudent Foreigner* (Sydney: Edward & Shaw, 1963).
11. Precisely what that position would come to be is itself of course a complex matter of debate which is reflected upon in various ways in, for example, Robert Manne, *The Culture of Forgetting: Helen Demidenko and the Holocaust* (Melbourne: Text Publishing, 1996); Judith E. Berman, *Holocaust Remembrance in Australian Jewish Communities, 1945–2000* (Nedlands, WA: University of Western Australia Press, 2001); Inga Clendinnen, *Reading the Holocaust* (Melbourne: Text Publishing, 1998) and a number of the essays in *Aboriginal History*, Vol.25 (2001).
12. See P.R. Bartrop, 'The Nuremberg Trials and the Holocaust: Crimes against Humanity as viewed from Australia (1945/46)', *Journal of the Australian Jewish Historical Society*, Vol.12, No.3 (November 1994), pp.606–18.
13. For contemporary (in 1960) awareness of the persistence of soft antisemitism see for example Baume, 'Baume Debunks Antisemitism'; and H. Wolfsohn, 'The Anti-Semites', *The Observer*, Vol.3, No.26, 1 October 1960, pp.11–12.
14. See generally Mark Johnston, *At the Front Line: Experiences of Australian Soldiers in World War II* (Cambridge: Cambridge University Press, 1996); and Mark Johnston, *Fighting the Enemy: Australian Soldiers and their Adversaries in World War II* (Cambridge: Cambridge University Press, 2000).
15. See the discussion of fighting the Japanese in Johnston, *At the Front Line* and *Fighting the Enemy*.
16. W.C. Wentworth (Mackellar), House of Representatives, 23rd Parliament, 3rd Session, First Period,16 March 1961, Hansard R.30, 1-1120 371-3, pp.371 and 373. Wentworth was a particularly strident anticommunist.
17. Menzies was elected in 1949 and remained in power until 1966.
18. By 1961, 79 per cent of households in Sydney and 78 per cent in Melbourne owned television sets: Colin Jones and David Bednall, *Television in Australia: Its History Through the Ratings* (Sydney: Australian Broadcasting Tribunal, 1982), p.5.
19. The summary is from America, but is no doubt true of Australia too: J. Shandler, 'The Man in the Glass Box: Watching the Eichmann Trial on American Television', in Barbie Zelizer (ed.), *Visual Culture and the Holocaust* (New Brunswick, NJ: Rutgers University Press, 2001), p.91.
20. 'Courtroom Films of Eichmann', *The Age Television and Radio Supplement*, 14–20 April 1961, p.1.
21. Peter Beilby (ed.), *Australian TV: The First 25 Years* (South Melbourne: Nelson, 1981), p.18.
22. 'They Said It in 1961', *The Bulletin*, 30 December 1961, p.10.
23. Peter Novick, *The Holocaust in American Life* (Boston: Houghton Mifflin, 1999), p.144.
24. Reuters or AAP. Editorial discretion was of course still exercised in the use of these reports. I have principally looked at *The Bulletin*, *The Sydney Morning Herald*, *The Melbourne Age*, *The Canberra Times* and *The West Australian*. The *Sydney Morning Herald* printed some articles written by Julius Stone who was at the trial – but he was not there as the paper's correspondent. The *Sydney Morning Herald* also ran articles by their staff correspondent in London, Walter Cronshaw, presumably because he was closer to Jerusalem than was head office in Sydney.

25. In general international press interest dwindled as time wore on. *The Age* reported on 8 May 1961 of 'Israeli Concern at Waning Trial Interest' because 'foreign news coverage of the trial' was 'becoming smaller': 'Israeli Concern at Waning Trial Interest', *The Age*, 8 May 1961, p.7.
26. 'Nazi Rise to Power Re-enacted', *Sydney Morning Herald*, 10 April 1961, p.10; 'Spotlight again falls on the Rise of Adolf Hitler', *The Age Television and Radio Supplement*, 7–13 April 1961, p.1.
27. Stone had been scheduled to visit Israel anyway to deliver some lectures to the Faculty of Law in the Hebrew University of Jerusalem on his way back from New York, so the few weeks at the trial represented an extension of an existing trip: Julius Stone, *The Eichmann Trial and the Rule of Law* (Sydney: International Commission of Jurists (Australian Section), 1961), p.1.
28. Leonie Star, *Julius Stone: An Intellectual Life* (Sydney: Sydney University Press, 1992), p.121 and passim.
29. Stone, *Eichmann Trial*, p.1; Star, *Julius Stone*, p.121. *The Eichmann Trial and the Rule of Law* was later republished as Ch. XI in Julius Stone, *Of Law and Nations: Between Power Politics and Human Hopes* (Buffalo, NY: W.S. Hein & Co., 1974). The International Commission of Jurists was founded in Berlin in 1952 with a membership composed of eminent jurists representing different legal systems dedicated to the primacy, coherence and implementation of international law and principles that advance human rights. Contemporary information about the ICJ can be found at www.icj.org/.
30. Julius Stone, *Regional Guarantees of Minority Rights: A Study of Minorities Procedure in Upper Silesia* (New York: Macmillan, 1933).
31. Stone, for example, had hated Oxford with a passion: see Star, *Julius Stone.*
32. The ICJ also commissioned a second rapporteur, without which Stone expressed doubt as to whether he would have accepted the assignment. Stone, *Eichmann Trial*, p.1. As a legal realist Stone was no doubt well aware of the role of subjectivity in perception.
33. 'Legal realism' refers to the proposition that the law, far from being a system of positively knowable external logic, is made by human beings and so conditioned by human subjectivities. As would be expected, Stone's report back to the ICJ is principally concerned with legal issues of jurisdiction, fairness and so on. Nevertheless, Stone did experience some grim bemusement at the preoccupation with legal issues, commenting that '[a] Rip Van Winkle who fell asleep in 1930 and awakened just before the Eichmann trial, would have rubbed his eyes at a most striking paradox ... that the most persistent vocal protests surrounding this case have been protests against the trial, rather than the fact that such hideous crimes were possible': Stone, *Eichmann Trial*, pp.6–7.
34. 'Accused Examined', *Canberra Times*, 15 April 1961, p.3. *The Canberra Times* ran many more photographs than (for example) either of the Melbourne or Sydney daily papers. Perhaps the larger number of photographs in the Canberra daily might be explained because its television channel was not launched until after the *Eichmann* trial had commenced, leaving a local market without the same degree of access to visual spectacle.
35. The classic account of Eichmann's 'ordinariness' is of course Hannah Arendt, *Eichmann in Jerusalem: A Report on the Banality of Evil* (New York: Viking Press, 1963). Arendt thought that Eichmann only became 'paler and more ghost-like' as the horrendous evidence unfolded, p.6.
36. 'Slave March "Eichmann's Sole Motive for Murder" Court is Told', *Sydney Morning Herald*, 19 April 1961, p.3; and J. Stone, '"Prophetic Mirror" Reflecting the Face of Mankind', *Sydney Morning Herald*, 28 June 1961, p.2.
37. The same description appears in 'Eichmann shows Signs of Strain', *The Age*, 19 April 1961, p.1; and 'Slave March "Eichmann's Sole Motive for Murder" Court is Told', p.3.
38. Stone, 'Prophetic Mirror', p.2.
39. Senator V.S. Vincent (Western Australia) and Senator J.G. Gorton (Victoria), Senate, 23rd Parliament, 3rd Session, First Period, 22 March 1961, Hansard S.19, 1-1222, pp.425–6.
40. Just as it had ignored Nuremberg: see Bartrop, 'Nuremberg Trials and the Holocaust'.
41. The actions of Viks were alleged to be more serious than 'just' having committed murder. Viks had served as the deputy chief of the 'Special Department' of the Tartu concentration camp in Estonia where he had ordered (at least) hundreds of Jews to their deaths and had personally been involved in brutalising internees: Mark Aarons, *Sanctuary* (Port Melbourne: Mandarin, 1990), pp.187 and 190–4.
42. G. Barwick (Paramatta), House of Representatives, 23rd Parliament, 3rd Session, First Period, 22 March 1961, Hansard R.30, 1-1120, pp.449–52, at p.451. The 'closed chapter doctrine' effectively remained in place until the Hawke Labor Government in the 1980s: see A. Menzies, *Review of Material Relating to the Entry of Suspected War Criminals into Australia* (Commonwealth Publishers: Canberra, 1986). Menzies recommended at p.180 that '[t]he Government make a clear and positive statement to the effect that, as regards serious war crimes, it does not regard the chapter as closed (contrary to the Barwick statement in 1961) and that it will take appropriate action under the law to bring to justice persons who

have committed serious war crimes found in Australia'. Following the Menzies Report, the Hawke Government introduced the *War Crimes Act Amendment Act (1988)* and established a special investigations unit. Three prosecutions were brought, but no convictions were obtained.
43. Barwick, House of Representatives, 22 March 1961, p.452.
44. See Janis Wilton and Richard J.B. Bosworth, *Old Worlds and New Australia* (Melbourne: Penguin, 1984), pp.17–18.
45. See for example Ronald Taft, *From Stranger to Citizen: A Survey of Studies of Immigrant Assimilation in Western Australia* (Nedlands, WA: University of Western Australia Press, 1965).
46. Which overlooked, of course, the violent dispossession of Australia's Indigenous peoples. See Wilton and Bosworth, *Old Worlds*, pp.151–2.
47. Barwick, House of Representatives, 22 March 1961, pp.451–2.
48. Ibid., p.450.
49. John McClaren, *Writing in Hope and Fear: Literature as Politics in Post-war Australia*, (Cambridge: Cambridge University Press, 1996).
50. For instance, although Stone asserted an 'enormous difference in legal and moral responsibility between using weapons of mass destruction in wartime against a combatant enemy people' and the crimes of the Nazis, his concern about nuclear proliferation indicates clearly that he was not an uncritical Cold War warrior: Stone, *Eichmann Trial*, pp.19 and 21.
51. Stone, 'Prophetic Mirror', p.2.
52. Ibid.
53. Ibid.; and Stone, *Eichmann Trial*, p.21.
54. Stone, 'Prophetic Mirror', p.2.
55. 'What Eichmann does not know', *The Bulletin*, 1 July 1961, p.3. After all, the editorial argued, 'communist totalitarians' had by the 1960s 'no doubt slaughtered more millions of human beings' if for no other reason than that 'they have had more time to do it in'.
56. Novick describes the same dynamic in America: Novick, *Holocaust in American Life*, p.134.
57. V. Bourke, 'Anti-Fascism is a Class Question', *Communist Review*, No.221 (May 1960), pp.196–8, at p.197. Although Bourke was discussing matters more generally, the statement would have obvious application to communist interpretations of the Eichmann trial.
58. J. Waten, 'The Cultural Commissar', *The Observer*, Vol.3, No.10, 14 May 1960, p.30.
59. H. Stein, 'Background to the Trial of Nazi Mass Murderer Eichmann', *Communist Review*, No.233 (May 1961), pp.188–90.
60. Ibid.
61. K. Thomas, 'Monopoly War Criminals', *Communist Review*, No.223 (July 1960), pp.284–6, at p.284.
62. Stein, 'Background to the Trial'.
63. See also E. Goldhagan, 'Communism and Antisemitism', *Quadrant*, Vol.5, No.1, Iss.17 (1960–61), pp.59–68.
64. 'Russian Jews in "Great Danger"', *The Age*, 13 July 1961, p.4. The airing of such opinions tapped in to grave concerns at the fate of the Jews of the Soviet Union that pre-dated the Eichmann trial, and is widely evident within the relevant Australian literature of the period. See for example ibid., and Isis Liebler, *Soviet Jewry and Human Rights* (North Melbourne: Human Rights Publications, 1965).
65. W.E. Gollan, 'Nazi Antisemitism', *Communist Review*, No. 220 (April 1960), pp.153–5, at p.153.
66. Ibid.
67. According to Bourke it was 'clear that the defence of the Jewish people against antisemitism [lay] not in race solidarity, but class solidarity': Bourke, 'Anti-Fascism is a Class Question'.
68. Between 1945 and 1954 Australia accepted about 17,600 survivors of the Holocaust: Rubinstein, *Jews in Australia*, pp.36–7. In relation to the scale of post-war immigration more generally see Wilton and Bosworth, *Old Worlds and New Australia*.
69. 'Nazi Hell Camp Victims Wait On', *Sun-Herald*, 18 June 1961, pp.72–3.
70. 'Nino Culotta' was the nom de plume adopted by the non-Italian writer John P. O'Grady who wrote a long series of pro-assimilation novels under the pseudonym, beginning with: Nino Culotta, *They're a Weird Mob* (Sydney: Ure Smith, 1957). Identified as 'one of Sydney's best cooks', it was clear that Markowski was making food that was sufficiently 'Australian' so as to be socially acceptable, while the un-named second survivor was described as getting both government and army contracts, clearly implying that he can be trusted.
71. 'Nazi Hell Camp Victims Wait On', p.73.
72. L. Kruszelnicki, 'What Eichmann Did Not Say', *The Bulletin*, 1 July 1961, p.16.
73. C. Williams, 'Karl Krusezelnicki', in C. Williams (ed.), *Fathers and Son* (Sydney: Angus & Robertson, 1996), p.149.

74. Kruszelnicki, 'What Eichmann Did Not Say'.
75. Kruszelnicki, ibid. The geographical emphasis was echoed by the editors of *The Bulletin* in both the by-line and editorial introduction to the issue.
76. Williams (ed.), 'Karl Krusezelnicki', p.156.
77. One of the few public comments made by any Australian Jew acting in a representative capacity to even implicitly refer to the goings on in Jerusalem was a paper given to the Australian Jewish Historical Society, the intent of which was to exculpate the Western democracies from any insinuation that they had stood idle while the genocide proceeded. It was not, according to the author, 'Australia's fault that her offer' to increase immigration 'could not be fully accepted' because of the outbreak of war and 'in making it too late she merely followed the rest of the world which must share with her the blame for the loss of Jewish lives which might have been saved: D.J. Benjamin, 'Australia and the Evian Conference', *Australian Jewish Historical Society Journal and Proceedings*, Vol.5, No.5 (1961), pp.215–33, at pp.231–2.
78. There were of course some prominent Australian Jewish communists including Judah Waten and Harry Stein who are mentioned elsewhere in this paper. One of the themes in the exchange in *The Observer* described at the commencement of this article concerned links between Australian Jews and communism.
79. See Novick, *Holocaust in American Life.*
80. Stone, 'Prophetic Mirror'.
81. J. Stone, 'What Does Eichmann's Fate mean to Civilisation?', *Sydney Morning Herald*, 7 July 1961, p.2.
82. Kruszelnicki, 'What Eichmann Did Not Say'.
83. D. Cusack, *Heatwave in Berlin* (Melbourne: Heinemann, 1961), p.169.
84. Berman, *Holocaust Remembrance*, pp.8–9.
85. D. O'Grady, 'The Practice of Hell', *The Observer*, Vol.3, No.18, 3 September 1960, pp.24–5. See also F.N.A. Flanagan, 'The Myth of Primo Levi: Understandings of Primo Levi in the English-Speaking World, 1945–2003', Unpublished Honours Dissertation, University of Western Australia, 2003.
86. See for example, contributions from Konrad Kwiet and Suzanne Rutland in this volume.
87. A. Stoller, 'Stress in Immigrants', in Harold Throssell (ed.), *Ethnic Minorities in Australia: The Welfare of Aborigines and Migrants* (Sydney: Australian Council of Social Service, 1969), p.164.
88. White remarked at the time: '[w]hether anybody reads them, is, of course, another matter.' This is described in Marr, *Patrick White*, p.368.
89. See for example Donald Horne, *The Lucky Country: Australia in the 1960s* (Ringwood, Vic: Penguin, 1964), p.94; and McClaren, *Writing in Hope and Fear*, p.177.
90. White even uses the term 'holocaust', albeit only in reflected metaphor. One of the other 'riders', the misanthropic Mary Hare who later befriends Himmelfarb has a pet goat (often used as an antisemitic symbol of the Jews), which is killed in a fire. 'Even on the morning of the mistress's severest trial, the abstraction of a goat's mask continued to communicate. Even though the goat itself had become a skull and a shred of hide in the ruins of the black and smoking shed. How she herself survived the holocaust of her discovery, Mary Hare could never be sure': Patrick White, *Riders in the Chariot* (London: Eyre & Spottiswoode, 1961), p.52. In White's earlier novel *Voss* he had already alluded to the extermination of the Jews. The eponymous protagonist, German explorer Johann Ulrich Voss, is in some respects a Hitler-like-figure, exhibiting Fuhrer-esque fanaticism, mysticism, absolute authority and charisma. Like Hitler, Voss seeks *lebensraum* (though to the West, not the East) and he too is stopped by scorched earth. When the great expedition across the country is under way, food falls short and the livestock in the procession begin to falter, whereupon Voss announces 'against the thunder', in a manner redolent of Hitler's oratory technique, that '[a]ll sheep must be sacrificed'. Once the slaughter has taken place, one of the men who has performed the butchery sings: '*A-jew, a-jew kind sheep / The fatal hour has come*': Patrick White, *Voss* (London: Eyre & Spottiswoode, 1959), p.76. The phonetic spelling adopted by White suggests that the sheep, slaughtered at the urging of the 'exultant' German explorer, are symbols of the Jews.
91. For an alternative interpretation of Patrick White's reactions to antisemitism, see John Docker's article in this volume.
92. White, *Riders*, p.184. In Australia, Himmelfarb is referred to as 'a blasted foreigner, and bloody reffo', who 'should have been glad he was allowed to exist at all': ibid., p.199.
93. The racist graffiti in 1960 had apparently confirmed in White's mind the plausibility of Himmelfarb's ultimate fate in Australia: Marr, *Patrick White*, p.368.
94. C. Wallace-Crabbe, 'Crucifixion at Sarsaparilla', *The Bulletin*, 25 November 1961, pp.35–6, at p.35.
95. White, *Riders*, p.184.

96. Ibid., p.183.
97. O.N. Burgess (Untitled Review), *Australian Quarterly*, Vol.34 No.1 (1962), pp.110–13, at p.113. For some other early reviews, see H.P. Heseltine, 'Fiction Chronicle', *Meanjin*, Vol.2, No.4 (December 1961), pp.474–91; M. Harris, 'Patrick White's Chariot', *Nation*, 21 October 1961, pp.21–2; M. Anrousseau, 'Odi Profanum Vulgus: Patrick White's *Riders in the Chariot*', *Meanjin* Vol.21, No.1 (March 1962), pp.29–31; J.D. Blake, 'Comment', *Overland*, No.25 (Summer 1962–63), pp.34–6, at p.35; and J. Beasley, 'The Great Hatred: Patrick White as Novelist', *Realist Writer*, No.9 (September 1962), p.11.
98. Cusack, *Heatwave*, p.164.
99. Norman Freehill with Dymphna Cusack, *Dymphna Cusack* (West Melbourne: Nelson, 1975), pp.131–2.
100. Cusack wrote a later novel on Nazis who had migrated to Australia: D. Cusack, *The Sun is not Enough* (London: Heinemann, 1967).
101. In the later novel, *The Sun is not Enough*, Cusack made reference to the change in awareness brought about by the Eichmann trial (see pp.165 and 228) making explicit her view that the Nazis crimes had previously been forgotten. See also Cusack, *Heatwave*, pp.131–2.
102. Cusack, *Heatwave*, p.92.
103. Ibid., p.147.
104. Ibid., p.173.
105. Ibid., p.178.
106. D. Malouf, 'Epitaph for a Monster of our Times', *Overland*, No.24 (Spring 1962), p.27.
107. J. Hanrahan, 'To Adolf Eichmann', *Poetry Australia*, No.15 (April 1967), pp.37–8.
108. Originally published in Peter Porter, *Once Bitten, Twice Bitten* (London: Scorpion Press, 1961).
109. Bruce Bennett, *Spirit in Exile: Peter Porter and his Poetry* (Oxford: Oxford University Press, 1991), pp.77–9.
110. P. Porter, personal communication to the author, 30 May 2007.
111. In a postscript, when Hannah Arendt's *Eichmann in Jerusalem* was published in Australia some years later, the book and the events it described had achieved sufficient notoriety to receive four lengthy reviews from established or emerging public intellectuals. These reviews have not been considered elsewhere in this paper. See J. Stone, 'Truth Distorted in "Report" on Eichmann Trial', *Sydney Morning Herald*, 18 January 1964, p.10; I. Liebler, 'Arendt's Eichmann', *Dissent*, No.11 (1964), pp.43–4; W.H.C. Eddy, 'A Question of Responsibility', *Quadrant*, Vol.8, No.1 (1964), pp.69–73; and G.J. Munster, 'Eichmann's Crime', *Nation*, 11 January 1964, pp.20–22.
112. 'Eichmann Story from his Cell', *The Age*, 25 April 1961, p.4
113. 'Eichmann Guilty of Jewish Killings', *Sydney Morning Herald*, 12 December 1961, pp.1 and 3.
114. Stone, *Eichmann Trial*, pp.16–18.
115. 'Israeli Agents track down most Hated Nazi', *The Age*, 25 May 1960, p.4. Novick has noted that sections of the press in America regarded the Eichmann trial as illustrating 'the difference between Christian forgiveness and "Jewish vengefulness"': Novick, *Holocaust in American Life*, p.129. See also 'Israelis Hide Nazi; Lynching Feared', *Sydney Morning Herald*, 26 May 1960, p.3.
116. 'Eichmann and the Jews', *The West Australian*, 1 June 1962, p.7.
117. 'Israelis Hide Nazi: Lynching Feared', *Sydney Morning Herald*, 26 May 1960, p.3. The article suggested that 'fears of a mob out-break' were 'well founded' and under the sub-heading 'Cage him!' recounted vox pops from the streets of Jerusalem, all suggesting various unpleasant ends for Eichmann. This was far from the only article on the theme.
118. Hanrahan, 'To Adolf Eichmann'.
119. The commentary is ambiguous, seeming to imply that Eichmann was himself Jewish (or did the writer mean that fellow Germans had been betrayed by Eichmann because they were Jewish?) and citing a 'betrayal' of 'thousands', rather than the organised murder of millions. More obvious and startling is that, in the midst of Eichmann's trial, a mainstream newspaper would question whether Hitler was correct in a hypothesis about 'racial science': 'Are the Jews a Race Apart?', *Sydney Morning Herald*, 3 June 1961, p.10.
120. Ibid.
121. The 'Report of the Committee on Physical Anthropology' in 'Report of the Conference' in William E.H. Stanner and Helen Sheils (eds.), *Australian Aboriginal Studies: A Symposium of Papers Presented at the 1961 Research Conference* (Melbourne: Oxford University Press, 1963), pp.462–5. See also for example: J. Le Gay Brereton, 'An Estimate of Assimilation Rate of Mixed-Blood Aborigines in New South Wales', *Oceania*, Vol.XXXII, No.3 (September 1961), pp.187–91; Marjorie Barnard, *A History of Australia* (Sydney: Angus and Robertson, 1962), pp.647–50, 659 and 666; A.A. Abbie, 'Physical Characteristics of the Australian Aborigines', in Stanner and Sheils, *Australian Aboriginal Studies*; and J.H. Bennett, 'Genetical and Biometrical Studies', in Stanner and Sheils, *Australian Aboriginal Studies*.

122. See Benzion Patkin, *The Dunera Internees* (Stanmore, NSW: Cassell Australia, 1979); and Cyril Pearl, *The Dunera Scandal: Deported by Mistake* (Sydney: Angus & Robertson, 1983).
123. See for example Paul Bartrop, *Australian and the Holocaust 1933–45* (Melbourne: Scholarly Publishing, 1994); and William D. Rubinstein, *The Myth of Rescue: Why the Democracies could not have Saved more Jews from the Nazis* (London: Routledge, 1997).
124. In 1995 the Commonwealth Attorney General requested the Australian Human Rights and Equal Opportunities Commission to inquire into the past laws, practices and policies which resulted in the separation of Aboriginal and Torres Strait Islander children from their families by compulsion, duress or undue influence, and the effects of those laws, practices and policies. Among numerous other findings, the inquiry found that the policies in question had amounted to 'genocide': Human Rights and Equal Opportunities Commission, *Bringing them Home, Report of the National Inquiry into the Separation of Aboriginal and Torres Strait Islander Children from Their Families*, Pt 4 (13) 'Genocide' (April 1997). *Bringing them Home* engendered a bitter backlash: see Robert Manne, *In Denial: The Stolen Generations and the Right* (Melbourne: Schwartz Publishing, 2001). More generally, controversy has raged over the nature and extent of violence on the Australian frontier, including the extent to which it was 'genocidal'. In relation to debates over genocide in Australian history, see for example Keith Windschuttle, *The Destruction of Aboriginal Society* (Sydney: Macleay Press, 2003); Robert Manne (ed.), *Whitewash: On Keith Windschuttle's Fabrication of Aboriginal History* (Melbourne: Black Inc., 2003); Bain Attwood, *Telling the Truth about Aboriginal History* (Crows Nest, NSW: Allen & Unwin, 2005); Ann Curthoys and John Docker, 'Special Section: "Genocide"?: Australian Aboriginal History in International Perspective', *Aboriginal History*, Vol.25 (2001); Henry Reynolds, *An Indelible Stain: The Question of Genocide in Australia's History* (Ringwood, Vic: Penguin, 2001); and A. Dirk Moses (ed.), *Genocide and Settler Society: Frontier Violence and Stolen Indigenous Children in Australian History* (New York: Berghahn Books, 2004).
125. See Tim Rowse (ed.), *Contesting Assimilation* (Perth: API Network, 2005).
126. P. Hasluck, 'The Problem of Administration', in Ronald M. Berndt and Catherine H. Berndt (eds.), *Aboriginal Man in Australia* (Sydney: Angus & Robertson, 1965), p.449.
127. See for example Bain Attwood, *Rights for Aborigines* (Crows Nest (NSW): Allen & Unwin, 2003); and Sue Taffe, *Black and White Together. FCAATSI: The Federal Council for the Advancement of Aborigines and Torres Strait Islanders 1958–1973* (Brisbane: University of Queensland Press, 2005).
128. William E.H. Stanner, *The Boyer Lectures 1968: After the Dreaming* (Sydney: Australian Broadcasting Commission, 1968).
129. Indeed it is telling that two public figures as intellectually dissimilar as Barwick and Cusack were able to share a partial understanding of the trial as emphasising the distinctness of the Australian nation with its fair and peaceable traditions.
130. Manne, *In Denial*, p.30.
131. R. Ward, 'An Australian Legend, *Royal Historical Society Journal and Proceedings*, Vol.47, No.6 (December 1961), pp.335–50, at p.350.
132. Russell Ward, *Australia* (Englewood Cliffs, NJ: Prentice-Hall, 1965), p.138.
133. C.M. Tatz, 'Aborigines – Equality or Inequality?', *Australian Quarterly*, Vol.XXVIII, No.1 (March 1966), pp.73–90, at p.73.

An Early Holocaust Novel: White's *Riders in the Chariot*, a Critique

JOHN DOCKER

> 'And so you killed the snake.'
> 'That is not killing,' said Mrs Jolley, propping the spade.
> 'That is ridding the world of something bad.'
> 'Who is to decide what is bad?' asked Miss Hare.
>
> (Patrick White, *Riders in the Chariot*[1])

Mark Levene uses the above quotation as an epigraph to introduce *The Rise of the West and the Coming of Genocide*, the second volume of his long and eagerly awaited *Genocide in the Age of the Nation State*.[2] Levene is signalling that the novel by Australia's Nobel Prize winning author Patrick White (1912–90), while well known in Australian literary history, is at last attracting attention as an early example of evocation of the Holocaust. *Riders in the Chariot* was published in 1961, the same year as the Eichmann trial in Jerusalem.[3] An important character in *Riders in the Chariot* is Mordecai Himmelfarb, a Holocaust survivor, who makes his way from Germany, via Palestine, to Australia. The novel evokes the Holocaust, and constructs Jewish identity, in Himmelfarb's German upbringing, journey to and imprisonment in a concentration camp, his escape, his passage across the hemispheres, and his survivor life in the antipodes. So far, however, it seems to have escaped the attention of the critical literature concerning Holocaust novels.[4]

In part this inattention is the result of how Holocaust literature is defined. For example, David Patterson, Alan L. Berger and Sarita Cargas write in the preface to their *Encyclopedia of Holocaust Literature* that the authors selected for the volume 'survived the Holocaust, perished in the Holocaust, or were otherwise closely connected to the Holocaust', and nearly all of them are Jewish. The editors contend that what distinguishes Holocaust literature is that it is the 'work of witnesses', witnesses who have undertaken 'a literary response to the Holocaust'. For this reason, the editors have excluded second-generation authors as well as writers who have 'merely incorporated the Holocaust theme into a work' – such as William Styron, Thomas Keneally and Sylvia Plath – and who have 'no other direct link to the Holocaust'.[5] Patrick White was not Jewish, nor was he connected to the Holocaust as witness and survivor. In these terms, White has 'merely incorporated the Holocaust theme into a work'.

Other critics argue that Holocaust literature is an inclusive, if always unstable, troubling, and controversial category that cannot be confined to witnessing by survivors or those closely linked to the Holocaust.[6] In his preface to *The Holocaust Novel*, Efraim Sicher writes that most discussion of Holocaust writing starts from 'the premise that testimony provides a primary source for witnessing, and all that follows must be secondary, inferior, or discredited'. He goes on to caution, however, that memory can be 'notoriously fickle' and that survivors tend to remember partially or from perspectives limited to their personal experience. Memory is always reconstructed, mediated and filtered through 'subjective hindsight', and he reminds us that no story can be told without being reordered and emplotted: 'Imagination and fantasy do not necessarily impair authenticity. Fiction and history are not exclusive. Both, in fact, are narrative constructions.' Sicher suggests that those who write Holocaust novels are not always connected to Holocaust survivors, and that like the 'second generation', they imagine a world they have not personally experienced. Sicher also argues that the Holocaust novel cannot be defined as or confined to a specific genre; rather it bursts the 'already fuzzy' generic boundaries of autobiography and fiction, memoir and fantasy, historical document and realist novel.[7]

In this essay I will follow Sicher's inclusive approach in referring to White's *Riders in the Chariot* as a novel that engages with the Holocaust and hence is broadly part of Holocaust literature. One of my aims, then, is to redress the neglect of *Riders in the Chariot* by a critical examination of its constructions of the Holocaust and Jewishness. Sicher concludes his preface by raising the question of literary quality, that any Holocaust novel must stand the test of whether it is good literature.[8] I will state at the outset that I am not an admirer of *Riders in the Chariot* as a novel, and another aim of my essay will be to explain why I think certain aspects of the text are dubious, objectionable and, sometimes, offensive.

I shall quickly outline the narrative. When he arrives in Australia, the now elderly Himmelfarb, who had been a university lecturer in Germany, chooses to travel to the outskirts of Sydney, where he humbly takes up work in a factory making bicycle lamps. The factory is owned by Harry Rosetree, formerly known as Haïm, who now wishes to be perceived and accepted as an assimilated migrant; he and his wife Shirl (once Shulamith) have converted to Christianity and attempt to lead ordinary suburban lives. By contrast, Himmelfarb is created as an outsider to Australian society, and we see him drawn to other outsiders who reside nearby: the eccentric Miss Hare, who lives in Xanadu, a decaying mansion she had grown up in and where she delights in the secret world of its wild garden (and where the conventionally minded Mrs Jolley is her housekeeper and would-be jailer); the kind-hearted fecund Mrs Godbold, a kind of earth mother at one with the eternal rhythms of procreation; and an Aboriginal artist Alf Dubbo, outsider by virtue of his Aboriginality and his art. The outsiders will often be mistreated, scorned, reviled, with Himmelfarb on one occasion being crucified by his fellow workers in the factory. Nevertheless, while strangers to the expectations of conventional society which they unwillingly antagonise, the outsiders form a kind of spiritual elite. The novel proceeds by constructing separate fictional biographies for each of them, as they come finally to connect and interact. They communicate, however, not by words or ordinary conversation, but by a kind of intuitive silence that recognises their shared fate as outsiders yet who also merit, by their being outsiders, a divine destiny. Himmelfarb, Miss Hare and Mrs Godbold are finally painted together by Alf Dubbo – recalling Ezekiel envisaging 'four living creatures' emerging from a holy whirlwind (1:3–6) – as riders in the chariot, blessed by God.[9] *Riders in the Chariot*, like other post-war White novels, was recognised as challenging traditions of secular realism in the Australian novel. Rather than displaying any conventional plotting, *Riders in the Chariot* is anti-realist and metaphysical, working often through metaphor and image and an active narrator's observations and comments. The novel helped bring modernist writing to Australia while contributing to modernism worldwide.[10]

It is also worth quickly sketching in Patrick White's biography. Born in Australia to a wealthy pastoral family, he chose not to continue his family's rural calling or to conform to what he saw as its stifling expectations of class and social behaviour; he was always attracted to those he recognised as outsiders and strangers, constituting a different kind of superior order, of sensibility, soul, spirit and imagination.[11] He spent much of the 1920s and 1930s in London's writing and artistic circles, and was shaped by, and shaped himself in, the modernist literary movement.[12] He was also influenced by the prophetic and pantheistic traditions of English romanticism; indeed he crossed romanticism's optimism about the nearness of plenitude, of unity of spirit with nature, with modernism's hard edges, its apocalyptic sense of history as probable disaster.

There was, of course, no single modernist literary aesthetic, and in this essay I will touch on differences between Himmelfarb in *Riders in the Chariot* and Leopold Bloom in James Joyce's *Ulysses*, Bloom as perhaps modernity's most famous literary creation of a Jewish figure.[13] *Riders in the Chariot* is an avowedly philosemitic novel, yet, disturbingly, I detect in phrases and images, and in interventions of its egregious narrator, attitudes more akin to the Judeophobia of another defining modernist text, T.S. Eliot's *Gerontion*.[14]

Joining the Royal Air Force, White spent much of the Second World War in Palestine, Greece and Egypt.[15] In Alexandria, he met Manoly Lascaris with whom he would form a lifelong relationship, and they decided to live in Australia after the war.[16] White's return to Australia after the Second World War was unusual; many intellectuals left in the 1950s for elsewhere (anywhere), regarding post-war Australian society as, impossibly and embarrassingly, politically conservative, censorious, narrow-minded, provincial, suburban, restrictive, racist, ethnocentric, unsophisticated, un-urbane, uncosmopolitan, anti-intellectual, uninterested in the life of the mind; a society where the intellectual could not breathe and certainly was not given an assured place as remotely important; a society of *ressentiment*, where the intellectual should be brought into the many folds of conformity; a society where difference inspired fear and threat.

The White we observe in his letters and in David Marr's massive biography *Patrick White: A Life* is a writer who saw himself as a permanent outcast to mainstream Anglo-Australian society. In the tradition of artist as prophet, as saviour, he would attempt to use his art to raise its spiritual level. Especially after his post-war return to this 'immense void of Australia' he felt driven, in a wonderful phrase, to 'fill the Australian vacuum'.[17]

Riders in the Chariot

In his biography Marr tells us that White spent the early 1930s almost untouched by European politics, unworried by fascism, and hardly aware of the fate of the Jews. Later, however, Marr says, White wished to make amends, particularly when living back in Australia. He now felt Jews were his fellows in exile, bringing European culture, sophistication and intensity to spiritually empty Australia. In the Castle Hill district on the edge of Sydney in the 1950s he and Manoly Lascaris got to know various Central Europeans and together they formed an outpost of Europe. Preparing to create the key character of Mordecai Himmelfarb for *Riders in the Chariot*, White began to study Judaism and the history of European Jews, and he was 'particularly keen to meet Jews'. The music of Bloch apparently helped him with Himmelfarb, for he had only to listen 'to know inside me what it means to be a Jew'.[18]

Riders in the Chariot, much of its action set in the philistine world of post-war suburban Sydney, is insistently structured in terms of a binary contrast: the unredeemed and the saved. On one side we observe with distaste the appalling surburbans themselves. In a dangerous chain of false being, the suburban host includes Mrs Jolley and her friend Mrs Flack – mother of the ringleader of the crucifixion of Himmelfarb in Rosetree's bicycle lamp factory – and indeed conventional respectability-seeking ladies of lower middle, middle, and upper middle class pretension generally. The chain extends to the mass of the horny-handed, female as well as male. When Himmelfarb is assaulted by his erstwhile colleagues, a group of drunken hands who had been celebrating a lottery win, they are eagerly encouraged by the women who work there in the office. Blue, the crucifixion party's leader, is somehow being controlled by, is the rough instrument of, the spirit of his mother Mrs Flack. In romantic and modernist terms, such characters belong to an external, practical, utilitarian world of superficial instrumental reason, using words as weapons, and they envy and wish to destroy those they feel are different, those they suspect possess a secret centre of true being, those who make them register their own, as it were, corelessness: 'To some it is always unendurable to watch the antithesis of themselves.'[19]

The suburban host also, alas, now includes Himmelfarb's employer Harry Rosetree along with Shirl Rosetree as they attempt to conform to what they think are the norms of respectable conventional Australians. But assimilation is hard if not impossible; they can never quite get it right, bringing their children up as Catholic in a largely non-Catholic area. Himmelfarb's face reminds Harry of 'the one great archetypal face' of his Jewish fathers. The factory owner recalls his childhood, when he was young Haïm and cherished religious tradition, knew the 'wisdom of the Torah and the teaching of the Talmud'.[20]

Just before his crucifixion Himmelfarb crosses Sydney Harbour by train and enters Harry and Shirl's home, situated in the wealthier suburbs where the Rosetrees try to blend into a life of 'ruthless materialism', of 'plastic ladies' and watering the lawn. Himmelfarb's sudden appearance is traumatic for Harry. Torn between his superficial social identity and his lost authentic Jewish essence, knowing always a 'latent misery', he breaks down, cries, and hangs himself. Shirl Rosetree is not, however, similarly moved. Shirl has lost her essence, that which she had been, Shulamith 'the black, matted girl' of her European past. She had never really loved Harry ('Mrs Rosetree had a secret longing for hard, blond men') and dedicates the rest of her life to trying ever harder to conform: 'She had a kind of gift for assimilation.' What were most important to her were the texture-brick home, the streamlined car, the advanced shrubs, the grandfather clock, the walnut-veneer radiogram, the washing-machine, and the mixmaster.[21] Women, the reader of *Riders* soon realises, represent the worst and the best of earthly creatures.

On the other side, there is the struggle and pain of a spiritual elite, indifferent to material reward and social conventions and status, they who will eventually ride in the chariot of illumination but who meantime are trapped amongst the unworthy. Miss Hare is created as an *Erdgeist*, an earth spirit daily reborn in the womb and birth canals of nature, nature as dark busy organic activity, as growth, decay, death and new growth.[22] Her friend Mrs Godbold lives not far away in a humble shed as a Gea-Tellus (as Mr Bloom in *Ulysses* in his final moments before sleep thinks of Molly)[23] ever bountiful with children and loving-kindness. Also nearby Himmelfarb, their leader, messiah, saviour, prophet, an Elijah, lives in an unpretentious house. Alf Dubbo paints the ascension of this elite of spirit just before he dies, his life's work arriving at its fruition as it performs this act of homage.

How does Mordecai Himmelfarb manage to avoid becoming another Harry Rosetree? The prehistory of Himmelfarb as a European Jew is evoked at some length in *Riders in the Chariot*. Although Haïm Rosenbaum unhappily lapsed into Harry Rosetree, he was always haunted by the female voices from his childhood ('the voices of the dark women continued to vibrate inside him'). It is 'dark' female presence and wisdom which had saved Himmelfarb as he grew up in Germany. *Riders*' narrator tells us that Mordecai was born in a north German town sometime in the 1880s. His father, Moshe, was a dealer in furs, and though the family had many kin connections with Jews from Eastern Europe and Russia, Moshe himself chose to identify with Germany and Western Europe, where Jews had been emancipated in the new age of Enlightenment and universal brotherhood. Moshe still went to synagogue, but regarded himself as a 'worldly Jew of liberal tastes', as 'the reasonable man'. Mordecai's father, then, has allowed himself to be seduced by an attachment to an 'outside world', a false Germany of apparent acceptance, culture ('the beauties of Goethe'), and prosperity. By contrast, Mordecai's mother felt that it was only in 'certain dark medieval streets' that she could escape from the oppressive material existence that so pleased her husband. The mother welcomed to their home cousins fleeing the pogroms back east, cousins 'orthodox' and 'dark' who embarrassed the father. The father will later convert to Christianity and leave the mother, his life declining into indifferent death as all around him, Christians and Jews, regard him with contempt.[24]

The son fortunately becomes increasingly drawn to his mother and her traditional values. Such was not clear at first or for many years, because Mordecai grew up a brilliant scholar, going to Oxford and returning to become a university teacher of English literature. But Mordecai as student and then academic increasingly senses the emptiness of the life of the mind, realises that 'reason is far too imperfect a weapon'. Living the life of reason means for Mordecai a 'shrivelling of the spirit in himself', that he had 'dried up'. He has to recover 'his faith' and the 'oil and spices of tradition' despite 'his rational self', and he effects this by studying mystical Kabbalistic texts and by drawing closer to the spirit of his mother. It finally becomes evident that his mother had 'given him her character', that he had been created out of the 'mother's silence and solitude of soul'. He rejects the spirit of his 'self-congratulating father', absorbing his mother's spirit by non-rational means, 'through the tips of her fingers or subtler colloquy of souls'. A distant cousin the mother had once welcomed to their home when he was a child, the 'Galician rabbi' whose hands were 'almost womanly', comes to supplant Mordecai's father as spiritual guide. The woman Mordecai marries, Reha, is like his mother reborn, devout, uninterested in scholarly knowledge, 'homely', even myopic like his mother, and similarly disliking 'worldly practices'. Reha is an 'initiate' of 'mysteries' chiefly because of her very 'simplicity'. She is devoted to Mordecai; every night while he does his academic preparation she keeps him company, sewing or knitting for poorer Jews. She is sure that he will become a saviour of his 'race' and of humanity, those Reha thinks of, including herself, as 'the ordinary ones'. She is privileged to keep him company on this part of his life's journey – 'with humility, conscious of the minor part she would be given to play'.[25]

Once Mordecai Himmelfarb has realised that he must go the way of his mother and Reha, of non-reason, he can strive for the simplicity and humility that accompany his fatedness as a saviour, a *zaddik*. It is a difficult and tragic journey that the narrator now has to trace for us in the midst of the Holocaust. Himmelfarb will lose Reha to the concentration camps; he himself will survive because of an uprising at the camp he is sent to, which allows him to drift with partisans in the forests and make his way to Palestine and eventually to Australia. It was expected by his conventional sponsors and advisers that as a former university professor he would apply for a post equal to his intellectual gifts. But Himmelfarb declares: 'The intellect has failed us.' He makes his way to the outskirts of suburban Sydney, 'the fringes of the city', away from any Jewish community or urban intellectual life, and here as if ordained he makes contact with Miss Hare and Mrs Godbold. After talking to Miss Hare and evoking his life's narrative, Himmelfarb tells her that she too is a redeemer, a 'hidden *zaddik*', one of those who in each generation go secretly about the world 'healing, interpreting, doing their good deeds'. Himmelfarb and Miss Hare realise that they along with Mrs Godbold will become riders in the 'Chariot of God', *zaddikhim* not confined to Jews but redeemers of humanity. Miss Hare and Mrs Godbold are riders because, like Reha, such women possess an 'extreme simplicity of soul' existing at a deep level below 'words'.[26]

Throughout *Riders* the elect desire to share a communion of silence, since words are the instrument of repressive reason; each enjoys or strives for unity with nature, that which reason cannot understand or reach, and each possesses a secret core, an essence, of true being. I will particularly critique such essentialising in this essay.

Jewish Identity, English Romanticism

In *Ulysses*, Leopold Bloom's feelings concerning Jewishness are bafflingly elusive, decentred, palimpsestial, fantastical, parodying and self-parodying. Bloom rejects any confining unambiguous identity. How Bloomean is Mordecai Himmelfarb, he who submits with an expression 'almost of contentment' to crucifixion in Harry Rosetree's bicycle lamp factory?[27] Is Himmelfarb an anti-Bloom?

Himmelfarb is constructed in *Riders in the Chariot* as embodying 'certain inherited truths'. He becomes a walking 'archetype', who would have 'shamed his apostate father'. In Australia, talking to Miss Hare, he presents himself as the essential Jew, the conscience of his people, wanderers who can only live in houses that are 'fragile and ephemeral': 'I am a Jew, you see.' He assumes that Jews are European. To Miss Hare he refers to himself as 'the Jew'. When he enters the Rosetrees' house, Shirl Rosetree sees Himmelfarb as representing the 'one Jew' of history.[28]

In this conception, identity has little to do with the 'outer man' that ordinary humans perceive. In his fragile house Himmelfarb humbly cherishes religious texts, and in such humility, unreachable by the arrogance of intellect, he comes ever closer to the 'centre of his being'.[29] This 'centre' of true Jewishness is in continuity with medieval Jewry (as was his mother) and with Eastern European and Russian Jewish experience. But it is not realisable by those Jews like his father who identify with the Enlightenment of Western Europe, and indeed Himmelfarb's own intellectual productions, as dutiful academic author of some literary critical analyses of mostly minor English literature, are derided in the novel.

Riders in the Chariot is a kind of riposte to *Ulysses*, for where Joyce's novel teases and revels in identities as plural, uncertain, slippery and opaque, *Riders* creates identity as the solemn reverse. Himmelfarb, having chosen not to go the way of Enlightenment Jewry, emerges as unified in his being, authentic, coherent, and certain of Jewish identity as religious, mystical, redemptive, messianic and traditional, organised around the 'certain inherited truths' that are apparently originary and should be telos for all Jews.[30] Yet we can have our doubts about this unitary identity, doubts inspired by certain textual stresses in the novel, excesses of meaning that undo the Himmelfarb-friendly narrator's attempts to present Himmelfarb as archetypal. In particular, there are tensions in the novel between Himmelfarb as ideal Jew yet where Jewish identity, especially after Himmelfarb reaches Australia, is increasingly *assimilated* to certain inherited English romantic ideals.

Himmelfarb is follower as well as leader. In Europe he learnt from his mother and wife how to be a proper Jew, to observe the single true way. In Australia he learns from Miss Hare certain other originary truths: in Propp's terms, she is a donor in the narrative, appearing at a crucial time to provide the hero with vital information that permits him to become seeker and quester rather than victim and defeated. When Himmelfarb meets Miss Hare he tells her, under a canopy of tree branches, that Jews, confined within ghettoes, were excluded from contact with the natural world. With the example of Miss Hare before him, he learns the reward of humble attention to nature, his core becoming, as he sits on his veranda at dusk, like 'some darker, greener flame'. While walking beside the 'green river' next to the factory, the water, in an epiphanic exchange, glistens for him, so that now a 'green effulgence ... emanated from, as much as it enveloped, him'.[31] In terms of romantic neo-platonism, Himmelfarb's inner core harmonises with a universal order of Nature.

In Himmelfarb's journey towards true knowledge, *Riders in the Chariot* is romantic *Bildungsroman*. His opposition to Jews being attracted to Enlightenment reason blends with a romantic opposition to the Enlightenment and instrumental reason. Himmelfarb's learning to listen to the inner self formed by religious tradition and throw off his outer self of reason and intellect joins a romantic binary, of social surface as against true inner being: the romantic core constituted in exchanges with natural processes, the green world. When, in a moment of negative epiphany, Himmelfarb crosses by train the city and the Harbour Bridge and registers Sydney as life denying and distorting, as inferno, as the grotesque garish future unless humanity can be redeemed by those who know, his mood of millenarial anti-urbanism inherits not only early twentieth-century modernism but canonical English romanticism as in Blake and Wordsworth, not least those long anti-urban passages *The Prelude* stages in London.[32] As with Wordsworth, there is in *Riders* a romance of the margins, valorising idiosyncratic characters – Miss Hare is a kind of Wordsworthian idiot woman or leechgatherer – existing apart from conventional superficial society.

Jewish Identity, Aboriginal Australia

What happens when English romantic concepts are transposed to a colonial-settler society like Australia? In a colonising way, *Riders in the Chariot* suggests that for those blessed by God and journeying towards God, where God (in pantheistic terms) is Nature, the passage can be smooth, direct and untroubled. Those touched with truth can, like Miss Hare and Himmelfarb, strive for a oneness with the antipodean natural world, a unity of whites with Aboriginal nature, whites who are the descendants of those who conquered, who dispossessed the Indigenous, whites who continue to be advantaged by that brutal dispossession. Indeed, in this romancing of the margins, the white heroes of the narrative are themselves insistently evoked as 'dark', from the right kind of Jew in the old world to the chariot riders of the new.[33]

In *Riders* the margins are unified, so unified that their romantic possession of the natural world in Australia is accepted, sanctioned and celebrated by the novel's Aboriginal character. In one of his culminatory paintings Alf Dubbo, the 'solitary blackfellow', evokes Himmelfarb as 'the Jew-Christ', portraying Christ 'darker' than is usual in convention. When Dubbo paints Miss Hare as the Second Mary, he evokes her as like a 'ring-tail possum' in a 'dreamtime womb of transparent skin'. *Riders* happily permits an Aboriginal character to enfold certain white characters into his own land and mythology, his own 'dreamtime', his own chronotopes. Here is romantic desire grounded indeed in white mythology. It is, however, an interesting textual trace of a different history that Alf Dubbo should regard Miss Hare as not only like the indigenous possum but as 'fox-coloured', an image that whispers of contradictory signification, of invasion and predation.[34]

Jewish Identity and Kabbalah

As the narrative increasingly maps Jewish identity onto romantic axes and axioms, the proposition that Mordecai Himmelfarb embodies 'certain inherited truths' of Judaism begins to look increasingly curious. The true Jewish way apparently is to strive (like Miss Hare, Mrs Godbold, Alf Dubbo) to abjure intellect, reason and words, to choose and enjoin 'silence'.[35] Yet such striving by Himmelfarb stands not only as a rejection of eighteenth and nineteenth century discourses of Enlightenment but also of long Judaic traditions of textuality, of Judaism as a religion of the book, of words, of textual commentary, of interpretation and reinterpretation, of writing, intellect, mind.

Derrida in his essay 'Edmond Jabès and the Question of the Book' writes of a 'certain Judaism as the birth and passion of writing', that there is a 'pure and founding exchange' between 'the Jew and writing', and that the 'situation of the Jew becomes exemplary of the situation of the poet, the man of speech and of writing'. For the Jew as exile, as wanderer, the 'necessity of commentary, like poetic necessity, is the very form of exiled speech', resonances which, says Derrida, are also to be found in the Kabbalah.[36] Ammiel Alcalay in *After Jews and Arabs* qualifies Derrida's argument here. Alcalay suggests that Derrida, in his writing on the poetry of Jabès, is not challenging the myth that the Jew is always pariah, outsider, wanderer and other, whose only house is that 'writing = Jew = Book'. For Alcalay, such a view of 'the Jew' totalises European Jewish experience as universal. It ignores another long and rich cultural history, that of Moorish Spain, North Africa, the Mediterranean, the Levant – the Islamic Orient where for more than 1,000 years 'the Jew *was* native, not a stranger but an absolute inhabitant of time and place', in occupations of all kinds, in cultural and intellectual life, participating in the very poetics of heterogeneity that constituted the Levant's distinctiveness. And he argues that the writing of Jabès, originally from Egypt, still signifies even in exile in France the collective duration of that Levantine history.[37] Alcalay disagreeing with Derrida's interpretation of Jabès' texts: such activity of writing, of movement of the word, Himmelfarb rejects in the name of an absolute and exclusive call to 'silence'.

Such a call to silence may indeed accord with Himmelfarb's supposed interest in Kabbalism. In *The Essential Kabbalah* Daniel C. Matt says of *The Zohar, The Book of Radiance*, that near the

> top of the sefirotic ladder, meditation reaches Binah. She is called *Teshuvah*, Return. The ego returns to the womb of being. Binah cannot be held in thought. … In the depths of Binah lies Hokhmah, Wisdom. The mystic is nourished from this sphere. Profound and primal, it cannot be known consciously, only absorbed. In the words of Isaac the Blind, one of the earliest kabbalists of Provence, 'The inner, subtle essences can be contemplated only by sucking, not by knowing'. Beyond Hokhman is the Nothingness of Keter, the annihilation of thought. In this ultimate sefirah human consciousness expands, dissolving into Infinity.[38]

Certainly there are affinities here with Himmelfarb and even more, perhaps, especially in the remarkable image of contemplation as sucking, with his friend and mentor Miss Hare. Yet the Kabbalists, as in the Book of Zohar, produced an immense body of writings. Himmelfarb's rejection of writing and his embracing of silence strike me as a strand of Kabbalah very much filtered through – assimilated to – English romantic discourses of desired moments of absorption in nature.[39]

Jewish Identity and Visuality

The Aboriginal artist Alf Dubbo paints Himmelfarb 'the Jew-Christ' as a 'flat, almost skimped figure, with elliptical mouth, and divided, canvas face'.[40] Yet that Alf Dubbo should paint Himmelfarb at all, with the full approval of the narrator, is also curious in terms of the novel's claim to anchor Judaism in 'certain inherited truths'. Judaism is very divided over the question of visual representation: there are no certain single truths, the inheritance is highly contradictory. In Exodus there is the injunction from God to Moses that there be no graven images; in particular, that there be no representation of God himself in figural form; Moses, on the other hand, is quite frequently in close visual contact with God. In *Tractatus Theologico-Politics* Spinoza sardonically points out that in many places in Scripture the injunction against visual representation does not hold, and God is often represented in highly anthropomorphic ways.[41]

Daniel Boyarin, in his essay 'The Eye of the Torah: Ocular Desire in Midrashic Hermeneutic', similarly argues that in the biblical texts and in later Rabbinic tradition there was an embracing of the visibility and corporeality of God. According to Rabbinic tradition, the moments in which God was held to have shown himself to the children of Israel were high points in Exodus, the crossing of the Red Sea and the giving of the Torah on Mt. Sinai. Boyarin notes that in Scripture one is not normally permitted to see God, and it may be dangerous to see God, and there is the taboo on images of God; but in Torah God most certainly can be seen and is seen. The memory of having enjoyed the sight of God in the Bible and the desire to have that experience again, Boyarin suggests, were a vital part of the study of Torah and making of midrashic commentary in Rabbinic religion. By the adoption of a hermeneutic method, the Rabbis hoped to recover the historical memory and original visions of God enacted in the Bible; a hermeneutic of recollected experience and visual perception, erotically charged.[42]

There is also the erotically charged Jewish mystical tradition, often drawing strength from the Song of Songs as well as the first chapter of the Book of Ezekiel, where the narrator begins by telling us 'the heavens were opened, and I saw visions of God' (Ezekiel 1: 1); and such reaching towards visions of God was certainly important in the medieval Kabbalists.[43]

Riders in the Chariot follows this mystical and Kabbalistic tradition, with its four riders in the chariot, as in the book of Ezekiel.[44] Himmelfarb 'the Jew-Christ' is painted as a 'figure'. Such visual representation is to be seen, *Riders* implies, as consonant with the only kind of Judaism that is proper, that of the Eastern European and Russian Jews and especially of the 'Galician rabbi', who inherited the medieval tradition cherished by Himmelfarb's mother.

Yet is the history of Judaism – as Daniel Boyarin says, the very name 'Judaism' is a 'reified fiction of four thousand years of a culture'[45] – so simple, so uncomplicated, so uncontradictory that there should be only one proper way?

The Shtetl

Should Eastern European Judaism be so innocently idealised as it is throughout *Riders in the Chariot*? In *The Non-Jewish Jew*, in the essay on Marc Chagall, a Russian Jew brought up in a shtetl and the great forerunner of Surrealism and Expressionism, Isaac Deutscher argues that 'Judaism's hostility towards the visual arts is notorious', and that rabbinical orthodoxy 'stunted' their growth 'far more cruelly than even Calvinism did'. The shtetl, the little town within the Jewish pale of Eastern Europe, would have its cantors and musicians, its bards, poets, and composers of folk tales; but it had 'no painters or sculptors'. Even the nineteenth century Hassidic revolt against Talmudic scholasticism, Deutscher feels, did not weaken the millennia-old abhorrence of the graven image, and Hassidic revivalism in any case quickly ossified into another rabbinical orthodoxy. It was 'in defiance of tradition', outside of the Synagogue (whose walls were 'bare and grim'), that the Russian or Polish Jew would paint. In and through Chagall, the 'long suppressed visual imagination of the Jew burst out like a volcano exploding in rainbows'.[46]

In *Riders in the Chariot* the narrator suggests that the traditional Jewish world of Eastern Europe, its present representative the 'Galician rabbi' whose hands were 'almost womanly', is a single world, unified across time (except for those Jews seduced by wealth who would migrate to contemporary America to absorb themselves in its 'nylon dream').[47]

Deutscher's *The Non-Jewish Jew*, calling attention to 'rabbinical orthodoxy', proposes otherwise, suggesting histories and stories of tension and conflict, of intolerance towards alternative identities. Deutscher's own ancestors, so Tamara Deutscher tells us in the introduction, came in the sixteenth century from Nuremberg to Galicia. Mainly printers, they originally bore the name of Ashkenazy. Isaac was named after his great-grandfather, a learned Talmudic scholar, a man of frightful temper and fanatic convictions, who became enraged that his son had turned to Hassidism, with its more joyous view of life and more lax discipline; he had his son persecuted by the non-Jewish authorities. In later generations, however, the family became Hassidic. When, nevertheless, Deutscher's own father wrote a history of the Jews in Germany, based on years of research, the manuscript was thrown into the fire by his father's mother, fearing that it might be heretical.[48]

In Arnold Zable's autobiographical *Jewels and Ashes* (1991), the Australian narrator writes of his return to ancestral sites in Poland, meeting the few Jews who survived Nazism in Bialystok and surrounding towns, places still imbued with traces of shtetl life for centuries. He hears stories of resistance to Nazi occupation forces and of the partisans in the forests: here *Jewels and Ashes* joins with *Riders in the Chariot* in disputing a narrative like Steven Spielberg's 1993 film *Schindler's List* that constructs Polish Jews as passive during the Holocaust. He meets and talks to Jews who appear desperate to escape from the confinement of small-town life and envy his diaspora state, growing up the other side of the world in a Yiddish-speaking community in Melbourne. The narrator, however, yearns to consecrate the memory of traditional Jewish life in pre-Second World War Poland as warm, spontaneous, cooperative, collective. At the same time he knows his own 'dream of the shtetl' is a 'fragile romance', and he recalls other stories, of his great-grandparents attempting to negotiate ancient quarrels that still simmered in the towns and hamlets of the pale; in particular the bitter conflict between older austere traditions of pious study and strict discipline, and, in the 1700s, the newly emergent Hassidic movement, with its emphasis on devotion, dance, and wonder-workers. The quarrel had split shtetl communities apart, and there were bans, book burnings, family feuds, denunciations to the czarist authorities resulting in imprisonment; marriage to Hassidim and assistance at their burials had been forbidden.[49]

In *Riders* Mordecai's father Moshe welcomes emancipation in Western Europe: it heralds that 'the Jewish soul was at last set free', that the 'walls were down, the suffocating rooms were burst open, the chains of observance had been loosed'.[50] But this whisper in the text, these suggestions of attempts to destroy dissent and difference within Eastern European Jewish history, have to contend with the crushing portrait of Moshe as contemptible in his delusions about enlightened Germany. By contrast, (supposed) Jewish tradition in Eastern Europe is admired in a fundamentalist way.

In 'Edmond Jabès and the Question of the Book' Derrida contrasts two kinds of interpretation as irreducibly different, that between the poet welcoming the 'adventure of the text', and the rabbi insisting on exegesis as Law.[51] In these terms, Mordecai Himmelfarb clearly becomes rabbi not poet; he is uninterested in the play of interpretation and any loosening of a particular kind of Jewish identity. He insists on representing himself as the true way, as archetypal, and he is disturbingly authoritarian in his relations with Harry Rosetree, like his father in his eyes an apostate. Himmelfarb refuses to accept Harry Rosetree's new identity ('We are Australians now'). In the factory Himmelfarb had already felt called upon to address Rosetree as Rosenbaum, and tried to get him to speak German with him and to admit he was Jewish – 'Surely you are one of us'. For all that Himmelfarb submits almost with 'contentment' to the crucifixion in the factory, and although he desires humility and simplicity, we see him hunting Harry Rosetree to his home, and, in a kind of stalking epistemic violence, refusing to Rosetree the dignity of choice, that Rosetree or anyone else's identity could be – as suggested throughout *Ulysses* – fragmented, contradictory and unknowable.[52]

That Narrator

In *Problems of Dostoevsky's Poetics* Mikhail Bakhtin, contrasting Tolstoy and Dostoevsky, argues that in Tolstoy's fiction the author dominates his texts in a monologic way, is all-knowing and all-controlling.[53] Here again *Riders in the Chariot* emerges as a kind of essentialising riposte to *Ulysses*. Where in *Ulysses* narration in a dialogic way is multiple and mysterious, *Riders* offers the perspectives of a single all-seeing narrator, whose knowledge of every character is exhaustive and complete. In *Riders* we are told that suburbia as in Mrs Flack and Mrs Jolley 'took for granted its right to pass judgement on the human soul, and indulge in a fretfulness of condemnation'.[54] Yet if the narrator, masculinist and aggressive, omnipresent and omniscient, omnipotent and omnivorous, does not like this or that character, those who fall on the wrong side of the binary divide of elect and non-elect, he will pursue and pursue them until revenge is enacted.

Throughout *Riders* the narrator himself is fretfully condemnatory, inducing a cumulative crudity of aesthetic effects. In particular, the narrator is unable to resist a dismissive damning mode, as in the continuous references to 'plastic ladies', accompanied by physical disparagement.[55] When Miss Hare was a child, her mother's lady friends, faced with oddity, knew 'firmly to suppress, like wind in company, the rise of unreason in their minds'. Mrs Jolley passes her tongue 'along her stripped lips'; eating, her face becomes a 'series of lumps'. When Himmelfarb's father Moshe marries a young Christian woman, Christel Schmidt, her hair is as 'heavy and yellow in its snood as horses' dung'; she is kind and capable, but 'of no further significance'. When Moshe dies 'of his young wife', he is buried 'by a priest with a stammer, and an acolyte with a cold'. A young German soldier stands 'holding a gun, and picking his nose'. On the train to the concentration camp, when Himmelfarb talks to a formerly wealthy Jewish woman, the Lady from Czernowitz, we learn of her 'floury breasts', though a little later we see that she has 'one dug'. When Himmelfarb arrives in Palestine, his brother-in-law Ari tries to convince him to stay and join the Zionist enterprise. In the exchange between Ari and Mordecai, Ari looks like he is 'trying to rid himself of phlegm' as he 'fidgeted about on his broad behind'. At Rosetree's Brighta Bicycle Lamps factory, the machinery 'hissed and pissed': 'Toothless lads hawked up mirthless laughter'. The men are 'pursy', or will loudly 'fart', while the ladies who work on the assembly line 'eased their plastic teeth' or 'shifted gum'.[56]

When Himmelfarb confronts Rosetree over Jewish identity, Rosetree is 'not only mentally distressed', he can 'not detach the pants from around his groin'. Talking of Himmelfarb to his wife, Rosetree 'had to belch'. Mrs Flack or Mrs Jolley at times would 'stare dreamily into her own bottomless mind, watching the cotton-wool unfurl'. Like Mrs Jolley, Mrs Flack can draw back 'her strips of palest lips'; or she will hiccup. At the end of a conversation with her friend, Mrs Jolley was 'perspiring uncomfortably behind the knees'. When Mrs Godbold, then Ruth Joyner, was young, she worked as a maid for Mrs Chalmers-Robinson, who might hold a lunch for ladies 'wearing monkey fur'; they quickly become 'monkey-ladies', or 'sick, drooping monkeys'. Ruth sees her mistress without clothes, the lady appearing like 'the sac of a slack, sick spider'. Later we see Mrs Chalmers-

Robinson at lunch at a restaurant with another lady, Mrs Colquhoun, a 'stream of melted ice-cream' threatening to 'spill from one corner of what had been' the latter's mouth. In the brothel scene one of the customers, Fixer Jensen, 'stood and picked his nose as usual'. Mrs Pask, Alf Dubbo's superficial foster mother, had on occasion to master 'her wind'. As the train passes through Sydney where the city's neon lights are a 'syrup' colouring the 'pools of vomit and the sailors' piss', Himmelfarb observes 'blue-haired grannies' whose breasts 'chafed to escape, from shammy-leather back to youth, or else roundly asserted themselves, like chamberpots in concrete'.[57]

In the factory, when news of the lottery win by the men gets abroad, Ernie Theobalds the foreman laughed 'as he played with the hair of his armpits'. When Himmelfarb is crucified by the drunken men led by Mrs Flack's Blue, Blue is so drunk the 'beer was running out of his navel'. Ernie Theobalds comes out to take a look, 'exploring the flesh under his singlet'. The policeman called to investigate is named 'Constable McFaggott'. While Alf Dubbo is on a bus, the conductor begins to 'clean his ears with a key'. When Dubbo dies, a bored young doctor is called, 'who was reading a detective story, and scratching himself through his flies'.[58] Such writing is tedious, tiresome, and unworthy. The judgement of the Australian poet A.D. Hope, a contemporary of White's, on White's writing as 'pretentious and illiterate verbal sludge' has considerable continuing merit.[59]

So judging and bludgeoning is the narrator that, in relation to Jewish characters he despises for not being truly Jewish, for not being graven in the image of Himmelfarb, he also cannot resist physical disparagement. When Nazi soldiers guard Himmelfarb's group of Jews before they enter the train, one guard 'inserted the blade between the great buttocks of a fat Jew'. We are to understand this as the Nazi guard's brutal perception, yet how different is this formulation from the narrator's notation of Himmelfarb's brother-in-law Ari in Palestine 'trying to rid himself of phlegm' as he 'fidgeted about on his broad behind'? There is the reference to the Lady of Czernowitz having 'one dug' that 'hung down beside the ancient scar which represented the second'. On the way to Palestine, there is a 'Jewess' supervising distribution of clothing, who 'wore a moustache', where 'little points of perspiration were clearly visible on the hairs'. In Jerusalem Himmelfarb runs into Appenzeller, someone he knew from student days, a physicist, a 'coarse-skinned, bristly individual' who 'laughed at his joke, and the pores round his nostrils oozed'. Indeed, we learn that advice would 'swim from Appenzeller's skin, of which the pores had always been conspicuously large'.[60] Such language is, I think, perilously close to the antisemitic, to Judeophobia.

Riders' narrator is not only Eastern European-centric about Jewish identity, but also Orientalist in relation to Palestine and the Levant. The narrator does not question the right of European Jews to colonise the 'stony soil' of Palestine, 'the Land', Jews who 'resisted the elements because there, at last, it was natural to do so': 'For the Jews were at last returning home. They would recognize the stones they had never seen, and the least stone would be theirs.' Ari and his *sabra* wife Rahel on their kibbutz 'belonged to their surroundings, like the stones, or the olive tree beneath which they were sitting'. The Arabs of Palestine are, however, almost invisible to the narrator, except for a 'couple of Arabs' who 'laughed' at Himmelfarb in Jerusalem: the Indigenous people of the land of Palestine are not evoked as belonging to its stones and olive trees; rather they are dismissed in a single contemptuous phrase.[61]

Nevertheless, Himmelfarb refuses to stay in Palestine. Himmelfarb perceives Ari as 'dangerously arrogant'. He feels that the Zionist focus on the 'National Home', on 'force', and 'work' as 'the panacea', ignores soul and spirit. Rahel the *sabra* already strikes Himmelfarb as merely 'practical'.[62] Here, then, is a similarity with *Ulysses*, in the way Leopold Bloom opposes Zionist nationalism, though Bloom thinks of the Levant, and especially Jerusalem, as proudly Oriental.[63]

Conclusion

Reading *Riders in the Chariot* this time, it struck me as a rather odious text, not least in being dominated by a narrator who is all too similar to Foucault's panopticon: that which sees and surveys all, but cannot itself be seen; positions itself beyond reflexive scrutiny, beyond the remotest self-parody. In *Riders* narration is a discourse of certainty, a relentless gaze that everywhere passes 'judgement' on the 'significance' of each 'human soul' that comes before it for sentencing.

The utopianism of *Riders* is rather chilling. In its final narrative segment there is not just a permanent opposition of two kinds of being, clearly inferior and superior. There is also an optimism about society as capable of change, where Himmelfarb has indeed proven a redemptive Jew-Christ. In these prefigurations of utopia, Mrs Godbold's earth-mother loving-kindness lives on in her daughter Elsie and Elsie's husband Bob Tanner. New ideal Australians are emerging, with Elsie as another earth mother, and Bob, an ordinary young Australian male, infused with a female spirit of loving-kindness; the loving-kindness that has its own lineage, in Himmelfarb's mother, his wife Reha, Miss Hare, Mrs Godbold, and now Mrs Godbold's daughter.

What a philistine Utopia this promises to be! It will be anti-intellectual, since Enlightenment values of reason have apparently failed absolutely: the brushstrokes that belittle Jews influenced by the Enlightenment as well as Enlightenment ideals in general are themselves derisorily crude.

It has always struck me as curious that White's writing has been so admired for so long. Criticism in Australia tends to construct literary history as a narrative of progress, with White as a pinnacle, a beacon.[64] But I cannot see White as a hero of Australian literary development, or of world literature. In terms of essentialising conceptions of ethnicity and identity, there is no vast difference between White's writing and the writings of Matthew Arnold and a host of English and European authors in the nineteenth century guided by a delusive obsession with relating culture to presumed ethnic essences. White's 1981 autobiography *Flaws in the Glass: A Self-Portrait,* for example, relishes a language of ethnic and racial insult, particularly towards those – Turks, Orientals generally, Slavs, Germans – he sees as threatening the true and essential character and traditions of the peoples he admires.[65] Criticism would do well to cease continuous celebration, and subject White's writings to searching critique.[66]

In these terms, I think *Riders in the Chariot,* as an early contribution to Holocaust literature, is certainly interesting, but also seriously flawed.

NOTES

1. Patrick White, *Riders in the Chariot* (1961; Harmondsworth: Penguin, 1964), p.83.
2. Mark Levene, *Genocide in the Age of the Nation State,* 2 vols. (London: I.B. Taurus, 2005).
3. I gain no sense from White's published letters, however, that he was interested in the capture of Eichmann and subsequent trial. See David Marr (ed.), *Patrick White: Letters* (London: Jonathan Cape, 1994).
4. There is, for example, no mention of *Riders in the Chariot* in Jacob Glatstein, Israel Knox and Samuel Margoches (eds.), *Anthology of Holocaust Literature* (1968; Philadelphia: The Jewish Publication Society of America, 1969) or in Lawrence L. Langer, *The Holocaust and the Literary Imagination* (1975; New Haven, CT: Yale University Press, 1977). In his introductory comments to the section 'Chariots' of White's letters for the period December 1958–February 1961, Marr notes that in *Riders of the Chariot* White, 'writing fifteen years after the revelations of Auschwitz ... was one of the first novelists to come to grips with this century's innovation in horror': *Patrick White: Letters,* p.151.
5. David Patterson, Alan L. Berger and Sarita Cargas (eds.), *Encyclopedia of Holocaust Literature* (Connecticut: Oryx Press, 2002), pp.ix–xi.
6. See the very interesting book by Sue Vice, *Holocaust Fiction* (London and New York: Routledge, 2000), which focuses on scandals concerning the Holocaust novels of Martin Amis, D.M. Thomas, Jerzy Kosinski, William Styron, Thomas Keneally and Helen Darville; in the conclusion on pp.163–4 there is discussion of Binjamin Wilkomirski.
7. Efraim Sicher, *The Holocaust Novel* (New York and London: Routledge, 2005), pp.xii–xiii, xviii, xxi.
8. Ibid., p.xxiii.
9. Concerning Ezekiel, cf. Karen Armstrong, *The Great Transformation: The Beginning of Our Religious Traditions* (New York: Knopf, 2006), pp.172–4.
10. Cf. John Docker, *Australian Cultural Elites* (Sydney: Angus & Robertson, 1974).
11. In his letters White reflects that in his conception of Himmelfarb in *Riders in the Chariot* 'what helped me most was the fact that throughout my life I have been an outcast myself'. See letter to his American publisher Ben Huebsch, Marr (ed.), *Patrick White: Letters,* p.180.
12. See White's autobiography *Flaws in the Glass: A Self-Portrait* (London: Penguin, 1981).
13. See John Docker, *1492: The Poetics of Diaspora* (London: Continuum, 2001), chs.4–7.
14. Cf. Maud Ellmann, 'The Imaginary Jew: T.S. Eliot and Ezra Pound', in Bryan Cheyette (ed.), *Between 'Race' and Culture: Representations of 'the Jew' in English and American Literature* (Stanford, CA: Stanford University Press, 1996), pp.84–93.
15. David Marr tells us that in the Second World War White, having joined RAF Intelligence, spent the winter of 1943–44 in Palestine interrogating refugees to find targets to bomb in the German towns from which they had fled. See *Patrick White: Letters,* p.55.
16. John Rickard, 'Clark and Patrick White', in Carl Bridge (ed.), *Manning Clark: Essays on his Place in History* (Melbourne: Melbourne University Press, 1994), pp.47–8.
17. David Marr, *Patrick White: A Life* (Sydney: Random House Australia, 1991), pp.312, 337. Cf. my review in *Australian Historical Studies,* Vol.99 (October 1992).
18. Marr, *Patrick White,* pp.225, 227, 332, 491, 523, 612.
19. White, *Riders in the Chariot,* p.402.
20. Ibid., pp.202–4, 376–7.

21. Ibid., pp. 382, 386–7, 402–3, 447, 450, 483.
22. Concerning Miss Hare as *Erdgeist*, see Marr (ed.), *Patrick White: Letters*, pp.153, 196.
23. James Joyce, *Ulysses* (1922), intro. and notes by Declan Kiberd (London: Penguin, 1992), p.870.
24. *Riders*, pp.96–9, 104, 115–16, 205.
25. Ibid., pp.96–7, 99, 103–4, 110, 113, 116, 123, 125–6, 129–30, 136, 140–42, 427.
26. Ibid., pp.97, 154–5, 198–9, 308, 427.
27. Ibid., p.409.
28. Ibid., pp.91, 144, 301, 307, 383–4, 387.
29. Ibid., pp.194, 198–9.
30. Ibid., p.387.
31. Ibid., pp.89, 197, 205.
32. The romantic and modernist trope of the city – in particular, London – as anti-life continues in W.G. Sebald; see *Austerlitz* (2001; London: Penguin, 2002), pp.48–50.
33. *Riders*, pp.99, 131.
34. Ibid., pp.434, 454–6.
35. Ibid., pp.22, 37, 99, 135–6, 169, 187, 311, 434.
36. Jacques Derrida, *Writing and Difference*, trans. and intro. Alan Bass (Chicago: University of Chicago Press, 1978), ch.3, 'Edmond Jabès and the Question of the Book', pp.64–7, 74.
37. Ammiel Alcalay, *After Jews and Arabs: Remaking Levantine Culture* (Minneapolis: University of Minnesota Press, 1993), pp.1, 64–5, 67–71, and passim.
38. Daniel C. Matt, *The Essential Kabbalah: The Heart of Jewish Mysticism* (San Francisco: HarperCollins, 1994), Introduction, p.11.
39. Gershom G. Scholem, *Major Trends in Jewish Mysticism* (New York: Schocken Books, 1954), Ninth Lecture, 'Hasidism: The Latest Phase', pp.325–50, evokes the history of Polish and Ukrainian Hasidism of the eighteenth and nineteenth centuries, its transforming of Kabbalistic tradition into an accessible and popular movement, and its offering of a new kind of leader, a prophet, an illuminate, a saint-mystic, blessed with charisma, as in the figure of the Zaddik. In Scholem's view, Hasidism, while being very creative in terms of its religious energy, offered no new religious or mystical principles and ideas in terms of the history of Kabbalism.
40. *Riders*, p.456.
41. Baruch Spinoza, *Tractatus Theologico-Politicus*, trans. Samuel Shirley, introd. Brad S. Gregory (Leiden: E.J. Brill, 1989), pp.70–72, 228, 233.
42. Daniel Boyarin, 'The Eye in the Torah: Ocular Desire in Midrashic Hermeneutic', *Critical Inquiry*, Vol.16 (1990), pp.532–50; in this essay Boyarin critiques the view that Judaism is the religion in which God is heard but not seen. Martin Jay notes, in *Downcast Eyes: The Denigration of Vision in Twentieth-Century French Thought* (Berkeley: University of California Press, 1993), pp.14–15, 549–50, that recent scholarship suggests that there is a tension in Jewish history between iconic and anti-iconic tendencies, and that at various times and places there were images of cherubim, funeral paintings, and synagogue decorations, and also iconic representation in the textuality of the late Kabbalah.
43. For the Song of Songs see Boyarin, 'The Eye in the Torah', pp.541–44; on p.534 note 5 Boyarin points to the continuity of Rabbinic tradition and the medieval Kabbalists in terms of embracing God's visibility and corporeality. Cf. Gershom Scholem, *Origins of the Kabbalah*, ed. R.J. Zwi Werblowsky, trans. Allan Arkush (Princeton, NJ: Princeton University Press, 1990), pp.238–44.
44. Cf. Peter Beatson, *The Eye in the Mandala. Patrick White: A Vision of Man and God* (London: Paul Elek, 1976), pp.111–13, 159–65.
45. Boyarin, 'The Eye in the Torah', pp.532–3.
46. Isaac Deutscher, *The Non-Jewish Jew* (London: Oxford University Press, 1968), ch.8, 'Marc Chagall and the Jewish Imagination', pp.155–6. I think that the massive involvement of Jews in the fantastical visual excess of Hollywood is also a release of the repressed; cf. Patricia Erens, *The Jew in American Cinema* (Bloomington: Indiana University Press, 1984).
47. *Riders*, p.143.
48. Deutscher, *The Non-Jewish Jew*, introduction by Tamara Deutscher, pp.3–4. Cf. Israel Shahak, *Jewish History, Jewish Religion* (London: Pluto Press, 1994), pp.14–20; John Docker, 'Orientalism and Zionism', *Arena*, Vol.75 (1986), pp.88–91. Cf. also E.J. Hobsbawm, 'Homesickness', *London Review of Books*, 8 April 1993, p.20: 'It is easier to sentimentalise the shtetl now that it no longer exists than it was when young men and women had to live in it.'
49. Arnold Zable, *Jewels and Ashes* (Melbourne: Scribe, 1991), pp.67–8, 91, 96, 100, 105, 144, 161–2.
50. *Riders*, p.98.

51. Derrida, 'Edmond Jabès', pp.67–8.
52. See Docker, *1492: The Poetics of Diaspora*, pp.85–6. In *Patrick White: A Life*, pp.145, 151, David Marr tells us that when young, in 1936, White read *Ulysses* and admired its technique, especially the way the author switches at will from the mind of one character to another, drifting with their thoughts; indeed, says Marr, Joyce became White's God and *Ulysses* his Bible. My argument, however, is that the essentialising of identity in *Riders in the Chariots* is the reverse of the anti-essentialising of *Ulysses* in the construction of Bloom.
53. Mikhail Bakhtin, *Problems of Dostoevsky's Poetics* (Manchester: Manchester University Press, 1984), pp.47–75.
54. *Riders*, p.211.
55. Ibid., p.382. In this aspect *Riders*' narrator reminds me of the egregious narrator of Peter Carey's *Oscar and Lucinda* (London: Faber and Faber, 1988).
56. *Riders*, pp.32, 77, 81, 120, 129, 169, 178, 184, 192, 200, 206, 216.
57. Ibid., pp.203, 210, 212, 246–7, 250, 282, 334, 391–2, 468, 484.
58. Ibid., pp.401, 405, 416, 424, 435, 460.
59. The phrase from Hope's review of *The Tree of Man* in the *Sydney Morning Herald*, 16 June 1956, is quoted in Hu Wenzhong, 'The Myth and the Facts: A Reconsideration of Australia's Critical Reception of Patrick White', *Australian Literary Studies*, Vol.16, No.3 (1994), p.335.
60. *Riders*, pp.175, 184, 189-90, 192.
61. Ibid., pp.143, 187, 189, 191–2.
62. Ibid., pp.191, 193.
63. Cf. Docker, *1492: The Poetics of Diaspora*, pp.66–8, 74, 77–8.
64. Cf., however, Simon During, *Patrick White* (Melbourne: Oxford University Press, 1996).
65. From David Marr's biography we learn that White's life had taken, by the time *Riders in the Chariot* was published, 'a new course and he was dispersing his Jewish friends'. He wished, in the early 1960s, to return to writing for the theatre. White now spoke of his old Central European Jewish companions as millstones. He broke with them 'brutally', justifying it on the grounds that he was an artist. Marr, *Patrick White: A Life*, pp.383–4, 455.
66. Cf. John Docker, 'Romanticism, Modernism, Exoticism: Patrick White in Biography and Autobiography', *Southern Review*, Vol.26, No.3 (1993), pp.358–76; 'White Mythologies: Ethnicity and Identity in White and Joyce', *Proceedings of the Sixteenth Annual Conference, Association for the Study of Australian Literature, 1994* (Canberra: Dept. of English, ADFA, 1995), pp.207–13; 'How Close Should Writers and Critics Be?' *Australian Book Review*, No.202 (July 1998), pp.25–6.

'Remembering for Us': The Transgenerational Transmission of Holocaust Memory and Commemoration

SHARON KANGISSER COHEN

One evening in 2005 the following incident was related to me by an old school friend. He recalled how during a recent Shabbat dinner at a friend's home he began speaking to her grandmother, a Holocaust survivor from Hungary. At one point the woman suddenly pulled up her sleeve and showed him the number tattooed on her arm. She asked, 'Do you know what this is?!' My friend is a well-educated Jew: he was brought up in a strong Jewish home, had a day school education and has always identified with and been active in the Jewish community. Having read extensively about the *Shoah*, he certainly knew what the number was, yet this woman was not convinced.

This incident is revealing on a number of levels. First, it demonstrates how trauma of the past lingers, to the extent that survivors, in an informal chance encounter, are compelled to speak about the past and identify themselves as survivors. Yet, perhaps more significantly, listening to this account I was struck by the knowledge that as recently as 2005 there could be a survivor of the Holocaust living in Sydney who was not convinced that young Jewish adults knew about the *Shoah*. Whilst it is difficult to ascertain the extent of this phenomenon, this incident does reflect wider, more complex issues relating to the transgenerational transmission of Holocaust memory and communal commemoration.

This article will consider these issues with specific reference to Sydney's Jewish community, focusing on the following questions: How do survivors view the younger Jewish generation's knowledge of and commitment to the past? Do survivors trust that this younger Jewish generation will be able to preserve the memory of the fate of those murdered and the stories of those who survived? Finally, how would they like the Holocaust to be remembered as it 'passes from living memory to History'?[1]

Background: Holocaust Remembrance in Sydney

In order to gain a fuller appreciation of these issues, it is necessary to outline how the Holocaust has been commemorated in Sydney over the past 60 years.[2] Generally, commemoration has moved from the periphery to the centre of Australian Jewish consciousness, a trend that is also discernable amongst Jewish communities in the United States, Canada, England and Israel. The Australian Jewish community is characterised by the strong presence of Holocaust survivors, with some 27,000 migrating to Australia after the Second World War.[3] On a pro rata basis Australia accepted more survivors than any other country outside Israel, but despite the large numbers of Holocaust survivors, it took almost 35 years 'from the end of the Holocaust for a commitment to remembering and recording to emerge'.[4] Researchers have attributed this public silence to the insular political outlook of the Jewish community, however, as has been discussed elsewhere in this volume, a lack of widespread public and popular recognition does not equate with total silence.[5] Memorial ceremonies began within the Jewish community while the atrocities were still being committed. The Warsaw Ghetto uprising of 1943 triggered communal public commemoration activities in Sydney and annual *Yom HaShoah* commemorative ceremonies have been organised ever since.

Public discourse about the Holocaust became more pronounced in the 1970s and 1980s, with the advent of the Holocaust denial movement and debate surrounding the War Crimes Unit being regarded by historians as crucial factors that broke the public silence. Together these continue to be cited as 'a key motive in the upsurge of publicity about the Holocaust', but they were not the only factors.[6] Multiculturalism, as the policy of the Australian government since the 1970s, also influenced and encouraged a more public expression of Jewish identity and Holocaust commemoration. Established in 1979, the Holocaust Remembrance Committee began to develop and run extensive activities relating to Holocaust awareness, commemoration and education; the first major Holocaust exhibition open to the general public was held in 1981 and attracted between 30,000 and 40,000 visitors; in 1982 the Australian Association of Holocaust Survivors was established; and in 1986 the Australian Institute of Holocaust Studies was born of the Association.

It was also during this period that the voice of the Holocaust survivor became more audible, as in different ways many survivors began to give testimonies of their experiences, often for the first time. The Dr Hans Kimmel Memorial Essay Competition, an educational programme established at a Sydney Jewish day school in 1976–77, required students to record their family's history. Because most of the students' grandparents were Holocaust survivors, the family's story was often connected to the Holocaust; by instigating the uncovering of their family's personal experiences, the students uncovered a Holocaust testimony. The programme demonstrated that it was the third generation, the survivors' grandchildren, who in many cases opened up inquiry into the survivor's wartime experiences, and encouraged survivors to retell their pasts to a wider public.[7] The Holocaust Remembrance Committee also began to recognise the importance of recording survivor testimony, and in the 1980s two oral history projects commenced in New South Wales.[8] More recent collections include the Spielberg interviews of the Shoah Visual History Foundation, for which 2,484 testimonies have been collected since 1994.[9]

Perhaps the most significant development in Holocaust commemoration in Sydney has been the establishment of the Sydney Jewish Museum (SJM). Envisioned and funded single-handedly by John Saunders, himself a Holocaust survivor, the Museum was officially opened in 1992, becoming, as Judith Berman has commented, 'a major success, attracting approximately 140,000 visitors in its first four years'.[10] The SJM has also provided an important place for survivors to gather and tell their stories, and many volunteer as guides to the historical exhibit. Today, 'testimony is to be a means of transmission to future generations'.[11] The centrality of survivor testimony in education and commemoration has transformed survivors' roles: no longer silent, they now guide Holocaust remembrance and captivate the younger generation with their personal stories of suffering and survival.

In recent years, the Jewish community has extended Holocaust awareness and its legacy to the wider Australian community. *Courage to Care* is an educational programme geared towards schools in regional and rural areas.[12] The programme focuses on the stories of 'Righteous Gentiles' who risked their lives and the lives of their families to save Jews during the Holocaust, and presents the Holocaust as an historical event that has universal lessons and implications. In another development, one which has already been mentioned in the introduction to this collection, the subject of the Holocaust was catapulted into the fore of Australian public debate with the publication in 1994 of Helen Demidenko/Darville's *The Hand that Signed the Paper*, a work controversial for its 'allegedly antisemitic and historically dubious thesis'.[13] According to Ben-Moshe, this debate commanded a significant proportion of Australian media headlines for much of 1995 and for some, particularly the Jewish community, the affair raised concerns regarding the presence of antisemitism within contemporary Australian society.

An important step in the development of Holocaust commemoration within the Australian Jewish community is Australian participation in trips to Poland and Eastern Europe, particularly 'The March of the Living'. For some survivors who accompany the groups to Poland, participation in the March is the first time they have retuned to former homes and sites of personal suffering and loss. Australian participation began informally in 1989, but it was only in 2001 that the community formally participated. Some community leaders and a number of survivors objected. For example, some members of the Association of Holocaust Survivors and Descendants were, 'strongly opposed to involvement with the March because its members believed that it was in bad taste, insensitive and was merely a Hollywood extravaganza'.[14] Furthermore, many survivors from Poland 'viewed the country as a cemetery and had vowed that they would never return to Poland after what had happened to them and their families'.[15] However, it can be argued that the March facilitates the building of the chain of an intergenerational memory that is formed as survivors pass on their stories to the younger generation at the sites of memory. It is clear that Holocaust education and commemoration in Australia will increasingly incorporate visits to Poland, a growing trend amongst Jewish communities all over the world.

In addition to the political outlook of the community that contributed to public silence about the Holocaust, Ruth Wajnryb, in her work *The Silence*, comments that 'there is a link between silence, the passage of time and healing'.[16] Silence was needed to rebuild one's life, home and community. Once survivors had indeed 'survived the survival', they could look back from the security of the life they had recreated and face the destruction. However, with the passing of time, silence is no longer healing or redemptive, and instead eventually threatens memory and commemoration.[17] Time, distance, aging survivors, and a greater preparedness to hear about the events of the *Shoah*, have helped survivors to overcome their silence and pushed commemoration to the fore of Jewish public life.

Today, the Holocaust is central to the public and private identity of the Sydney Jewish community. *Yom HaShoah* is commemorated annually and a week-long series of educational and commemorative activities are organised around the memorial day. Most significantly, survivors are at the forefront of the commemorative activities and their individual stories, representing a myriad of different experiences, are central to Holocaust education. At present the issue that confronts the Sydney Jewish community is no different from the questions facing other communities. How is memory of the Holocaust to be kept alive and vibrant as survivors' voices begin to recede and as the past passes from 'living memory to history'?[18]

The Future of Holocaust Memory and Commemoration

In order to understand how survivors want the Holocaust to be remembered in the future, I conducted a number of discussion groups with Holocaust survivors living in Sydney. The discussion groups took place over a period of two weeks, and 11 survivors participated. Responses were also gleaned from personal interviews conducted with Australian survivors over the past year. Most of the participants were child survivors. They varied in terms of their country of origin, age and experiences during the war. Many spent the war in hiding, others in ghettos and in death and labour camps; one was saved on the *Kindertransport*. There were five females and six males. Their level of involvement with Holocaust commemoration and education varied. Most participants had told their stories publicly for educational purposes; some volunteered as guides at the SJM. Others told their stories to school-age students as part of a wider range of educational activities. The following relates to the salient issues that emerged from the discussion groups, which shed light onto this sensitive and important issue. It is important to add that these discussions do not represent the views of all survivors, rather this article needs to be seen as a microcosm of a larger debate.

'Only those who were *there* know'

It was clear from the discussion groups that all the participants were acutely conscious of their aging and mortality. They felt that the nature of Holocaust memory and commemoration would change significantly once they were no longer around. Once they have passed on, they felt that people will know 'less and less'. For Kathy, one respondent, survivors are the transmitters of information and access to correct and accurate information will not be guaranteed without them. She raised this concern while relating her experience of an encounter with a group of students during a recent visit to Bergen-Belsen, the camp from which she was liberated in 1945:

> KATHY: 'I have met a group of students with two teachers. And that teacher was talking about nonsense, and I asked her, "Where do you get your information from?" … and she said, "Well, I attend workshops." Big deal, workshops. Who knows what they are teaching them there?'
>
> DAVID: 'Where was she from?'
>
> KATHY: 'German … they were German teachers, German students and they get a worksheet and then she goes "blah, blah, blah" … Complete nonsense. And then I interfered, I didn't want to do that because I felt embarrassed, I didn't want to … but it made my blood boil and I couldn't listen to what she was talking about and I interfered, and I said, "excuse me please" …'
>
> ADRIAN: '…I was here.'
>
> KATHY: 'Yes, "I was here." And the students couldn't believe it and they begged me to stay with them to take them around, but I couldn't because I was committed …'

Hearing teachers give what she believed to be wrong information disturbed Kathy and she felt bound to step in and tell the students of her experience. She was the authority; she had been there and was encouraged by the students' seemingly positive response to her. The students were apparently moved by the 'unique, irreplaceable and deeply disturbing contact with a person who could say: "I was there and it happened".'[19]

Kathy's trip to Poland and Germany reinforced her feelings that she, having survived the Holocaust, was best equipped to know and tell what had happened. She found it very difficult to listen to others, especially those who had not experienced the Holocaust. In our discussion she explained that on her visit to Auschwitz:

> I met a very nice man who is not Jewish, he is the curator, very knowledgeable. That man actually emphasized the importance to remember their own Polish people. Which is alright, but … [they] are not to be compared to our victims, with our people who were killed.

For Kathy, the survivor is most qualified to transmit accurate information and her position is understandable in light of her work as a volunteer guide for the SJM. At the Museum, survivors act as guides and through their guiding they weave their personal stories into the narrative of the general historical exhibition, acting as both historical witness and 'witness historians'.

Rosa, a participant from a different group, acknowledged that whilst there is much written about the Holocaust, she was aware of the precious role of the survivor who is able to add to the historical narrative. She explained that as students ask her questions, she is able to draw from her own individual experience and add something that they may not have known before. Thus, without survivors, the ability to glean new information of this kind will be lost.

Preserving Memory

Kathy, significantly, felt that survivors not only transmit memory but they also preserve it. She expressed these concerns as she spoke about the state of Holocaust memorials and former sites of destruction in Poland and Germany:

> These places are so vast, I am talking now about Birkenau and about Auschwitz – the places are so vast. And they are not surrounded by fences or by any ropes – they are not roped in areas. People actually walk on human bones. And I was disgusted, my daughter picked up a piece of a human bone … I mean how bad is that? How can this be eliminated or overcome? … There are rabbits running through and deer and there are people who are come from one side of the camp where there is an open road, people live there actually … they go across [the camp] to the other side of the city, wherever this place is and they took their bicycles and bicycle through. It disturbed me greatly, you know, these places should … not be open for public *spatzieren* [spazieren gehen] whatever, and these places should have memorial stones erected … Unless we do something while we are alive, believe me … there will be very little done after.

Kathy's comment reflects her main concern about the future of Holocaust commemoration: she does not want the camp to become overgrown and disregarded by the younger generation. For Kathy, the next generation is preoccupied with their own reality and the Holocaust is not their priority. Furthermore she is concerned for the physical remains and memory of the dead, for whom she feels responsible. Many survivors contemplate who will take over this obligation once they are no longer able to do so, even wondering if they have done enough themselves.

As they think about the future, survivors are troubled about the fate of Holocaust memory and commemoration. They are concerned that the next generation has neither the ability nor interest to maintain memory and commemoration and combat denial. For many survivors in Sydney, it was the rise of Holocaust denial which pushed them to break their silence around their past and speak publicly. David, one of the more vocal participants, explained: 'I have two sons, I didn't talk to them about my experiences. I only talked to them when it became … when there were people that came out and tried to deny that the Holocaust ever happened.' Thus for most of his adult life he kept silent about his past and only spoke up when he felt that this past was challenged. Researchers have argued that there is a strong relationship between the denial movement and heightened public awareness of the Holocaust.[20] The discussants explained that despite radical advancements made in Holocaust education and awareness over the past two decades, survivors still feel threatened by the denial movement. Unease over denial can be understood in light of its continued presence, despite the plethora of historical writing on the Holocaust and the massive amount of survivor testimony that has been collected and recorded. Their worry is heightened when they think about a future in which they will no longer feature as 'living proof' – a future in which Holocaust memory and commemoration will be in the hands of people who may not have the same commitment and interest in keeping Holocaust memory alive.

While the issue of denial was worrisome to all participants in the discussions, there was disagreement amongst them as to the best way to deal with it. One survivor I interviewed presented himself as a 'watchdog' for any misinformation being disseminated on the Holocaust, even by his fellow survivors. Over the past few years this individual has devoted a huge amount of time and energy to exposing a particular survivor who, he believes, has been fabricating their past.

Tom, another discussion participant, argues that in the face of the denial movement there are limits to what may be considered 'freedom of speech': 'There is nothing wrong with freedom of speech as long as it does not lead to conflict and hatred and violence' and misinformation. David disagrees with Tom and retorts, 'Yeah, but you can only do it by education and you can only do it by bringing up another argument. If you want to shut up everybody they will want to shut up us as well'. Kathy, in response to this exchange, once again returns to her main anxiety: 'As long as we are around, but what happens after?' David puts his faith in the younger generation, he comments: 'Well, that's why you educate the kids – that's why you educate the kids…'

What to Remember?

Holocaust commemoration involves more than a decision to remember: it also requires a decision about *what* to remember. Meaning attributed to the event is usually motivated by the individual's or group's own concerns or ideological agenda. For David, sharing the past with the younger generation is the best way to keep the memory of the Holocaust alive. He believes 'that the only way that I have really achieved is if the kids ask me questions. If they don't ask me question, I feel that I have failed'. David wants, as Inga Clendinnen puts it, 'increasing understanding'.[21] Throughout his story, David tries to challenge the students, he tries to make them empathise with the decisions he had to make – to make them feel what it was like to be in his situation. He explained to us that after relating a certain episode in which he had to make a difficult choice, he would turn to the students: 'Now I tell them, "What would you do? Now that you've heard my story … what would you do?"' David wants the younger generation to *feel* what it was like during the period, to identify with him and his predicament. Kathy, however, explains: 'I don't want them to feel because that would be very cruel … and I definitely wouldn't want them to be in my shoes … But I want their understanding.'

Individuals like Kathy and David not only want their audiences and the next generation to listen to their stories and be interested in what they are saying; they also want them to understand what they have been through. For these survivors, keeping the story alive is important, but it is also important for students to know with what these individuals have had to grapple – their emotional and physical struggles. Such survivors want their experiences acknowledged, preserved and even honoured. In response to my question, 'When you speak to students, when do you think you have achieved what you have wanted to achieve?' Kathy replied, with a twinkle in her eyes, bringing her hands up to clap, 'When you get an ovation and when they are quiet'.

Whilst all of the participants felt that education is the key to Holocaust remembrance, there was no consensus regarding what the message or focus of that education should be. In one of the groups, Tom was adamant that educationally the Holocaust should be taught as a deterrent. He believes that the lesson of the Holocaust is 'not to discriminate again because Jewish people were victimized, dehumanized and vilified. And hate-mongering is going on, a lot of it is out of misinformation and ignorance, and somehow or another we need to project what this sort of thing leads to'.

Tom's comments express his own attitude to his experiences during the war. In numerous conversations, Tom has stressed the need to 'move on' from the past, to 'look forward' and use the past as a message for the future. Even professionally, as an active member of B'nai B'rith and participant in the *Courage to Care* programme, he directs his past towards creating a better Australia, a more harmonious and tolerant society. Similarly, Irwin believes that the role of Holocaust education is 'to develop a keen sense of compassion, to develop a more human attitude to one another, if that would have existed in the war years, history would have perhaps taken a different course. Right?'

Not all of the participants hold these views. Other survivors felt that Holocaust education is about retelling their unique past, to make sure it is not forgotten. David remarked that the SJM was a better place for him to tell his story so that he 'could speak about my … my … me'. Adrian exclaimed that, for him, the Holocaust should be remembered, 'If for no other reason, for the honour of souls that have perished'.

These opinions reflect part of wider debate regarding the future direction of Holocaust memorialisation in Sydney. The SJM was 'built by survivors and in memory of those who did not survive, the initial memorial intent of the SJM was clearly defined'.[22] *Zachor* was the imperative. 'The SJM exhibition does not attempt to recast the Holocaust experience into either a humanist or nationalist mould.'[23] The Museum defines as its mission to 'Tell the story of the Holocaust simply, truthfully and honestly so that it would never happen again'.[24]

In a recent article that is echoed in her essay in this collection, Avril Alba, the SJM's education manager, argues for a more universal dialect that will 'enable the SJM to continue to imbed Holocaust memory with both integrity and relevance into Australian public life'.[25] Leaning towards such a 'universal dialectic' might be more appropriate for the next generation. It may empower them to feel more qualified to speak about contemporary issues of 'unreason' and 'inhumanity' than about the experience of the Holocaust itself.

The Next Generation: How to Remember?

The issue of how to remember the Holocaust is connected to the wider question of Holocaust representation, a topic that has occupied the minds of writers and researchers across many disciplines.[26] It is beyond the scope of this article to present the concerns relating to this complex field. Suffice to say that since Theodor Adorno's statement that 'to write poetry after Auschwitz is barbaric', artists and scholars have faced the question 'if we are able to represent the Holocaust at all'.[27] Are there certain aesthetic methods or genres 'out of bounds' for writing about or representing the Holocaust, and to what degree are artists restrained by the 'actuality' of history? These questions are not only debated in artistic and scholarly circles, but were raised in the discussion groups. The question of 'limits' in respect of how individuals respond to and commemorate the Holocaust was mentioned in relation to the behaviour and activities of the younger generation on 'The March of the Living'. Kathy was particularly perturbed by their behaviour in Poland:

> Our own children who are being taken there now on the March of the Living, our own groups are dancing in Auschwitz and in little villages in synagogues. They are dancing there the *hora* to celebrate life. I was disgusted with that … I said this is not a place to dance, this is a place to say *kaddish*, this is a place where to say *Yizkor*, you go to Israel where you are debriefed and this is where you dance the *hora*, not in Auschwitz.

For Kathy, Holocaust commemoration is clearly not about celebrating life and survival, it is about mourning the dead. On another level, Kathy's comments can be interpreted as her questioning 'Who is the commemoration for?' Is it for the victims and the survivors, or is it for the young adults themselves? The younger generation may have the *need* to dance in Auschwitz, to reaffirm life and survival, but should this be the focus of commemoration? Is it appropriate to dance in Auschwitz?

Furthermore, Kathy's observations reflect a deeper issue, the conflict between generational memory: what the victims wanted those who did not experience the Holocaust to remember, what survivors want the second and third generation to remember – and the appropriate way of remembering; what the second and third generation feel is important to remember – and the manner in which they chose to do so. Kathy's attitude to 'dancing in Auschwitz' highlights the potential conflict between the survivors' own sensibilities and the younger generation's understanding and needs. It is not surprising that this 'tussle' exists between generations, particularly as the past gradually moves from 'living memory to history'. Yet, it is an issue that needs to be dealt with sensitively. For survivors like Kathy, the younger generation still has an obligation to be guided as to the purpose of commemoration, how to remember, and the appropriate way to do so. Yet there were other participants in the group who felt that it was entirely up to the younger generations to determine how they wanted to commemorate. Vera exclaimed, 'I don't think we can dictate to other generations how to commemorate this'.

Adrian vocalised an intermediate position. He likened the transition to knitting a jumper:

> You start knitting a jumper … or a shawl and you start off with a orange colour and then you flow into a red and then into a blue and from there into green. Multi-coloured like Joseph's coat. But it is the changing of the colours as you have the transition, which is the most important point. You don't have one colour and then stop and start and have another colour. That's aggressive, that's ugly, that's disharmonious. You melt in, you take over in the nicest sense of the word.

Whilst Adrian empowers the next generation to fashion their own form of commemoration, he wants it to be informed by the tradition established by the survivors. His words are a plea for respect and sensitivity, of knowing what came before and appreciating the legacy that has already been created.

Entrusting Memory

Whilst there was considerable discussion in all the groups regarding the issue of how survivors want subsequent generations to remember the Holocaust, it was clear that many of those present agreed that young people were generally not able or willing to remember the Holocaust effectively. There was an overwhelming sense amongst all participants that the second and third generation would not rise to the occasion and are not sufficiently interested in the past. Pauline commented that she had taken the trouble to make copies of her own, her mother's and her husband's video testimony for each of her children, and yet not one of them had watched them. However, during the interview she related that when visiting her son it became clear he had shared her past with his friends. This was quite surprising and revealing for her: what she may have interpreted as lack of interest may not have been. The interesting questions that arise are: Why cannot Pauline's son convey his interest in her story to her? Has Pauline failed to recognise his interest because of her own expectations?

In contrast, Irwin blamed himself for his children's lack of interest in the Holocaust and in his past:

> To be awfully honest, the buck stops with us, because we cannot blame it on the children. It is one of our many failings that we didn't [talk] … now there are a number explanations for it. You ask, 'how often can you talk about it?' It's like a wound; if you keep on digging that it won't never heal, will it? We wanted to bury [it].

In one group, I asked the participants why they felt that the younger generation was not interested. They pointed to the lack of attendance at the communal *Yom HaShoah* ceremonies. I asked why they thought this was the case, to which Josie replied: 'I still think that people find it unpalatable. I think they find it … you know, and I mean the last one was very lovely, they did a very … it was quite a sort of uplifting evening. I think that if we continue to do that then people may come.' Josie's comment suggests she thinks it might still be too difficult for those who have not experienced the *Shoah* to hear and cope with what transpired. Adrian was less understanding of the sensitivities that the younger generation might have towards confronting the Holocaust. During his discussion group, he turned to me as the 'representative of the next generation' and spoke determinedly about his position:

> You young people. How about you getting involved now! Not in ten years to come. Now! How much are you part of the *Shoah*? … This is important to us. We will be here for a year, two years, five at most and then we are off. It's entirely up to you and I say, and I am sorry to sound presumptuous, that it is your sacred duty to take over from us. To get involved now! Not tomorrow! Not yesterday.

Adrian was clearly disappointed about the level of involvement the younger generation has in commemoration of the *Shoah*. This was a difficult encounter for me as I was saddened by his feelings of disappointment, but also quite taken aback by the force of his speech and moved by the intensity of his plea. Adrian, together with the other participants, feels that the next generation has recoiled from the *Shoah*. They think that they have retreated in order to protect themselves and their parents from terrifying memories, images and open wounds.

Ritualising Memory

In reaction to their feelings – their lack of confidence in the next generation to support the memory of the Holocaust effectively – there was a clear sentiment amongst all the groups that one of the only ways the memory of the Holocaust can survive is by being cast as a religious act, duty and obligation, to be codified in the Jewish religious calendar. James Young explains:

> As ordered by the Jewish calendar, time offers itself as an insuperable master plan by which Jewish lives are lived, past history remembered and understood. For only time, when patterned after the circular movements of earth around the sun, and the moon around the earth, can be trusted to repeat its forms perpetually.[28]

To repeat perpetually is how these survivors want the Holocaust to be remembered. They want the *Shoah* to fit into a day whose 'form' inevitably recurs.

Most of these survivors do not trust that this will happen if left to the will and inclination of the next generation. Thus they feel that memory and commemoration of the Holocaust needs to be beyond individual or collective will, and rather be institutionalised and codified as a religious ritual. Mark Baker has asserted that if Holocaust memory is to be preserved for generations, a liturgy and a distinct set of rituals need to be developed, which would be performed in every Jewish home.[29]

Adrian felt the *Shoah* needs to be remembered as a communal *yahrzeit*, 'a point where you arrive every year'. In all the discussion groups, the participants looked towards the Pesach story as the 'most appropriate' model. It is a compelling model, because it has been remembered so well for thousands of years. There was much discussion about where to situate commemoration of the *Shoah* in the *seder* Pesach. Pauline suggested writing a text that would be added to the end of the *Haggadah*. Vicki even suggested that I should write this addition, 'and at Pesach time, right before Pesach it should be sent out to every Jewish family to be added'. Josie then suggested introducing the text 'with the bitter herbs'.

Adrian also spoke about how central the Pesach ritual is to Jewish life, how well it has been remembered for so long. 'If the Pesach story can be remembered so well, how much more so should the *Shoah* be remembered?' he asked. After all, he argued, the Jews during the *Shoah* suffered more than the Jews did as slaves in Egypt.

David, a participant in another group, is a deeply secular man who, because of his experiences during the war, no longer believes in God. Even so, he argued that religion should play a bigger role in commemoration of the Holocaust:

> Religion is not involved in the way that it should be involved with the Holocaust. Because I will tell you what, I get so angry. You go on, on, on, on Pesach, you read the *megillah* … and you read the story that you're going to take literally, that somebody took Jews out and it took you forty bloody years to get from Egypt to the land of Canaan … and we read the story to our children, we take it as the Gospel. Here you have the Holocaust, where so many Jews have been killed ... They are on the pulpit and they tell about Shavout, about Pesach, about Yom Kippur, about Rosh Hashanah … we should talk to them, to commemorate the *Shoah*, they should bring it out. Because you know, the last one [student group he spoke to], the non-Jewish one, she [one student] said, 'You know, that was a miracle that you survived, that was a miracle'. 'Why a miracle?' I asked. 'My parents were killed. 6 million Jews were killed. I survived and you think that I feel that it is a miracle?' I said. 'I felt guilty for a long time, that I was not able to join my mother. I feel guilty because I came in from work and my father was already gone.' So I said, 'There were no miracles'.

Each participant had their own story of survival, of rebuilding, and of understanding of their experience. They have disparate memories, yet together they shared a commitment to commemorating the Holocaust, to finding some way to ensure that the *Shoah* lives on in Jewish memory and tradition. They are searching to find a 'unified form of commemoration' that transcends the individual's own will and capacity to remember. They seek it in the model of Jewish tradition and ritual, which is familiar, intimate and successful in sustaining Jewish traditional and cultural memory. They all face the future with trepidation as they know that, once they go, they will take with them the memories and stories of those who did not survive. They are witnesses to both the victims' lives and their brutal deaths, and, as Kovner writes, witnesses to the '"other planet" which was none other than our own!'[30] As they grow older, they realise that they are reliant on the next generation to preserve their memories, the story, and to maintain remembrance of those souls who perished. In these discussions they articulated their anxieties over the ability of future generations to do so. They do not feel that the next generation is willing or able to look at the *Shoah* closely and squarely without recoiling from it.

Reflections

This issue over *what* and *how* to remember the Holocaust as it passes from 'living memory to history' can also be understood by locating it within the discourse of generational effects on memory. Howard Schumann and Jacqueline Scott argue that 'people will tend *not* to recall as important those events and changes that preceded their own lifetime. As Karl Mannheim stated it, 'only knowledge gained in real situations … sticks'.[31] Autobiographical memory is seen as richer and more meaningful to the individual than historical memory. Therefore, memory of the Holocaust is essentially different for survivors than it is for those who have inherited the memory.

As the nature of memory differs between different generations, so too does the meaning of the event: 'Younger people must base their knowledge of earlier events on what they have heard or read, which may have the advantage of greater perspective but it less likely to be personal or concrete'.[32] The tussle between the generations over the *meaning* of the event is inevitable because it is the individual's lived experience that will determine the meaning. As Schuman and Scott point out, 'those whose own youth occurred in a period different from that of the event they mention [or remember] show a tendency to contrast the event implicitly with events from their own adolescence'.[33]

Therefore it is reasonable to see Holocaust memory moving in the direction of a more universal dialectic.[34] The struggle between the generations is a predictable dynamic and will undoubtedly produce friction and unease, yet potentially it can enrich the discussion and thereby keep Holocaust memory alive. If the next generation has a different vision of commemorating the Holocaust, it does not imply that they do not care. Some survivors may view dancing at the site of Auschwitz as inappropriate, but they should not view it as wrong. If anything they need to recognise the effort these students made in making the trip and their commitment to learning about the past. And the students need to hear and respect the sensitivities and opinions of survivors. A dialogue, albeit a fiery one, can only lead to a path of growth. For survivors, the dialogue may help them feel more secure, that the younger generation is committed to remembering and commemorating the past, and that the 'autobiographical memory' of the survivors continues to inform the 'historical memory' of the younger generation.

Another way of understanding the tussle between survivors and the next generation is to consider the issue of communicating trauma. Ruth Wajnryb claims that many survivors misread their children's responses: 'They were quick to interpret as indifference that which – it is entirely (and tragically) possible – was actually the face of their own silence, reflected back to them.'[35] Survivors sent the message that 'none of us who came after could understand what they went through'.[36] Wajnryb comments that survivors were right; yet 'the prediction was peculiarly unhelpful'.[37] It was unhelpful because it became an obstacle to genuine inquiry. It served to protect survivors against retelling for remembering is a painful process. 'If it's impossible for anyone else to understand, if I tell people that it is impossible, I will so deter them so that they won't press and probe in all the places that resonate in pain and grief.'[38] In this sense Wajnryb has offered a profound understanding of how the message, delivered unconsciously on the part of the survivors, may have disempowered the next generation.[39]

It could be argued that by insisting the Holocaust be inscribed within traditional Jewish ritual and ceremony these survivors look towards a tradition that successfully sustained Jewish history for thousands of years. It is tradition that (whilst reliant on individual acts of remembering) is commanded and demanded by a higher authority, and is thus not reliant on the will and inclination of individuals. Inscribing Holocaust memory in Jewish tradition and ritual guarantees that it inevitably recurs. However, in terms of ritualisation of memory, the Holocaust resists integration into a religious mythic framework. '[T]here were no miracles', David cried. Even though David finds the religious model compelling and is prepared to contemplate it as a sure custodian of Holocaust memory, he cannot fully come to terms with it. Furthermore, as David Golinkin has argued, '[in terms of the] connection between the Holocaust and Pesach. There is none. Pesach is a festival of redemption and triumph; the *Shoah* was our hour of greatest destruction and despair'.[40] The difficulties of using a unified religious narrative/ritual to remember the Holocaust would thus betray the theological crisis that the Holocaust represents.

The Holocaust is undeniably a part of modern Jewish history, but it is not a part of Jewish religious tradition and culture. It was a fate imposed by the perpetrators on its victims; it was not the product of Jewish creativity, intellect and spirituality. It needs to be remembered, in the same way as other historical events must be remembered. Its victims need to be mourned. Yet it needs to be commemorated within Jewish historical memory and alongside Jewish religious and cultural tradition. It needs to be remembered in its own right, as a period of grave suffering and distress from which there was no redemption. The Holocaust needs to inform our behaviour.

James Young in his reflections on the future of Holocaust memory and commemoration differentiates between 'unified forms of commemoration' and 'the unification of memory': 'For despite unified forms of commemoration, memory in these shared moments is not necessarily shared, but in fact varies from person to person. This is not a day of shared memory, but rather a shared time of disparate remembrance.'[41] The ability to facilitate and contain disparate remembrance is an honest reflection of the event and the deep questions that it raises for its victims, survivors and the next generation.

Perhaps most significantly what this article has tried to show is how concerned some survivors are over the future of Holocaust memory and commemoration. From the discussion groups it was clear that most of these survivors are unsure the next generation possesses the inclination and ability not only to remember the Holocaust, but to remember it *well*. One way to understand this is connected to considering the survivors' own difficulties in facing their stage in life. They may feel reluctant to hand over Holocaust memory to the next generation as it implies their own mortality. Furthermore, their uncertainty arises from the nature of the tragedy itself; the Holocaust is an irreparable wound that no commemorative activity can 'heal' or repair. As mentioned previously, during one of the interviews Adrian challenged me: 'You young people. How about you getting involved now!' I was taken aback by the tone and force of his reprimand, and also felt unjustly accused. As a Holocaust researcher, I believe that I do make a contribution to Holocaust memory. I wanted him to see that, yet I did not respond to his outburst. Despite its awkwardness, this episode gave me greater insight into the issues of Holocaust commemoration. On one level Adrian's comments reflect a deep disappointment with the next generation, but on another they embody his anger over the irreconcilable loss inflicted by the *Shoah*, and his sense of powerlessness in the face of such a tragedy. From this dramatic and uncomfortable encounter I came to understand that perhaps whatever we do – and by 'we' I mean the subsequent generations and the survivors themselves – will never be enough. As James Young writes, 'All of us wish we could bring the victims back to life, to repair the terrible wound' – obviously an impossible task.[42] Remembering will always be accompanied by grief, anger and pain: one cannot bring consolation to those whose grief cannot be consoled.

NOTES

1. J. Young, 'Toward a Received Memory of the Holocaust', *History and Theory*, Vol.36 (1997), p.21.
2. For an in-depth description of the development of Holocaust memory and commemoration in Australia refer to J.E. Berman, *Holocaust Remembrance in Australian Jewish Communities 1945–2000* (Crawley: University of Western Australian Press, 2001).
3. S. Rutland and E.S. Caplan, *With One Voice: A History of the New South Wales Board of Jewish Deputies* (Darlington: Australian Jewish Historical Society, 1998), p.318.
4. Ibid., p.318.
5. According to historian William Rubinstein, the political orientation of Australian Jewry from the 1950s moved towards the right and has since been predominantly 'inward looking, concerned almost solely with its own future, with Jewish issues and an exclusively Jewish agenda, and if the term is not too extreme, voluntarily reghettoized'. See W.D. Rubinstein, *The Jews in Australia: A Thematic History*, Vol.2 (Melbourne: William Heinemann Australia, 1991), p.6.
6. Ibid., p.457.
7. Owing to its success, this type of project has since been duplicated in other Australian Jewish day schools. This phenomenon corroborates Dan Bar-On's *Fear and Hope: Life-Stories of Five Israeli Families of Holocaust Survivors, Three Generations in a Family* (Cambridge, MA: Harvard University Press, 1995) in which he stresses the importance of the birth of grandchildren for survivors as having enabled them to reach new levels of self-confidence and self-awareness in their newfound homes which ultimately led to their desire and sometimes compulsion to remember and articulate their *Shoah* experiences.
8. The first project is the Caplan/Kwiet project which was started in 1980 and continued for a period of eight years. The second, the 'Twelfth Hour project', recorded oral testimonies from 1988 until about 1990.
9. Available at www.vhf.org (accessed 21 March 2005).
10. Berman, *Holocaust Remembrance*, p.130.
11. A. Wieviorka, 'On Testimony', in G. Hartman (ed.), *Holocaust Remembrance: The Shapes of Memory* (Cambridge: Blackwell Publishers, 1994), p.24.
12. To date, the exhibition has been visited by approximately 178,550 visitors including 83,500 school-aged students.
13. In 1995, Demidenko won the Miles Franklin Award, Australia's top literary prize for her work, a 'novel' about a Ukrainian immigrant tried for war crimes in Australia. Her thesis in the book 'contends that Ukrainians killed Jews during the Holocaust in revenge for the killing of Ukrainians by communist Jews

during the famine of the 1930s'. D. Ben-Moshe, 'The Demidenko/Darville Controversy', *Without Prejudice* Australian Institute for Jewish Affairs (1996), p.33.

14. Rutland and Caplan, *With One Voice*, p.342.
15. A. Klein, 'March of the Living: Active Holocaust Commemoration in the Landscape', *Australian Journal of Jewish Studies*, Vol.18 (2004), p.31.
16. R. Wajnryb, *The Silence: How Tragedy Shapes Talk* (Sydney: Allen & Unwin, 2001), p.78.
17. Not all survivors have chosen to speak about their experiences. There are those who continue to keep their pasts to themselves. Silence still seems to have 'survival value' for them.
18. Young, 'Toward a Received Memory of the Holocaust', p.21.
19. S. Veil, 'Teaching about the Holocaust and Artistic Creation', Colloquy and Ministerial seminar, Strasbourg, 17–18 October 2002. See www.coe.int/T/E/Com/Files/Events/2002-10-*Shoah* (accessed 17 September 2007).
20. For more on this issue see J. Berman, 'Holocaust Museums in Australia: The Impact of Holocaust Denial and the Role of the Survivors', *The Journal of Holocaust Education*, Vol.10 (2001).
21. I. Clendinnen, *Reading the Holocaust* (Melbourne: Text Publishing, 1998), p.198.
22. A. Alba, 'Integrity and Relevancy: Shaping Holocaust Memory at the Sydney Jewish Museum', *Judaism*, Vol.53 (2004), pp.108–9.
23. Ibid., p.110.
24. Sylvia Rosenblum quoted in Berman, *Holocaust Remembrance*, p.155.
25. A. Alba, 'Integrity and Relevance: Shaping Holocaust Memory and the Sydney Jewish Museum', *Judaism*, Vol.54 (2005), p.109.
26. For more on the issue of Holocaust Representation refer to S. Friedlander (ed.), *Probing the Limits of Representation: Nazism and the 'Final Solution'* (Cambridge, MA: Harvard University Press, 1992); B. Lang, *Holocaust Representation. Art within the Limits of History and Ethics* (Baltimore, MD: Johns Hopkins University Press, 2003).
27. T. Adorno, 'Commitment', in Andrew Arato and Eike Gebhardt (eds.), *The Essential Frankfurt School Reader* (New York: Continuum, 1982), p.312.
28. J. Young, *The Texture of Memory: Holocaust Memorials and Meaning* (New Haven, CT and London: Yale University Press, 1994), p.263.
29. M. Baker, 'From Commemoration to Ritual: The Future of the Holocaust', *Generation*, Vol.2 (1991).
30. A. Kovner, E.A. Levenston and I. Greenberg, *Scrolls of Testimony* (Philadelphia: Jewish Publication Society of America, 2001), p.xxxvi.
31. K. Mannheim, quoted in H. Schuman and J. Scott, 'Generations and Collective Memories', *American Sociological Review*, Vol.54 (1989), p.360.
32. Schuman and Scott, 'Generations and Collective Memories', p.371.
33. Ibid., p.378.
34. However, it is also interesting to note that some of the survivors themselves see the Holocaust as a lesson against intolerance and racism, and not through their own lived experience. A partial explanation for this dynamic could be attributed to the impact that collective memory of an event has on effecting and shaping autobiographical memory.
35. Wajnryb, *The Silence*, p.316.
36. Ibid., p.317.
37. Ibid., p.317.
38. Ibid., p.318.
39. From my own previous research, whilst I have found instances whereby survivors have not been able to share their past because of this message, generally I have found that since liberation survivors have been searching for an empathic other who is willing and able to listen and contain their story. Whilst my research has been conducted in Israel, perhaps the Australian post-war environment was indeed different. The differences between the two communities, is a subject for further inquiry.
40. D. Golinkin, '*Yom HaShoah*; A Program of Observance', *Conservative Judaism*, Vol.37 (1984), p.54.
41. Young, *The Texture of Memory*, p.280.
42. J. Young, 'The Holocaust as Vicarious Past: Restoring the Voices of Memory to History', *Judaism*, Vol.51 (2002), p.84.

Memory-Work: Video Testimony, Holocaust Remembrance and the Third Generation

AMELIA KLEIN

> From a really young age, going to a Jewish primary school … it was quite traumatising seeing those horrific images … I understand that the Holocaust is a traumatic thing … I suppose the focus should be more acknowledgment of the effect that it has had as opposed to actually going into that trauma again. I have a real difficulty with the whole 'Remember Remember Don't Forget' because I think that can be unhealthy or dysfunctional.[1]

Introduction

This article explores the attitudes of grandchildren of Holocaust survivors towards Holocaust remembrance. The paper argues that viewing video testimony facilitates memory-work and can influence the third generation's attitudes towards Holocaust remembrance.[2] Memory-work, a process involving reflecting and questioning one's relationship in the present to the past, takes place as viewers form their own responses to the video testimonies without being limited in a particular way to remember, and without becoming pressed into existing Jewish communal rituals.[3]

The paper begins by arguing that Holocaust remembrance is intertwined with the Jewish obligation to remember. When Holocaust survivors are no longer alive to personally give their testimony, video testimonies will become the sources used in Holocaust remembrance and commemoration rituals. Interviews with members of the third generation reveal that Holocaust remembrance practices are not fixed but rather are fluid and changing. Grandchildren's responses contribute new insights into the dilemmas surrounding the Jewish communal obligation to remember for the third generation and emphasise the important position video testimony occupies in shaping new approaches towards remembering the Holocaust.

Responsibility to Remember

Remembrance is a key concept in Judaism.[4] There are many days in the Jewish calendar dedicated to remembering historical events.[5] Throughout the Jewish Bible, Jews are commanded 'to remember their history and to 'observe the rituals of faith through remembrance'.[6] Furthermore, in Judaism the commandment of *Zachor* 'does not end with the cognitive act of memory – it must be connected to both intention and action'.[7] So for Jews following the tradition, remembrance in general and Holocaust remembrance in particular involves action on the individual's part, through learning, teaching, keeping or preserving the memory that has been passed on.[8]

Commemorating the Holocaust, then, is enveloped within a strong history and tradition of remembering. Acknowledging the role that memory of historical trauma plays in the personal and communal consciousness of Jewish people assists in understanding the prominence of Holocaust remembrance in Jewish communities.[9] Since the end of the Second World War, Holocaust remembrance has taken place in the personal, familial, public and communal arenas. Unlike other events commemorated in Jewish history, remembering the Holocaust has yet to assume a fixed ritual or liturgy. At present many different configurations and formats exist.[10] Aspects of this remembrance may include oral, written and video testimonies, education and research programmes, fiction and documentary films, as well as commemorative rituals and community liturgies.[11] According to Judith Berman, '*Yom Hashoah* commemorations in Australian Jewish communities have not been under the control of a centralised remembrance authority' and have often 'been the occasion of intense debate about the appropriate institutional form that the act of remembering should take'. In order not to exclude members of the community, the ceremonies have generally been secular in form with religious elements, taking place in 'civic venues'.[12]

Throughout the world, Holocaust survivors testify in public as part of educational and commemorative programmes. When there are no longer any living witnesses to fulfil this task, video testimonies may be utilised for this purpose. In fact one of the main objectives for establishing the video testimony project at the Jewish Holocaust Museum and Research Centre (JHMRC) in 1992 was to videotape Holocaust survivors' testimonies in the hope that these videos would become sources for the legacy of the Holocaust for subsequent generations – both within the families of survivors and within the Jewish and wider communities.[13] It is also important to note that the Melbourne Jewish community has proportionally the highest number of Holocaust survivors of any Jewish diaspora community. The JHMRC collection has over 1,300 video testimonies reflecting a wide diversity of experiences.[14]

Survivors, museums and educational institutions have proclaimed that it is the responsibility of subsequent generations to continue the activity of remembering the Holocaust. Many survivors feel an obligation to testify publicly as they promised those who did not survive that they would bear witness to the events of the Holocaust and remember all those who died.[15] This obligation to remember extends from the survivor generation to their children and grandchildren, and potentially beyond to all subsequent generations. This responsibility was publicly declared at the first world gathering of Holocaust survivors in Israel at Yad

Vashem in 1981. Australian Holocaust survivors attended this gathering. It was a pivotal point in the development of consciousness regarding an Australian survivor community. The emergence of a survivor community meant that many survivors began to openly and publicly identify themselves particularly by testifying about their experiences. At this gathering members of the second generation were described as 'the bearers of the legacy'. Communities and commentators often refer to this obligation and responsibility as a part of 'Holocaust legacy'.[16] In 1983 the 'Passing of the Legacy' was introduced into Holocaust commemorations in Sydney. Later, the third generation was incorporated into this symbolic transmission which takes place during Holocaust remembrance ceremonies.[17]

To date, little research has been conducted on the reactions of the third generation towards Holocaust remembrance activities. The perspectives of the third generation will almost certainly contribute to shaping the future way in which the Holocaust is remembered. Whilst questions of 'obligation' and 'responsibility' are sensitive areas to broach, enquiry is necessary if individuals and communities are to work through and understand their relationship to this traumatic past. The complexity surrounding the issue of remembering and of communal obligations relating to memory is revealed in the following discussion through the voices of the third generation and their responses to Holocaust video testimonies.

Holocaust Remembrance, Video Testimony and the Third Generation

The phrase 'Remember, Never Forget' is one of many similar phrases commonly employed as a primary post-Holocaust message by educators, communal leaders, politicians and survivors who claim that remembrance is necessary in order to prevent genocide from recurring.[18] These formulaic phrases are often quoted like religious chants. In fact these injunctions may actually conceal questions that involve thinking about the meaning of remembrance and the challenges that remembrance poses.[19] Concerns about the simplistic nature of phrases like 'Remember, Never Forget' have led to calls for their underlying assumptions to be 'examined and unpacked'.[20] Concern relates to a lack of clarity about what exactly subsequent generations are being asked to remember – was it the fact that Jews survived? That the threat of tyranny requires eternal vigilance? That they must continue to bear witness so the dead did not die in vain or to counter Holocaust denial? Interviews with the third generation suggest that although some adhere to the mantra of 'Remember, Never Forget', others have begun to question the existing communal obligations surrounding Holocaust remembrance.

Recall that one reason for studying the role of video testimony in Holocaust remembrance is that for future generations video testimonies will replace the voices of living survivors as the primary eyewitness sources to the Holocaust.

Whilst much emphasis has been placed on recording, archiving and digitising Holocaust video testimonies, few qualitative studies have been conducted on responses to viewing video testimonies.[21]

Members of the third generation highlighted concerns regarding the future uses of video testimonies to 'keep the memory alive'. For example, interviewee Natalie had not attended a Jewish day school but had learnt about the Holocaust at the Jewish youth movement she attended. Her grandfather was born in Breslau, Germany. He was sent to Buchenwald concentration camp after Kristallnacht, was released and managed to emigrate to Shanghai in 1939. Natalie wished all future viewers of her grandfather's testimony to become new witnesses, to 'carry the torch'.[22] But she was concerned that even though 'the fourth generation may get the understanding from the videos and documents … they don't have the direct relation' to the survivors that the third generation does. In her article in this volume, Sharon Kangisser Cohen reflects that many Holocaust survivors 'are troubled about the fate of Holocaust memory and commemoration'. According to Natalie, when the survivors are no longer alive, there will not be the 'direct emotional impact' which may lead to a diminished effect: 'Out of sight, out of mind'. In this way, she reinforced the fact that connection to the material will change over time. Kylie[23] expressed a similar concern, comparing her experiences and close connections with survivors with the potential experiences of future generations: 'I think it's going to be very difficult for students to have a connection and to remember … when all we have are the testimonies to use as first-hand footage'.[24] Like Natalie, Kate believed that while future Holocaust remembrance would draw on video testimonies, it is difficult to predict their impact on subsequent generations.[25] She was also worried about desensitisation and stated that she herself felt saturated by Holocaust-related material: 'another story, another testimony … there's a potential to switch off … it's horrible to be feeling like that … you become so immune to it'.

Other respondents also mentioned the issue of 'saturation'. In many instances, forceful language was used to describe these feelings: 'Drummed into my head; forced upon me; drilled into us; brought up with it; pushed in our faces; never going to choose to look at it; shoved down our throats; overdosed on it.'[26] It has been suggested that the effect of Holocaust testimonies and visual material can be 'blunted by over-familiarization'.[27] Previous exposure to Holocaust-related material, together with degree of connection to the survivor generation, may affect responses to video testimonies. The future role of video testimonies in education and commemoration will be influenced by these factors.

Viewing video testimony influenced some interviewees' attitudes towards Holocaust remembrance. Maya, a 23-year-old orthodox university student, had not previously viewed her grandfather's video testimony. Although Maya recalled participating in Holocaust remembrance ceremonies every year at school and singing in the choir, she stated that until she watched the video testimony:

'It doesn't really hit you … it's too overwhelming, you don't know what to do, it's sad and awful.' Maya said she 'had a feeling of upholding the legacy … if you go on with your life, you forget about the Holocaust and how important it is to think about it. The testimony reactivates it in you.' Viewing the video testimony inspired a connection for her that had been missing from her formal school commemorations and she made the commitment to pass on her grandfather's testimony.[28] As a result she was able to recognise more clearly her own responsibility in remembering the Holocaust.

Natalie's response was similar. After the viewing Natalie wholeheartedly believed it was her 'job' to 'remember what happened' and 'pass the testimony down' to future generations. Natalie considered being part of the third generation 'unique' and felt privileged to be able to 'witness the survivor, learn their story and pass it on'. Both Natalie and Maya accepted the communal responsibility to ensure that subsequent generations remember the Holocaust.

It is interesting to consider the reasons why Maya and Natalie may have taken an approach that involved reiterating the standard phrases often used in relation to remembering the Holocaust. Perhaps they felt obligated to respond in the way their Jewish day school or youth movement had educated them or as their families would have expected. Maya and Natalie's commitment to remembering corresponds with existing communal expectations that the third generation will become the next generation of Holocaust memory carriers.

After viewing his grandfather's testimony, Jason's perspective on Holocaust remembrance shifted dramatically. Before viewing the video testimony Jason said that he had never been to a Holocaust commemoration and that remembering the Holocaust was not a priority in his life. He was one of the few interviewees who had never heard the word Zachor. This may be because he did not attend a Jewish day school and was not closely affiliated with the Jewish community. After viewing the testimony Jason reflected: 'I suppose I have never even thought about the Holocaust too much before … wasn't really something on my mind'. He was glad the video testimony had been made 'so when my grandfather goes … it won't be forgotten what's happened'.[29] Jason's viewing experience inspired him to consider such issues further.

All four of Peter's grandparents are Holocaust survivors.[30] He attended a Jewish day school but is no longer involved in the Jewish community. In his pre-interview Peter stated that Holocaust remembrance was significant for him. After the viewing, he commented: 'I think it's quite important to sometimes have a reminder … you can sort of get preoccupied and lost in the mire of daily life … it was a little bit of a wake up call.'

The aforementioned responses show that viewing video testimony can motivate in some descendants the personal desire to continue Holocaust remembrance, as in Maya and Natalie's case, or become a springboard for further thought, as in the case of Jason and Peter. In contrast, viewing their grandparents' testimonies did not alter Deborah and Anne's attitudes towards Holocaust remembrance.[31] In the pre-interview, they both stated that remembrance was 'very important' and after the viewing, reiterated the same sentiments. In the post-viewing interview, Deborah intimated that remembrance would become 'more important when she had children', as if to imply that it was not a focus for her right now and Anne suggested that Holocaust remembrance was 'not really something she thought about daily'. It is possible that Deborah and Anne would have liked to explore further the issue of responsibility or obligation to remember but were hesitant about how this subsequent discussion would have been received by the interviewer who was researching questions relating to Holocaust video testimonies and remembrance.

Mark focused more on the historical and familial aspect of remembering rather than the broad canvas of collective Holocaust remembrance. He had not attended a communal commemoration because he was not Jewish and did not identify with the community.[32] After viewing the testimony he stated: 'I don't commemorate the Holocaust … it kind of passed me by … I don't really know why.' Not identifying with the Jewish community could be the reason why Mark's approach to remembrance was different. He advocated the importance of video testimony and viewing for family history but did not link this to the standard Jewish communal expectations of 'Remember, Never Forget'. He believed that whilst the Holocaust would never be forgotten, it would recede into history and be studied as an historical event. As the only non-Jew interviewed, Mark's responses contrast with Deborah and Anne's, suggesting that communal and cultural expectations can influence Jewish viewers' responses.

In a similar way to Mark, Jane felt the necessity to remember in order not to become complacent and take her life for granted; however, in terms of Holocaust commemoration she stated: 'It is going to have to dilute. The actual loss of survivors will result in remembrance filtering out over time.'[33]

On the other hand, Taryn challenged the expectation that Holocaust remembrance would result from the viewing experience. She criticised the idea of Holocaust remembrance and felt that 'Holocaust acknowledgement' was more appropriate.

> From a really young age, going to a Jewish primary school … it was quite traumatising seeing those incredible and horrific images … being really young and being told, 'be careful … remember you're Jewish' … it kind of freaked me out a bit … remembering forced upon me. I understand that the Holocaust is a traumatic thing … I suppose the focus should be more acknowledgment of the effect that it has had as opposed to actually going into that trauma again and seeing all those images and remembering it in that way. I have a real difficulty with the whole 'Remember Remember Don't Forget' because I think that can be unhealthy or dysfunctional.

According to Taryn, the non-interactive nature of the video-testimony medium proved to be beneficial:

> I know for me, I can read an encyclopaedia, I can get information … but the thing that is going to affect me and get me understanding is actually seeing someone … that authenticity of a human response … Being able to stop the tape, rewind … watch in my own space … and see my grandfather's response again.

The video testimony allowed her to acknowledge her grandfather's experiences during the Holocaust without the pressure of feeling forced to become a link in the chain of remembering (an expected outcome of many Holocaust commemorative ceremonies and education programmes). Instead, the non-interactive medium of video testimony enabled Taryn to take a more objective position in relation to her grandfather's testimony. Her comments indicate her desire to question and reflect on her own response to the Holocaust. According to second-generation author Eva Hoffman, the capacity to conceptualise the past is paramount if subsequent generations, born in the aftermath of the trauma of the Holocaust, are to live in the present without the past consuming them.[34] It appears that Taryn is striving to achieve this position. Her insightful comments provided a springboard for considering further the existing Jewish communal paradigms of remembrance and the position of video testimony within this framework. These issues are investigated in the next section.

The above comments of viewers of video testimony indicate that their relationship towards Holocaust remembrance and to the notion of 'Remember, Never Forget' is not fixed, but rather occupies a dynamic, shifting space.

Video Testimony and Memory-Work

For the third generation, formulating their own perspectives towards Holocaust remembrance involves memory-work – that is, developing their own perspectives in relation to viewing the video testimonies and their own 'attitudes' towards Holocaust remembrance. Such memory-work has been linked to the psychological process of 'working through'.[35] This term has been employed by researchers studying the Holocaust to frame the ways in which survivors, their children and grandchildren may 'cope with the traumas originating in the Holocaust'.[36]

Researcher Agata Kula concluded that her third-generation interviewees 'reveal a common tension between their belief in the importance of perpetuating a memory of the Holocaust on the one hand and, on the other, their desire to move forward and celebrate more positive aspects of Judaism'.[37] According to Björn Krondorfer, young American Jews as 'a post-Shoah generation … can also move toward a "post-victim" discourse and ethos without betraying the memory of the Holocaust'.[38] The burden of remembering is also highlighted in other research on the third generation.[39] These studies confirm that subsequent generations struggle to find their position in appropriately remembering the past and simultaneously establishing their identity in the present.[40]

For the third generation, working out their attitudes towards Holocaust remembrance is a complex issue, one that may take a lifetime to resolve. Viewing video testimony has the potential to both help and hinder this process. On the one hand, a surface viewing of video testimonies without any preparation beforehand or discussion afterwards may perpetuate the clichéd message of 'Remember, Never Forget' and thus hinder the process of memory-work and working through one's relationship to the past. LaCapra suggests that people may resist the process of working through due to a 'fidelity to trauma, a feeling that one must somehow keep faith with it'. That is, if working through leads to a different relationship to the past, those involved may feel they are 'betraying' the dead and feel that they want to 'remain within trauma'.[41]

On the other hand, the video testimony may lead a viewer to take a different position, which may not involve a token act of remembrance but rather actively engage him/her in forming a personal response. Such a response depends on the individual viewer, their background and connection to the survivor. It is clear from the statements of respondents that some are questioning their role in the chain of remembrance. The baton of remembrance may thus not be passed on smoothly from Holocaust survivors to their grandchildren.

One reason for this could be that video testimony provides a potential way of engaging with Holocaust history and memory that does not involve the traditional elements of Jewish remembering, re-enactment and re-narration. Traditionally, Jewish memory is accessed through the channels of 'ritual and recital'. These 'rituals of remembrance' involve a group of practices focused on re-enacting, reciting and reconnecting with religiously significant historical events.[42] The rituals take place through annual acts of commemoration which link the memory of the past with the present.[43] The very medium of video testimony, with limited possibility of interaction, challenges the existing paradigms of Jewish remembrance practices of re-enactment and re-narration.

Nevertheless, the third-generation responses discussed above show that the non-interactive aspect of video testimony may actually be beneficial for subsequent generations of viewers. The video testimony can become an anchor for the survivor's experience and the place where later generations begin to navigate an otherwise inaccessible terrain of family Holocaust history and memory. Instead of reliving the past, 'as if you yourself were there' (which some forms of Holocaust remembrance encourage such as the international experiential March of the Living – a programme that takes students to the sites of Holocaust trauma[44]), the viewer has time to digest the information and to consider their response. The viewing takes place alone and there is physical space between the grandchild who is watching and the survivor on screen who is testifying.

The viewing may not result in a grandchild 'reliving' or 'valorising' the trauma of the Holocaust but rather may allow the viewer some degree of distance from the testimony and its messages.

As seen in the case of Taryn, members of the third generation may develop a new perspective towards Holocaust remembrance after viewing video testimony. This could mean engaging in the fourth stage of Bar-On's working-through process that focuses on forming attitudes towards the past and assessing the implications of what has been learnt in relation to the present and future.[45] According to LaCapra: 'The extent one works through trauma … one is able to distinguish between past and present and to recall in memory that something happened to one (or one's people) back then while realizing that one is living here and now with openings to the future.'[46] The third-generation viewer of video testimony does not have to adhere to an institutionalised formula for commemoration or remembering. Instead, viewers have the choice to decide how and in what way they wish to remember. Viewers have the opportunity to move beyond the position of a becoming 'witness to the (survivor) witness' to a new location where their attitudes can be reconfigured in line with what is authentic for them. That the choice lies with the individual has important repercussions for Holocaust education in general and for the future role of the video-testimony archive in particular. As an 'active agent'[47] in determining how the past is perceived, a viewer may be released from a formulaic, prescribed response, and therefore be able to make their own active choice about how to remember the Holocaust.

The potential exists then for the video testimony to become a very significant medium for the Jewish community with respect to communal remembrance. This would involve engaging with video testimony in a new way. Roger Simon and Claudia Eppert suggest forming 'communities of memory' with the purpose of discussing responses to testimonies through 'performative re-tellings' and the writing of 'shadow texts'.[48] In such communities, members would discuss the difficult aspects of the testimonies and decide which parts should be re-told and in what context. Facilitators of such discussions would need to take into consideration the problems of desensitisation and saturation mentioned by respondents earlier in this article. Simon and Eppert recognise that part of the process of responding to testimony may be 'painful' and that dealing with the information can be considered part of a '"working through" of the materials of remembrance in a way that produces something new'.[49] They believe that such communities of memory (whether initiated in schools, universities or adult study groups) can create a space where the 'practices of remembrance are contested, shaped, and deepened by consideration of the shared significance of what has been heard, seen, or read'. Such meetings may involve 'struggle', 'conflict', 'argument' and 'deliberations' about the issues of transmission and witnessing.[50] Video testimonies may be a central place for such contested spaces of communal remembrance. These discussions could also assist in the collective memory-work and communal working through of the Holocaust.[51] Each generation will find an alternative way to respond to the Jewish communal obligation to remember the Holocaust.[52] Hass' suggestion that Holocaust commemoration in the second generation will be different from the survivors can be extended to apply to the third generation. These ideas are reinforced by Paul Valent's comments about the changing nature of Holocaust remembrance: 'The way the Holocaust will be absorbed and made meaning of, will depend on the inherited reverberations of the Holocaust at any one time, and the circumstances and needs of those times that the Holocaust is required to inform.'[53] Valent indicates that Holocaust remembrance is still developing, and asserts that the events will be remembered 'according to [their] perceived relevance at any one time'.[54] This idea was echoed by interviewee Danielle, a direct descendant whose grandparent had not made a video testimony:

> I believe that Jewish people need to deal differently with grief. There is so much grief and negativity within the older generation that it causes enormous suffering for younger generations. This angers me. Yes, we need to experience grief but we must empower ourselves to overcome this so that it is not so deeply engrained in the hearts and souls of Jewish youth. Perhaps it is incumbent on the third generation to approach commemoration differently so that we stop feeling so much pain, so that we realise our role in speaking out against other genocides. At the same time we must ensure that we acknowledge the atrocities that were committed against our people, our families and unite in ensuring it never happens again. This is a difficult task – it involves a delicate balancing act that will ultimately give us greater freedom of expression and peace in a world full of different religions, cultures and people.

In this statement, Danielle expresses her desire to move beyond the mourning to a point of resolution. She suggests converting the position of victimhood into affirmative action, for example campaigning for the rights of other oppressed peoples.[55] Perhaps if Danielle participated in a community of memory and viewed survivor video testimonies, she, like Taryn, would have the opportunity to work through her 'grief' and 'pain' and achieve her goal of a new 'approach to commemoration' and 'greater freedom of expression'.

Like Danielle, other third-generation interviewees without video testimonies expressed similar concerns about the future of Holocaust remembrance. Brett found formal commemorations 'difficult to connect to' and 'unappealing'. Nevertheless he observed that 'there's still something inside me, this sort of brainwashing thing that has been passed on to me … we are told "Don't Forget, Don't Forget"'. He stated emphatically:

> Whether your grandparents went to a camp or not … everything our community is built on comes from the Holocaust … I don't want to sound

> clichéd but I really believe that Holocaust remembrance is part of our community whether we like it or not … it is sort of a blanket over us … even if you try to throw the blanket off … it's like rebelling against the mainstream.

Brett's opinion highlights the way in which the obligation to remember the Holocaust is interwoven into the fabric of the Melbourne Jewish community.[56]

Similarly, Tamara did not like the way the community commemorates the Holocaust and felt the ceremonies were repetitious:

> Our generation is to some extent letting go of it … healing … that's quite controversial to say … in order for people to heal themselves when something traumatic has happened, they tend to forget a little … People in the second generation would be devastated to hear that and say 'you've got to keep the memory alive' but you can't. You can't keep a second-generation memory, third-generation even fourth-generation memory as strong as the first.

In this statement, Tamara challenges the communal expectation to 'keep the memory alive'. Similarly, Isabel thought Holocaust remembrance ceremonies would change over the next 100 years. She observed that until now commemorations had followed a formula established by survivors, involving lighting candles and singing specific songs:

> I feel like I have heard all the stories before and I know the stories and I know the reaction in me … we shouldn't hold a torch for the sake of it … we need to deal with it in a way that enters the younger consciousness. But that's scary as well because you can create a split between the generations.

Holocaust remembrance is a contested area for these individuals. They are thinking about new ways of conceptualising their responsibility as members of the third generation as well as expressing the need to move beyond the formulaic communal obligations to remember. The opportunity to view video testimonies and participate in communities of memory may provide these descendants with an avenue to discuss their concerns relating to the burden of remembrance and enable them to begin their own process of memory-work.

That the nature of Holocaust commemorations is problematic is a view that is held by both respondents and other researchers. For example, Krondorfer believes that Holocaust remembrance ceremonies and educational programmes that follow a 'certain ritualistic quality', rather than being innovative, may 'alienate' participants.[57] In Australia, Holocaust commemoration ceremonies have been described as 'bankrupt' in the context of over-saturation of society with Holocaust images.[58] Judith Berman has suggested that the future of Holocaust remembrance in Australia will depend on the 'commitment' of Jewish day school students to 'carry the legacy'.[59] For the memory to hold meaning it needs to be reshaped by each generation, not remain fixed and formulaic. It is clear that forums need to be established to create and generate such 'reshaping'.

An ongoing interaction between the past and present will influence the way the Holocaust is remembered. The significance of remembering is located 'not in the past events themselves, but in the past events as they exist in relation to our contemporary and future concerns'.[60] Writing 'shadow texts', initiating a dialogue with family members, creating communities of memory or being part of a discussion group before and after the viewing of video testimonies will help to facilitate the formation of new ways of relating to the obligation to remember. But such relationships will always depend, of course, on the 'discourse community' in which viewers are situated.[61] Dan Stone proposes that 'memory-work', in his words, 'a process in which continually thinking about what is being commemorated is part of the commemoration itself' and where 'people emerge from the commemoration feeling that they have questioned their own presuppositions', is a necessary part of Holocaust memorial days. What is needed are 'forms of commemoration that are based around questioning both the events and our understanding of them ... [those that do] not offer final answers, achieving closure'.[62]

Video testimony plays an important role in memory-work. This discussion has suggested that for the third generation the viewing experience can lead to further questioning of 'presuppositions' about the obligation and responsibility to remember. According to Stone, 'When the memory-work is itself called into question, only then is it possible to respond to the Holocaust without incorporating it into traditional modes of memorialisation'.[63] Video testimonies can facilitate such self-reflexive acts of remembrance, especially when forums are created for viewers to process their experience. These forums will have reverberating effects on the wider community, leading organisers of the large formulaic communal commemorations to begin to shift their outlook about the most effective ways to engage the community audience in the activity of Holocaust remembrance.

This shift in the dynamics of remembering could ultimately result in a community that moves beyond the cycle of remembrance which has until now been immersed in the trauma of the Holocaust to a position where the Holocaust is remembered in a different way. From this new standpoint community members could understand, acknowledge, and work through the effects of the Holocaust on their lives and subsequently be 'free' to live in the present without the overarching pressure of always remembering the past.

Conclusion

The qualitative data showed that for members of the third generation the meaning of Holocaust remembrance is neither pre-constituted nor predictable. This article has suggested that video testimonies have a role to play which the creators of the JHMRC archive were unaware of when they began the collection process – that is, video testimony can assume a pivotal function in both individual and communal working-through processes. Post-viewing discussion forums may facilitate new understandings, attitudes and emotional responses towards remembering the Holocaust.

Interviews with the third generation revealed that they are beginning to re-conceptualise the meaning of Holocaust remembrance. The third generation's temporal distance from the Holocaust and access to information, such as that encapsulated in a video testimony enables them to make novel decisions about their role in remembering.[64] Viewers are not merely passive recipients but active participants who think about the ways they want to remember the past. Holocaust remembrance practice is not only about following the injunction 'Remember, Never Forget' or the dictum 'Keep the memory alive' (as expounded by the JHMRC archive or individual survivors or the Melbourne Jewish community) but rather it also depends on how individuals choose to engage with and incorporate the memory of the Holocaust into their own lives.[65]

Watching video testimony can shift the focus of Holocaust remembrance away from the existing formulaic programmes and ceremonies (which the third generation find 'unappealing' and 'repetitious') and, instead, empower viewers. From this position of empowerment, the viewer is able to create and articulate an alternative approach to Holocaust remembrance. This new approach replaces normative rituals of remembering with an acknowledgement of the impact of the Holocaust in the individual's life and a separation from the binding communal obligation to become a link in the chain of remembering. Ultimately this allows the viewer to envision a future that is not overshadowed by a perceived burden to remember. In facilitating memory-work and the creation of such reflective spaces for viewers, video testimonies therefore make a significant contribution in forging new ways to approach Holocaust remembrance.

NOTES

The views expressed in this article are the author's own and as such do not represent the policies of the Jewish Holocaust Museum and Research Centre, Melbourne.

1. Taryn, granddaughter of Mr H. She watched her grandfather's video testimony archived at the Jewish Holocaust Museum and Research Centre, Melbourne, Australia.
2. Throughout this article, the term 'third generation' refers to the generation of the grandchildren of Holocaust survivors. The research was conducted as part of my PhD between 2003 and 2006. Participants were interviewed before and after they viewed their grandparent's Holocaust video testimony. All respondents were over 18 years old and lived in Melbourne, Australia. Ten grandchildren were interviewed on their responses to their grandparents' video testimonies. Eight grandchildren whose grandparents chose not to make video testimonies were also interviewed for comparative data. Two Jewish individuals from the same generation as the grandchildren were also interviewed about their responses to Holocaust video testimonies. To ensure confidentiality, all interviewees were assigned pseudonyms.
3. This term is used by Dan Stone in D. Stone, 'Day of Remembrance or Day of Forgetting? Or, Why Britain Does Not Need a Holocaust Memorial Day', *Patterns of Prejudice*, Vol.34, No.4 (2000), pp.58–9.

J. Young also employs this term; see James Young, *At Memory's Edge: After-Images of the Holocaust in Contemporary Art and Architecture* (New Haven: Yale University Press, 2000), p.4.

4. The Hebrew word for remembering is *Zachor*. *Zachor*, is not only associated with Holocaust commemoration. It also has other connotations and refers to remembering the *Shabbat* (Hebrew word for Jewish Sabbath), remembering the exodus from Egypt and other significant events in the history of the Jewish people.
5. For example, the destruction of the First and Second Temples are commemorated together on the ninth of the Hebrew month *Av*.
6. Yosef Haim Yerushalmi, *Zakhor: Jewish History and Jewish Memory*, 3rd edition (Seattle: (University of Washington Press, 2002), pp.5–26; J. Young, *The Texture of Memory: Holocaust Memorials and Meaning* (New Haven, CT: Yale University Press, 1993), p.209. For example, in the Passover ritual, commemorating the exodus of the Jews from Egypt, the individual involved in the commemoration is instructed to consider that it was he who had personally left Egypt. As it states in Exodus 13.3, 'remember this day on which you departed from Egypt'. Rabbi N. Scherman, *The Torah: Haftaros and Five Megillos with a Commentary Anthologized from the Rabbinic Writings, The Stone Edition* (New York: Mesorah Publications, 1993), p.361.
7. Z. Gill, 'Our Living Legacy: A Message from Holocaust Survivors for All Generations', *Yad Vashem Quarterly Magazine* (2002), p.4.
8. Roger Simon, 'The Paradoxical Practice of Zachor: Memories of "What Has Never Been My Fault or My Deed" ', in Roger Simon, Simon Rosenberg and Claudia Eppert (eds.), *Between Hope and Despair: Pedagogy and the Remembrance of Historical Trauma* (Lanham, MD: Rowman & Littlefield Publishers Inc., 2000), p.11.
9. Young, *The Texture of Memory*, pp.210–17.
10. The reasons for this lack of consensus shed light on the dilemmas associated with Holocaust remembrance. According to Young, 'each commemoration reflects the ethos and tradition, the piety or politics of a given community'. Young, *Texture of Memory*, p.272. For discussion of the conflicts and issues in relation to establishing formal Holocaust remembrance proceedings in the Australian Jewish community see Judith Berman, *Holocaust Remembrance in Australian Jewish Communities, 1945–2000* (Crawley: University of Western Australia Press, 2001), Part I: *Yom Hashoah* Commemorations, pp.15–78. Avril Alba's article in this volume, 'Displaying the Sacred: Australian Holocaust Memorials in Public Life', provides insight into the complicated place of Holocaust memory 'both within and beyond' the Australian Jewish community.
11. Isabel Wollaston, *War Against Memory? The Future of Holocaust Remembrance* (Great Britain: Society for Promoting Christian Knowledge, 1996), p.35.
12. Berman also describes specific tensions erupting between Orthodox and Liberal congregations in Perth and Sydney. J. Berman, '*Yom Hashoah* (Holocaust Day) commemorations in Melbourne, Perth and Sydney 1945–1996: Debates Concerning the Date, Scope, Location, Nature and Rituals', *Australian Jewish Historical Society Journal*, Vol.15 (1999), pp.84–90.
13. Phillip Maisel, 'The Holocaust Testimonies', in Stan Marks (ed.), *10 Years: Jewish Holocaust Museum and Research Centre, Melbourne, 1984–1994* (Melbourne: Jewish Holocaust Museum and Research Centre, 1994), p.24. The Museum was established in 1984. The JHMRC Testimony Department uses a broad definition of 'Holocaust survivor' including anyone 'who lived under the German sphere of influence during World War II, from Hitler's rise to power in 1933 to the end of the war in 1945' as eligible to record a video testimony. The Department also accepts testimonies from refugees from Nazism who left Germany and Austria prior to 1933. Jewish Holocaust Museum and Research Centre Video Testimony Project Advertisement, *Centre News*, Vol.12, No.1 (April 1995), p.6. The video testimony interviews are structured around a set of questions. The interviewers are expected to cover three stages of survivors' lives: their background, childhood and perception of events leading to the Holocaust; a detailed description of their experiences during the Nazi occupation; their experiences upon liberation and how their life was affected by the Holocaust. The final section of the interview deals with post-war life in Australia. See Amelia Klein, 'Community and Remembrance: The Role of Melbourne Holocaust Survivor Testimonies', in G. Pass and D. Woods (eds.), *Alchemies: Community Exchanges* (Perth: Black Swan Press, 2004), pp.179–83.
14. Berman, *Holocaust Remembrance*, pp.5–6.
15. Ruth Wajnryb, *The Silence: How Tragedy Shapes Talk* (Sydney: Allen & Unwin, 2001), p.80. Also see SSVHF and the Fortunoff Archive, www.usc.edu/schools/college/vhi/, www.library.yale.edu/testimonies/ (viewed 22 July 2006); G. Hartman, 'Learning from Survivors: The Yale Testimony Project', *Holocaust and Genocide Studies*, Vol.9, No.2 (1995), pp.192–207.

16. Suzanne Rutland and Sophie Caplan, *With One Voice* (Sydney: Australian Jewish Historical Society, 1998), pp.320–21. For a history of the survivor community and the development of Holocaust education in Australia, see S. Rutland's article in this volume, 'In the Shadow of the Holocaust: The Development of Moriah College'. Henry Greenspan, 'Imagining Survivors: Testimony and the Rise of Holocaust Consciousness', in Hilene Flanzbaum (ed.), *The Americanization of the Holocaust* (Baltimore, MD: The Johns Hopkins University Press, 1999), pp.60–61. This is also described by Alan Berger, *Children of Job: American Second-Generation Witnesses to the Holocaust* (Albany, NY: State University of New York Press, 1997), p.7; and Natasha Burchardt, 'Transgenerational Transmission in the Families of Holocaust Survivors in England', in Daniel Bertaux and Paul Thompson (eds.), *Between Generations: Family Models, Myths, and Memories, International Yearbook of Oral History and Life Stories*, Vol.11 (Oxford: Oxford University Press, 1993), p.134.
17. Berman, *Holocaust Remembrance*, pp.42–3. In the USA, third generation groups for direct descendants of Holocaust survivors have started. No groups have officially started yet in Australia, though different workshops for the third generation have been conducted by Jewish Care, Melbourne, the JHRMC and the Sydney Jewish Museum. N. Krasnostein, 'Third Generation Workshops at Centre', *Centre News*, Vol.28, No.1 (April 2006), pp.23–4.
18. Wollaston, *War Against Memory?*, p.7.
19. Eva Hoffman, *After Such Knowledge: Memory, History and the Legacy of the Holocaust* (New York: Public Affairs, 2004), pp.156, 176.
20. Oren Baruch Stier, *Committed to Memory: Cultural Mediations of the Holocaust* (Amherst, MA: University of Massachusetts, 2003), p.19.
21. Several studies have specifically focused on analysing Holocaust video testimonies. For example, see Shoshana Felman, 'Education and Crisis, or the Vicissitudes of Teaching', in Shoshana Felman and Dori Laub, *Testimony: Crises of Witnessing in Literature, Psychoanalysis, and History* (New York: Routledge, 1992), pp.1–56; G. Hartman, 'Preserving the Personal Story: The Role of Video Documentation', *Dimensions: A Journal of Holocaust Studies*, Vol.1 (Spring 1985), pp.14–18; Geoffrey Hartman, *Scars of the Spirit: The Struggle against Inauthenticity* (New York: Palgrave/Macmillan, 2002); Dominick LaCapra, *Writing History, Writing Trauma* (Baltimore, MD: The Johns Hopkins University Press, 2001); Lawrence Langer, *Holocaust Testimonies: The Ruins of Memory* (New Haven, CT: Yale University Press, 1991); Laub, Chapter Two: 'Bearing Witness, or the Vicissitudes of Listening' and Chapter Three: 'An Event Without a Witness: Truth, Testimony and Survival', in *Testimony*, pp.57–92; D. Laub, 'Testimonies in the Treatment of Genocidal Trauma', *Journal of Applied Psychoanalytic Studies*, Vol.4, No.1 (January 2002), pp.63–87; Stier, *Committed to Memory*, Chapter Three: 'Framing Memory: Videotestimonies and the Transmission of Holocaust Remembrance', pp.69–109; James Young, *Writing and Rewriting the Holocaust: Narrative and the Consequences of Interpretation* (Bloomington: Indiana University Press, 1990). To date, most of the discussion on viewer responses has taken place in the absence of empirical data and case studies on viewer responses.
22. The question as to whether the viewer of video testimony becomes a new 'witness' to the survivor witness is an important and necessary area for investigation. See A. Klein, 'Third-generation Responses to Holocaust Video-testimony', unpublished PhD thesis, Deakin University, Melbourne, Australia, 2006, especially Chapter Four: '"Witnessing", Video-testimony and the Third Generation', which explores the relationship between the notion of witnessing and viewers of Holocaust video testimony.
23. Kylie's grandparents are not Holocaust survivors. Kylie is Jewish and from the same generation as the grandchildren of Holocaust survivors interviewed.
24. LaCapra's classroom experiences revealed that in general students are only able to watch an hour of video testimony. LaCapra, *Writing History, Writing Trauma*, p.216. See especially Chapter Three: 'Holocaust Testimonies: Attending to the Victim's Voice'. It is important to note that the majority of Holocaust video testimonies in the JHMRC archive range in length from approximately two to eight hours. This raises the question of editing full-length video testimonies for the purposes of museum exhibitions and educational programmes. Viewing an edited segment of a video testimony will obviously affect the nature of viewer responses as well as the future function of video testimonies in these institutions and programmes. These issues need to be addressed by researchers and the museum community.
25. Kate is a grandchild of Holocaust survivors. Her grandparents chose not to record Holocaust video testimonies. As part of the research, Kate watched a video testimony from the JHMRC archive.
26. Burchardt also identifies the theme of saturation in her interviews with the second generation. For example, one interviewee speaks of having the survival story '"rammed ... down my throat"'.

Burchardt, 'Transgenerational Transmission', p.128.

27. Hoffman, *After Such Knowledge*, p.172.
28. Her grandfather, Mr W., was born in Sosnoweiz, Poland – he experienced the ghetto, and was also sent to Auschwitz and Blechammer. He was liberated at Buchenwald.
29. Jason's grandfather, Mr F., was born in Berlin, Germany. During the Holocaust, he was sent to Schoenfelde Labour Camp in Germany, and then to Auschwitz-Monowitz, Gross-Rosen and Dachau.
30. Peter viewed the video testimony of his grandfather, Mr D., who was born in Danzig, Germany. Mr D. joined the French army under false papers and later worked for the French resistance.
31. Deborah is a traditional Jew who learnt the Holocaust at school and a Jewish Youth movement she attended as a teenager. She viewed the video testimony of her grandmother, Mrs R. Mrs R. was born in Oppeln, Germany. She lived in Berlin from 1937 to 1939 and remembers *Kristallnacht*. She managed to emigrate to Britain in May 1939. Her parents died in the Holocaust. Anne is not an observant Jew, however she culturally identifies herself as Jewish and is a member of the Australian Union of Jewish Students. She learnt about the Holocaust from Jewish newspapers, family conversations and movies. Her grandfather was born in Eldagasen, Germany. After *Kristallnacht*, he was taken to Buchenwald. He managed to leave Germany on a Jewish welfare permit and later travelled to Australia on the Dunera.
32. Mark has a Jewish father and a non-Jewish mother. According to Orthodox Judaism, a child is Jewish only if the mother is. Reform Judaism adheres to a broader definition. If the mother of father is Jewish then the child is considered Jewish. Mark did not identify as Jewish. Mark's grandfather, Mr H., was born in Euskirchen, Germany, he emigrated to the United Kingdom and came to Australia on the *Dunera*. Mr H. rejected his Jewish identity in Australia.
33. Jane and Taryn are sisters. They are both traditional Jews who studied the Holocaust at primary school level. They viewed their grandfather's video testimony. Mr H.M. was born in Berlin, Germany. He left Germany by himself in August 1938 and went to London. He then went by ship to Australia.
34. Hoffman, *After Such Knowledge*, pp.74, 190.
35. The concept of working through was initially developed by Freud to 'describe the process between patient and therapist' in which the patient comes to terms with repressed childhood memories. Sigmund Freud, 'Remembering, Repeating, and Working Through', in Sigmund Freud, *Beyond the Pleasure Principle and Other Writings*, translated by J. Reddick with an Introduction by M. Edmundson (London: Penguin Books, 2003), pp.31–42. However, the idea of working through has extended beyond the context of psychoanalysis and has been applied to cultural memory studies on social and historical traumatic events. For use of this concept in Holocaust research see for example, A. Lazar, J. Chaitin, T. Gross and D. Bar-On, 'A Journey to the Holocaust: Modes of Understanding among Israeli Adolescents who Visited Poland', *Educational Review*, Vol.56, No.1 (February 2004), p.18; D. Bar-On and P. Hare, '"Working Through" the Holocaust? Comparing the Questionnaire Results of German and Israeli Students', *Holocaust and Genocide Studies*, Vol.7, No.2 (1993), pp.230–46; N. Fresco, 'Remembering the Unknown', *International Review of Psycho-Analysis*, Vol.11 (1994), pp.417–27; S. Friedlander, 'Trauma, Transference and "Working Through" in Writing the History of the *Shoah*', *History and Memory*, Vol.4, No.1 (1992), p.51; Caroline Weidmer, *The Claims of Memory: Representations of the Holocaust in Contemporary Germany and France* (Ithaca, NY: Cornell University Press, 1999). For other research in the field of cultural memory utilising the 'working through' principle see Judy Atkinson, *Trauma Trails: Recreating Song Lines: The Transgenerational Effects of Trauma in Indigenous Australia* (Melbourne: Spinifex, 2002); Dominick LaCapra, *History and Memory After Auschwitz* (Ithaca, NY: Cornell University Press, 1998), p.195; Dominick LaCapra, *Representing the Holocaust: History, Theory, Trauma* (Ithaca, NY: Cornell University Press, 1994), pp.169, 187–8, 213; Simon *et al.*, *Between Hope and Despair*.
36. Dan Bar-On, 'Transgenerational Aftereffects of the Holocaust in Israel: Three Generations', in Ephraim Sicher (ed.), *Breaking Crystal: Writing History and Memory After Auschwitz* (Urbana: University of Illinois Press, 1998), pp.96–7. According to Bar-On, the third-generation working-through process includes the following five stages: Knowledge; Understanding; Emotional responses; Attitudes and Behaviour. See Dan Bar-On, *Fear and Hope: Three Generations of the Holocaust* (Cambridge, MA: Harvard University Press, 1995), pp.17–18. Elsewhere I have argued that viewing video testimony enables grandchildren to gain new knowledge and understanding and work through their emotional responses to the Holocaust in general and their grandparents' experiences in particular. See A. Klein, 'Filling in the Gaps Through Holocaust Video-testimony: What Do Grandchildren Learn?', *Cahier International Etudes sur le témoignage audiovisuel des victims des crimes et génocides nazi/International Journal Studies on the Audio-visual Testimony of Victims of the Nazi Crimes and Genocides*, Vol.13 (June 2007),

pp.101–16.

37. A. Kula, 'Cohabiting the Present with Ghosts of the Past: Holocaust "Memories" of Third Generation Jewish Australians', unpublished essay for Honours course, History Department, Melbourne University, 2002, pp.13–14.
38. Björn Krondorfer, *Remembrance and Reconciliation: Encounters between Young Jews and Germans* (New Haven, CT: Yale University Press, 1995), p.233.
39. Maria Nooke and Christine Müller, 'The Kubiak/Grunwald family Dialog: Blocking Out the Theme of Migration from Israel to East Germany', in Gabriele Rosenthal (ed.), *The Holocaust in Three Generations: Families of Victims and Perpetrators of the Nazi Regime* (London: Cassell, 1998), p.137. For example, one of their respondents states, 'it's always hanging over everything like a shadow'. Similarly, Bar-On highlights this tension in the analysis of the life stories he conducted with three generations of Holocaust survivor families. Bar-On, *Fear and Hope*, pp.92–3, 334. See also Ephraim Sicher, 'The Burden of Memory: The Writing of the Post-Holocaust Generation', in Ephraim Sicher (ed), *Breaking Crystal: Writing History and Memory after Auschwitz* (Urbana, IL: University of Illinois Press, 1998), pp.19–87.
40. Bar-On, *Fear and Hope*, p.42. Wajnryb expresses similar ideas in *The Silence*, p.150.
41. LaCapra, *Writing History, Writing Trauma*, pp.22, 70.
42. Yerushalmi, *Zakhor,* pp.11, 40. An example of the set ritual practices of remembering can be seen in the case of *Tisha B'Av*, the day in the Jewish calendar that commemorates the destruction of the First and Second temples. There are set rituals to follow for this day of commemoration, including the reading of the Book of Lamentations, fasting, wearing non-leather shoes and sitting on low stools. Rabbi S. Ganzfried, *Kitzur Shulcan Oruch: The Classic Guide to the Everyday Observance of Jewish Law*, Vol.II (New York: Moznaim Publishing Corporation, 1991), pp.508–15; David Roskies, *Against the Apocalypse: Responses to Catastrophe in Modern Jewish Culture*, 2nd edition (New York: Syracuse University Press, 1999), pp.37–8.
43. M. Baker, 'From Commemoration to Ritual: The Future of the Holocaust', *Generation*, Vol.2, No.2 (1991), p.25. For example, the Passover ritual involves a family meal, where the story of the departure of the Israelites from Egypt is recounted. All family members participate in reading the narrative, accompanied by a series of rituals involving eating and drinking as well as singing, reciting and discussing parts of the Passover *Haggadah* text. Rabbi J. Elias, *The Haggadah: with translation and a new commentary based on Talmudic, Midrashic and Rabbinic Sources* (New York: Mesorah Publications, 1988).
44. The primary aim of the March of the Living is *Zachor*, keeping the memory of the Holocaust alive. Goals of the March of the Living, www.marchoftheliving.org/ (viewed 25 July 2006). The focus is on active commemoration, encompassing education and remembrance activities at different Holocaust-related sites in Poland. For an in-depth discussion of the programme, see Stier, *Committed to Memory*, Chapter Five: 'Performing Memory, Tourism, Pilgrimage, and the Ritual Appropriation of the Past', pp.150–90. Every year it attracts increasing numbers of students and this experiential ritual has now become part of the Australian Jewish community's commemoration of the Holocaust. For participants in such a programme there is an obligation to become a link in the chain of remembering – this is a direct outcome of the recitation of the March of the Living pledge 'to always remember'. Avenues are not necessarily available for individuals to form their own relationships to the sites or think for themselves about the way they would choose to remember. For detailed discussion of Australia's involvement in this programme see A. Klein, 'March of the Living: Active Commemoration in the Landscape', *Australian Association of Jewish Studies Journal*, Vol.18 (2004), pp.25ff. Also see Sharon Kangisser Cohen's article in this volume, '"Remembering for Us": The Transgenerational Transmission of Holocaust Memory and Commemoration'.
45. Bar-On, *Fear and Hope*, pp.17–18.
46. LaCapra, *Writing History, Writing Trauma*, p.22.
47. This term is used by Rosenthal in her studies with the third generation. See *The Holocaust in Three Generations*, p.2.
48. R. Simon and C. Eppert, 'Remembering Obligation: Pedagogy and the Witnessing of Testimony of Historical Trauma', *Canadian Journal of Education*, Vol.22, No.2 (Spring 1997), pp.178, 184, 186. Emphasis in original.
49. Ibid., p.180.
50. Ibid., p.186.
51. Ibid., pp.186, 187. For Kellerman, the issues of Holocaust commemoration and legacy are linked with a 'collective working through'. N. Kellerman, 'The Long-Term Psychological Effects and Treatment of Holocaust Trauma', *Journal of Loss and Trauma*, Vol.6, No.3 (July–September 2001),

p.204.

52. Aaron Hass, *In the Shadow of the Holocaust: The Second Generation* (New York: Cornell University Press, 1990), p.165. Hass' thoughts concur with Fine's thesis that 'each individual must read the past and relate to it from the perspective of his or her own circumstance'. E. Fine, 'Transmission of Memory: The Post-Holocaust Generation in the Diaspora', in Sicher, *Breaking Crystal*, p.186.
53. P. Valent, 'Holocaust: One of History's Greatest Teachers', *Centre News*, Vol.27, No.1 (April/May 2005), pp.24–5. For example, the Passover seder takes on new meaning after the Holocaust. See for example, Samuel Touster (ed.), with an introduction and commentary, *A Survivors' Haggadah* (Philadelphia: Jewish Publication Society, 2000).
54. Ibid., p.26.
55. Several grandchildren of Holocaust survivors confirmed this view. They stated that being involved in community activism and human rights was a positive way in which they were able to translate their responsibility to remember the Holocaust into active involvement with contemporary events in society.
56. For an overview of Holocaust commemoration in Sydney see Sharon Kangisser Cohen's article in this volume.
57. Björn Krondorfer and Christian Staffa, *Living in a Post-Shoah World: Reflections of American, German, Jewish and Christian Students*, 4th Summer Program on the Holocaust (Berlin: Evangelische Akademie Berlin Brandenburg, 1995), p.13.
58. M. Fagenblat, 'Rituals of Remembrance', *Generation*, Vol.4, No.2 (June 1994), pp.10–11. S. Ser emphatically suggests 'we have saturated the world with Holocaust movies, books, museums … memorials … their sheer volume has also diluted Holocaust commemoration, making it less significant, and therefore less effective … we can start by looking afresh at the way we choose to remember the Holocaust'. S. Ser, 'The Downside of Holocaust Remembrance Day', *The Australian Jewish News*, 3 February 2006, p.16.
59. Berman, *Holocaust Remembrance*, p.101.
60. Ernst van Alphen, *Caught by History: Holocaust Effects in Contemporary Art, Literature, and Theory* (Stanford, CA: Stanford University Press, 1997), pp.63–4. This idea is also articulated by Baum who argues: 'If memory of the Holocaust is to be preserved and handed down, each generation must articulate its own particular relationship to the event'. R. Baum, 'Never to Forget: Pedagogical Memory and Second-Generation Witness', in R. Simon, S. Rosenberg and C. Eppert (eds.), *Between Hope and Despair: Pedagogy and the Remembrance of Historical Trauma* (Lanham, MD: Rowman & Littlefield Publishers, Inc., 2000), p.95.
61. Simon and Eppert, 'Remembering Obligation', pp.181–2.
62. Stone, 'Day of Remembrance or Day of Forgetting?', pp.58–9. Friedlander echoes Stone's comments in a similar way stating, 'if we make allowance for some sort of ritualised form of commemoration, already in place, we may foresee, in the public domain, a tendency towards closure without resolution, but closure nonetheless'. S. Friedlander, 'Trauma, Transference and "Working Through"', p.54.
63. Stone, 'Day of Remembrance or Day of Forgetting?', pp.58–9.
64. Perhaps it takes three generations to work through the original trauma. Wajnryb states: 'A Buddhist saying has it that after a time of killing, it takes three generations for the healing to happen'. *The Silence*, p.55.
65. This concurs with Langer's idea that 'every future generation will have to be educated anew in how to face the historical period we call the Holocaust'. Lawrence Langer, *Admitting the Holocaust: Collected Essays* (New York: Oxford University Press, 1995), p.180.

Displaying the Sacred: Australian Holocaust Memorials in Public Life

AVRIL ALBA

Introduction

Will Australian Holocaust museums and memorials remain relevant in Australia's shifting political and cultural landscape? Internationally, Holocaust museums and memorials have sought to reach beyond their home constituencies, to inform and influence the broader communities in which they are situated. This same impulse also animates Australia's Holocaust museums, but in addition they contain a strong intra-communal focus, one that emphasises Jewish collective loss and mourning.[1] This emphasis is most clearly evident in the memorial spaces contained within Australian Holocaust museums as purpose-built spaces for ritualised commemoration. This dual focus results in an in-built tension within these institutions, as a memory considered sacred to a particular, albeit diverse community, is placed in public space intended to engage a broader audience. This positioning has the effect of linking Jewish and non-Jewish understandings of Holocaust memory in a dialectical relationship, as change within effects change without and vice versa, resulting in a syncretism of theological forms and associated rituals. In laying bare this dynamic process, a clearer outline of the 'shape' of sacred Holocaust memory in Australia can be ascertained.

If abroad Holocaust museums and memorials are seldom solely Jewish – in fact, more often than not they are funded and run by state authorities – in Australia, they were founded and funded by Jewish survivors as centres for Holocaust research and remembrance. The survivors' choice to situate communal remembrance in a museum/memorial context distinguishes it from traditional Jewish commemorative forms which have historically been centred in text and ritual and enacted largely in the synagogue and home. In this public commemorative space traditional Jewish responses to destruction are reformulated from a lay perspective, informed more by personal and communal loss than commitment to a particular theological worldview. This sacred memory is conveyed to the broader public through built structures and associated commemorative days that originate within the Jewish tradition but undergo modification in order to engage a wider audience. These 'scared spaces' and the commemorations enacted in and near them provide an ideal case study through which to explore the contemporary sacralisation of Holocaust memory within the Australian Jewish community and also to ascertain how this memory is transformed as it enters the public sphere.

In exploring exactly what kind of 'sacred memories' are being constructed in Australian Holocaust memorials, we are also asking about the utility of these memories as they enter into the public realm. For whom do these memories become sacred and why? Dan Stone argues that assessing the historiography of the Holocaust is important because 'to imbed the Holocaust in a given theory of history is immediately to provide it with a moral purpose that the mere record of events does not suggest'.[2] Memory, perhaps even more so than history, has a deep influence on how historical events are instrumentalised in order to influence the present, and as such it is important to understand the sacred meanings that are being given to Holocaust memory. In outlining the sacralisation of Holocaust memory in the Sydney Jewish Museum's (SJM) Sanctum of Remembrance, the aim of this article is to provide a more comprehensive understanding of what this memory entails both within and beyond the Australian Jewish community and assess its influence with regard to contemporary causes and concerns.

The form and function of sacred Holocaust memory in the Australian context is examined in this article through the following framework. First, the question of why Holocaust memorials have evolved as alternative 'sacred spaces' *within* the Jewish world is addressed. Second, the form and utility of this sacred memory *beyond* the Jewish world is explored by examining the connection between sacred and traumatic memory. In the third and central section, these theoretical frames provide a backdrop for an exploration of sacred Holocaust memory in the SJM's Sanctum of Remembrance. Through this prism, the particularistic emphasis of sacred Holocaust memory existent in Sydney's Jewish survivor community is identified and the argument advanced that this emphasis must be re-thought if Holocaust memory is to retain currency in contemporary debates beyond the Jewish community. Finally, an alternative framework is offered in which sacred Holocaust memory retains an intra-communal commemorative focus, while concurrently promoting relevancy in the Australian public sphere.

Extraordinary History, Inadequate Theology

> [I]n our time, Jewish life is in advance of Jewish thought … Jewish life itself ... is in the grip of, and responding to, epoch making events.
>
> Emil Fackenheim[3]

Emil Fackenheim's prescient observation, made over a quarter of a century ago, still holds true for Jewish life and thought today. In particular, the poignancy of his statement is evidenced in the broad variety of Holocaust 'memory forms' existent within the Jewish world. There is no consensus within modern Jewish thought on the theological meaning(s) of this 'epoch making event' and hence liturgical responses to the Holocaust remain largely unsystematic in content and form.[4] On the one hand, a diversity of response might well be expected from so heterogeneous a people; on the other, this variety is indicative of a dilemma that continues to confound modern Jewish thought in general, but most starkly post-Holocaust theology, namely, does the historical experience of the Holocaust negate the covenantal relationship between Israel and its God and if not, how does (and, indeed, how can?) the tradition reconcile the events of the Holocaust within pre-existing notions of covenant?[5]

As Jewish thought is yet to respond fully to the enormous theological challenges posed by the Holocaust, those active in Jewish life today continue, as Fackenheim suggests, to create Holocaust remembrance forms largely independent of any conscious theological framework. For example, there are many fine liturgies for Holocaust remembrance, some drawing upon works that emerged throughout the Holocaust, others hearkening back to prior destructions;[6] there are others still that have transformed traditional liturgical responses in line with what some consider a *novum* in Jewish history.[7] Yet the majority of Holocaust commemorations do not utilise the traditional liturgy and are not enacted in solely Jewish ritual spaces. In light of these developments, a broader lens is necessary to understand how the Jewish world continues to understand and assimilate the Holocaust into its sacred memory and connected memorial practices. Subsequently, existing studies concerned with these broad issues have reached beyond traditional forms of liturgy to consider literary and artistic responses in general – aiming in particular to understand how these responses form both continuations and departures from traditional Jewish responses to destruction.[8] What remains largely unexplored, however, is the relationship of memorials and memorial spaces to the Jewish commemorative tradition.[9] So ubiquitous are these 'memory forms' that their presence is rarely questioned, much less examined in-depth in relation to traditional Jewish responses to destruction. Such spaces provide a case in point vis-à-vis Fackenheim's observation. Emerging out of deeply felt need rather than systematic theological deliberations, these spaces run ahead of systematic Jewish thought and provide an important but as yet under-explored framework through which to delineate and explore the nature of sacred Holocaust memory within the Jewish world.

Holocaust Memorials as Sacred Spaces

Due to their public setting and mission, Holocaust memorials also provide a forum for exploring how Holocaust memory is conceived of as sacred memory *beyond* the Jewish world. As public memorials are built, understandings of the sacred that were once confined within a discrete religious tradition are modified and expanded, resulting in a syncretism of commemorative forms. Further, what may or may not be deemed 'sacred' in largely secular Westernised societies is itself a point of contention and therefore what constitutes sacred Holocaust memory and sacred space must be clarified.

With regard to the broad concept of sacred space, the work of Mircea Eliade remains instructive. According to Eliade, a sacred place is a site that has been *consecrated* by a hierophany, that is, the manifestation of a higher being.[10] The place where the hierophany occurs becomes a sacred place. The nature of a hierophany in Eliade's formulation allows us to discover two aspects of the sacred: first, a 'modality of the sacred' and second a 'moment in history'.[11] In other words, by examining the creation of sacred space we can evaluate how the sacred is both constructed and understood in distinct historical periods, from the perspective of the respective religious community and/or individual believer. Similarly, as Eliade sought to examine hierophanies to understand the nature and function of the sacred at particular moments in history, so too does the following examination of the construction of the sacred in the SJM's Sanctum of Remembrance seek to reveal the nature and function of sacred Holocaust memory in the present.

If the usefulness of Eliade's approach for determining the form and function of sacred Holocaust memory in memorials and museums is apparent, the limits of his definition are equally clear. First, the explicit lack of a deity ostensibly precludes secular spaces such as memorials from being classified as sacred spaces according to this definition. Second, Eliade's notions of the sacred are based upon studies of cohesive and traditional religious communities but, as noted, in modern ethnically and religiously diverse societies the notion of the sacred exists within the context of secularisation. The concept of the 'sacred' may be considered independent of the 'Divine' because what is deemed sacred holds widely divergent meanings for a variety of groups and individuals. However, if the sacred is no longer dependent on the Divine, then what do contemporary notions of the sacred encompass?

Increasingly, understandings of the sacred are linked to concepts of traumatic memory. For example, Barbara Misztal argues that the contemporary preoccupation with traumatic memory is illustrative of a 'sacralisation of memory'.[12] Misztal posits that the 'decline in national and religious memories as stable sources of identity reopens the space to search for both authentic identities and useable pasts' and understands this situation to be the result of 'two trends of a paradoxical nature':[13] the need for memory in essentially 'amnesiac' modern societies and the emergence of new forms of spirituality.[14] This definition of the sacred is intimately linked to the human need to confront ultimate questions, particularly those pertaining to suffering and mortality. In this characterisation of the sacred, the Holocaust is increasingly cast as the paradigmatic 'sacred' historical event – the ultimate 'trauma drama' to which all others are compared.[15]

If traditional religious paradigms cannot contain concepts of the sacred in contemporary societies, then how is the sacred memory of the Holocaust to be conveyed? Daniele Hervieu-Leger points out that in modern societies a clear distinction must be made between the 'immediate experience of the sacred and that of the religious administration of the sacred'.[16] The 'immediate experience' is individual and therefore largely immeasurable. The 'religious administration' is more often institutional, and in modern and ostensibly secular societies this distinction allows for the 'administration of the sacred' by institutions and frameworks other than those of traditional religious structures. The modern memorial, and in particular the war memorial, provides perhaps the most ubiquitous contemporary example of the 'administration of the sacred' outside of traditional religious institutions.[17] In these spaces a variety of individual and communal rituals are enacted that, while lacking a cohesive theological worldview, do function to mediate the sacred memory of a traumatic past. In a similar vein, while Holocaust museums and memorials cannot be understood to replace or even serve to replicate synagogues, they can be considered as forms of 'administration of the sacred' that exist outside of traditional structures. Both within and beyond the Jewish world therefore, Holocaust memorials function as important mediators of sacred Holocaust memory – a traumatic memory that has resisted containment into traditional theological forms.

Moreover, Holocaust memorials serve to mediate the sacred memory of a traumatic past *in public space* – not in a private communal environment. As such, the sacred memory housed in these spaces contains another dimension – a public and hence political one. Mark Chmiel examines a similar connection between sacred Holocaust memory and the political sphere in his study of Elie Wiesel's deployment of sacred Holocaust memory. Chmiel examines Wiesel's use of 'sacred Holocaust remembrance as solidarity with its victims, patriotic legitimation of the state, and ultimate end'.[18] His analysis is grounded in a broad understanding of the political that encompasses not only participation in explicitly political organisations, but also the methods through which 'persons can translate private grievances into public issues' and how 'persons can handle, or mobilise others to handle social or private issues by having recourse to general or universal political ideas, rights and democratic norms'.[19] Holocaust memorials, and the rituals performed in or near them, provide a physical embodiment of this political process. The following exploration of the form and function of sacred Holocaust memory in the SJM's Sanctum of Remembrance provides a microcosm through which to chart this complex progression in which an internal communal need to mourn and remember is transformed into an external forum for political and social engagement.

The Sanctum of Remembrance: History and Design

The Sanctum of Remembrance at the SJM was established two years after the museum was opened in 1992. Since then it has inhabited several different places and was only placed in its current position in October 2004. Located adjacent to the final section of the permanent exhibition, *Long Journey to Freedom* – an exhibition outlining the migration of Holocaust survivors to Australia – the Sanctum space 'completes' the visitor experience and is strategically located to allow the visitor space for contemplation after the confronting content of the Holocaust exhibit.

The design and creation of the Sanctum space were both motivated by the SJM's volunteer survivor guides, in particular those active at a board level. The space would serve, in the survivors' words, to 'remember the victims and honour the survivors'. The founder of the Sanctum, Holocaust survivor Marika Weinberger; considers the Sanctum to be the defining element rendering the SJM a memorial as well as a museum.[20] Speaking on behalf of the Australian Association for Jewish Holocaust Survivors and their Descendants (AAJHS&D), she describes the aim of the project: 'The Sanctum was not to be a cemetery but it does serve a similar function for those who have no graves to visit. It is a place of remembrance and as such its goal is to bring peace if not closure.'[21] The initial conception of the Sanctum therefore was as a largely private space, dedicated to the commemorative needs of the survivor community.

The Sanctum in its current form is largely the result of the work of Melbourne designer Bryon Cunningham, who redesigned the space as part of a refurbishment of significant sections of the SJM completed in October 2004. During the refurbishment, at the urging of the survivors, a dedication to those individuals who saved Jews throughout the Holocaust – commonly referred to as the 'Righteous Among the Nations' – was added. The Sanctum was moved and enlarged but the essential elements of the memorial remained intact, namely: individual commemorative plaques, an eternal flame, inscriptions and a selection of commemorative sculptures (see Figures 1, 2 and 3). A recording of the *kaddish* (mourner's prayer) is played continuously in the Sanctum and there are copies of the prayer available for those who wish to recite individually as well.

In 2006, the SJM commissioned Sydney designer, John Cabello, to create a Menorah specifically for the space (see Figure 4), which through its design and placement in the middle of the rear wall has the effect of drawing together the disparate elements of the Sanctum as well as providing a focal point for reflection. Despite its now more prominent position and increased physical space, the Sanctum remains the domain of the survivors, epitomised in the following inscription: 'The voice of the survivor is the authentic voice of the Holocaust. It speaks for the victims, living and dead.'[22] The particularistic emphasis of the Sanctum is clearly apparent, begging the question of why this memorial was placed in the public space of a Museum, rather than the 'Jewish' space of a synagogue, or even a cemetery. The answer lies in the perceived need for the Sanctum in the Sydney survivor community and its current commemorative function.

Constructing the Sacred

The creation of the Sanctum space is, in itself, an acknowledgement that Sydney survivors felt that existing traditional modes of commemoration were in some sense inadequate to contain and relay their experience. For example, the most recent benefactor of the Sanctum, Dr. Bronia Hatfield, commented in her 2005 dedication speech that her family now had a 'resting place', referring to the Sanctum as her family's 'graveyard' and noting that she now had a physical space to visit and recite *kaddish*.[23] Indeed, many survivors speak of 'visiting' the Sanctum when they come to the museum – even some survivors who have renounced traditional forms of Jewish worship in light of their Holocaust experiences will visit the Sanctum to 'pay their respects'.[24] The Sanctum is clearly a place in which the survivors feel they can mourn and remember those who perished.

FIGURE 1
Individual Commemorative Plaques (SJM, Sydney)

As one survivor notes: 'We need the Sanctum. None of us are sophisticated enough to say "it is enough if I think about it" … it may not be a traditional space but in many ways it is a better space.'[25]

FIGURE 2
The Eternal Flame (SJM)

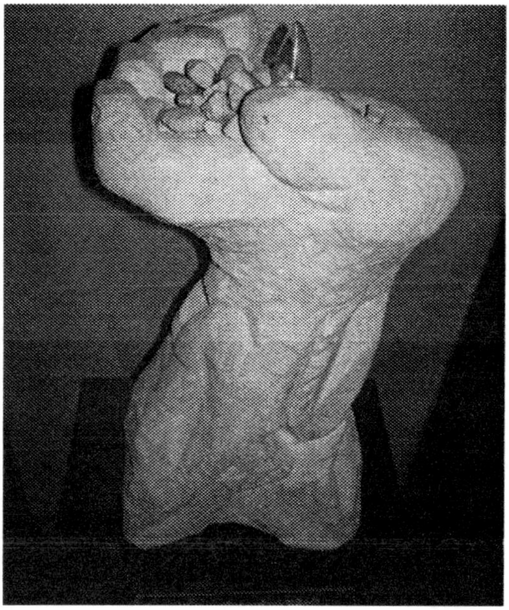

FIGURE 3
Commemorative Sculpture (SJM)

Survivors who were questioned as to whether it was more important to visit the Sanctum on *Yom HaShoah* (Holocaust Remembrance Day) rather than traditional places of worship answered resoundingly in the affirmative.[26] Yet while the Sanctum provides some reassurance for the survivors that the Holocaust will be remembered in a manner they deem appropriate, they also acknowledge that the Sanctum space will change over time and that the rituals enacted in and near it will also undergo modification. One survivor felt that this propensity for change was a dangerous aspect of the choice to house Holocaust memory in museums and memorials and that until the Holocaust was firmly entrenched in the refrains of daily Jewish prayer it may not yet be remembered with integrity and for perpetuity. While another survivor felt that such changes were 'natural' as succeeding generations should not remember the Holocaust in the same way, she too expressed a desire to 'keep it Jewish' maintaining that a connection to tradition would ensure ongoing commemoration.[27] The same survivor was adamant that in the fullness of time, when the survivor generation had passed, the Sanctum space would have increased meaning. Referencing the resurgence of ANZAC (Australia New Zealand Army Corps) Day commemorations in contemporary Australian life and the 'poppy wall' at the Australian War Memorial in particular, she maintained that once the generation of witnesses was no more, the need for new vessels of memory would ensure that the Sanctum would be increasingly utilised on both an individual and communal level.[28]

The survivors' need for the Sanctum and its associated rituals are indicative of a larger issue at stake with regard to the construction and transmission of sacred Holocaust memory within the Australian Jewish community. The survivors' strong desire to keep this memory connected to traditional Jewish commemorative strategies is at odds with their equally firm insistence on maintaining the Holocaust's 'exceptional' status in contrast to earlier destructions in Jewish history. Sharon Kangisser Cohen's article in this volume clearly demonstrates that while some survivors feel that their experience should become part of the traditional liturgy, they are also wary of it becoming 'just another destruction' in Jewish history.[29] For example, Kangisser Cohen notes that despite the fact that some survivors favour the inclusion of Holocaust remembrance in the Passover *seder* they are keenly aware that in their story, as opposed to the Exodus narrative, there is no redemption – 'there are no miracles'.[30] Their desire, therefore, to see the Holocaust remembered as 'exceptional' stands in contradistinction to traditional Jewish liturgical commemorations such as the *Tisha B'Av* (9th of Av), in which distinct historical tragedies are 'collapsed' into an undifferentiated typology of destruction and redemption.[31]

The Sanctum space therefore allows survivors to connect Holocaust memory to traditional Jewish responses to destruction but also extend beyond them. A case in point is the rituals performed as part of annual remembrance days for which the Sanctum provides a focal point. The most significant of these is the

FIGURE 4
John Cabello's Menorah (SJM)

observance of *Yom HaShoah*. While this day (27 Nissan) has gained widespread acceptance in the Jewish world as an appropriate day for commemoration, some commentators argue that *Tisha B'Av*, the traditional day of mourning for all catastrophes in Jewish history, would be more apt.[32] Subsequently, observance of *Yom HaShoah* remains a national rather than religious holiday, sanctioned by the State of Israel. On *Yom HaShoah* a daylong programme of events at the SJM[33] centres on the 'Reading of the Names' ceremony in which names of Holocaust victims are read continuously, a ritual that has become a regular part of *Yom HaShoah* observances throughout the world.[34] A powerful ceremony, in which dignitaries from both the Jewish and broader Sydney communities are asked to participate, it departs from traditional Jewish commemorative strategies in both content and form.

Firstly, the commemoration takes place in an ostensibly secular institution on *Yom HaShoah*, which, as already noted, is a secular remembrance day. These factors ensure that the ceremony is not invested with the same liturgical 'weight' as *Tisha B'Av* or even the traditional *Yizkor* service which is recited as part of High Holiday services and on each of the three pilgrimage festivals – *Pesach*, *Shavuot* and *Sukkot*. Secondly, the Reading of the Names ceremony is resoundingly 'individualistic' at its core. While individuals do remember and 'name' the deceased as part of a traditional *Yizkor* service, the emphasis in the Jewish commemorative tradition is on communal remembrance. Finally, the Sydney community expressly invites non-Jews to take part in this ceremony. In 2007 the honour of the first reading was given to New South Wales Governor, Marie Bashir, a woman of Christian Lebanese origin – an indication that sacred Holocaust memory is not solely an internal concern. What these examples make clear is that in the development of the Sanctum space and performance of these commemorations Jewish symbols and rituals are transmitted but also extended, they provide points of connection but are set aside when deemed inadequate in remembering and relaying the 'extraordinary history' at hand.

Similarly, the co-option, extension and transformation of traditional commemorative strategies is evident in the built structures of the Sanctum, epitomised in the Menorah – the central sculptural figure in the Sanctum space. Again, the desire for and development of the Menorah was a lay-led initiative by SJM survivors. Central to their vision was the concept of death and regeneration. Directed by the survivors' vision, John Cabello created a sculpture that, while drawing upon traditional symbols, also extends and subverts them and, in so doing, creates a symbolic structure encompassing connection and disjuncture, continuity and change (see Figure 4).

Cabello's Menorah utilises an ancient Jewish symbol to reorient Jewish history from the perspective of the Holocaust. The Menorah (seven-stemmed candelabra) has its roots in the Hebrew Bible where the Israelites are commanded to 'make a candlestick of pure gold' (Exodus 25:31). Brought through the wilderness to the Land of Israel, the Menorah is eventually placed in the Temple in Jerusalem and so becomes the central symbol of ancient Israelite civilisation. However, the most famous ancient depiction of the Menorah is in its appearance in the Arch of Titus.[35] Here it is no longer a symbol of sovereign strength and power; rather it depicts the greatest calamity in Jewish history prior to the Nazi Holocaust – the destruction of the Second Temple by the Romans in 70 CE. In the arch relief the humiliation of the destruction is epitomised in the looting of the Temple. Taken as one of the spoils of war, the fate of the Menorah mirrors the dispersion of the Jewish people. With the establishment of the State of Israel in 1948, the Menorah is re-established once more as a symbol of nationhood, embossed on the Israeli coat of arms.

Historically, therefore, the Menorah is understood both as a symbol of destruction *and* redemption, and as such it falls neatly into traditional theological paradigms. Yet for both Cabello and the survivors who influenced the design of the Menorah, the deliberate configuring of a six, rather than seven-stemmed candelabra ruptures the traditional theological paradigm. At first reading the choice of six is easily identified with the six million. While this choice is certainly a deliberate reference, there is an additional element at play. The absence of the seventh candle may also be read to underscore the idea of 'void' – one that immediately connects the knowledgeable visitor with the concept of the 'counter-memorial' pioneered by German artists Jochen Gerz and Esther Shalev-Gerz in the late 1980s.[36] The emphasis is on absence rather than presence, rupture rather than reconciliation. Understood theologically, the significance of the design lies in its refusal to submit to traditional paradigms of destruction and redemption.

This emphasis on rupture is underscored in the other key elements of the sculpture. A circle holds the Menorah together – reminiscent of an egg – a traditional symbol of life in the Jewish tradition. The cycle of life is compromised, however, by the uneven positioning of the candlesticks. Their deliberate intrusion into the circle serves a reminder of the precariousness of this cycle in the post-Holocaust world. The differing heights of the candlesticks are intended to represent the individual experience of each of the victims. This emphasis on individuality is reminiscent of the impulse underlying the 'Reading of the Names' ceremony. Finally, the placement of the Menorah in a public space is also significant, as a once particularistic religious and national symbol, now located in a public setting, comes to embody diverse meanings. In employing these strategies, Cabello's Menorah transforms and reinterprets a traditionally redemptive symbol, simultaneously connecting and distinguishing the Holocaust from prior destructions in Jewish history.[37]

As evidenced in these two examples, the Sanctum provides a forum in which to enact uneasy theological compromises. For the survivors it allows for a clear distinction between *this* tragedy and other Jewish tragedies. As such, the symbols contained within the space and the rituals performed in or near it begin within the Jewish tradition but end beyond it – embodying Fackenheim's observation that it is indeed the demands of Jewish life that precede Jewish thought with regard to contemporary forms of Holocaust remembrance. However, *beyond* the Jewish community, the question remains as to whether the survivors' insistence on the exceptional nature of the Holocaust experience must necessarily relegate the sacred memory housed in the Sanctum to a purely internal, Jewish concern. Does this particularistic focus sit in opposition to the Sydney Jewish Museum's self-declared mission 'to inspire mutual respect and cross cultural understanding in our society', or can this emphasis be retained but recast to allow the universal resonance of Holocaust memory to be felt beyond the confines of the Sydney Jewish community?[38]

Conveying the Sacred: Holocaust Memory in Australian Public Life

Within the Australian setting, Holocaust museums and memorials were created in a Jewish community that has been historically non-universalistic in its outlook.[39] In the words of the SJM's first curator, Sylvia Rosenbaum, 'One cannot use the Holocaust to tell other stories'.[40] While this outlook still dominates within the Australian Jewish community, Neil Levi argues that just the opposite has occurred in the broader Australian public sphere. Indeed, so pervasive is the explicit use of

Holocaust memory as a comparative tool in Australian public discourse that,

> the Australian case poses a problem for the widespread critique of transnational Holocaust remembrance as a form of what is known as 'screen memory': the claim that the Holocaust is remembered in order to displace, repress or 'screen' other, perhaps more traumatic, local events or histories.[41]

Levi cites numerous examples of such explicit comparisons in both public discourse and 'built references' in major Australian cultural institutions such as the National Museum of Australia. In Australian public life the Holocaust *has* been used to 'tell other stories', its moral weight buttressing both liberal commentators who would liken aspects of the Australian experience to that of Nazi Germany and more conservative voices who would use it to disavow – 'whatever we have been, we were never that'.[42] In a cultural landscape in which museums and memorials are increasingly understood as reflections of and contributors to issues of national import, a framework for grappling with the meaning of Holocaust memory in the Australian context must be found if the SJM is to retain its self-proclaimed mission of 'contemporary relevance'.[43]

This challenge is not unique to the Australian experience and it is well documented that the 'shape' of most major Holocaust museums and memorials is deeply influenced by either nationalistic or humanistic imperatives.[44] Judith Berman notes that the 'universalisation' of Holocaust memory may take several different forms: it may be 'nationalised' and made relevant to other historical experiences of the nation in which it is placed; its 'moral, political and social implications' may be focused upon to highlight contemporary political causes and concerns; or the more 'humanistic' aspects of Holocaust memory can be invoked, where a 'consideration of the universal humanistic lessons of the Holocaust' is undertaken 'to fight against prejudice, discrimination and racism'.[45]

While Berman's distinctions are useful, her overall conclusion that the 'universalization of the Holocaust ... inevitably turns attention away from the destruction of European Jewry' is open to question.[46] If a shallow universalism may lead to a 'blurring of distinctions', a collapsing of distinct experiences of persecution into more generalised categories of loss, emphasising the *universality* of a particular experience only amplifies its resonance. Its invocation can serve to illuminate a variety of historical instances, political and social causes and moral and ethical dilemmas *without* betraying its particular identity. In such a definition, the application of Holocaust memory to highlight other instances of genocide and mass trauma serves only to augment, not to diminish Holocaust memory, to extend empathy and identification with victims of persecution rather than detract and obscure.

Literary critic Ruth Wisse makes a similar distinction between universalism and universality in reflecting upon the universal appeal of modern Jewish literature:

> Some critics have mistaken the broad appeal of Jewish writing for proof that it belongs to no particular people, but this is to confuse universalism, which seeks to eliminate tribal categories, with universality, which is the global resonance of a tribal work. The Hebrew Bible is a tribal document that became one of the world's most influential works of literature.[47]

Wisse's astute observation also has application to current uses of Holocaust memory, wherein the Holocaust is understood both as a specific historical event – the genocide perpetrated against European Jewry – and a universal symbol – a paradigm of 'radical evil'. The complex process through which this transformation has occurred is explored from a sociological perspective in the work of Jeffrey C. Alexander. He argues that the Holocaust, 'a specific and situated historical event', has become,

> transformed into a generalised symbol of human suffering and moral evil, a universalised symbol whose very existence has created historically unprecedented opportunities for ethnic, racial and religious justice, for mutual recognition, and for global conflicts to become regulated in a more civil way.[48]

Alexander makes the point that at the time of the liberation of Europe's concentration camps, the genocide of European Jewry was subsumed within the broader picture of Nazi atrocities. Through a multitude of examples from film to literature, Survivor testimony and the development of international law, Alexander charts how, in the 60 years since the liberation of Europe's concentration camps, the Holocaust was 'particularised' and then paradoxically 'universalised' as the archetypical example of 'ontological evil'.[49] In so doing, Alexander provides a sociological framework for understanding how Jewish suffering has come to be a 'universal' reference point in diverse communal and national settings. His analysis is therefore extremely useful in tracing how Holocaust memory has become a moral touchstone for a diverse array of political and social causes. While Alexander conflates the universalisation (blurring of historical distinctions) of Holocaust memory in the immediate post-war period with the universality (global resonance of a particular historical experience) of Holocaust memory in the present, his work provides a useful 'secular' template with which to examine how Holocaust memory acts as a sacred memory that is at once particular and universal – a memory that both retains and points beyond its particular historical circumstance.

The construction of Holocaust memory charted by Alexander demonstrates that just as Holocaust memory is both particular and universal, so is it 'unique and not-unique at the same time'.[50] In using such terminology, Alexander is pointing to the power of Holocaust memory as a sociological 'bridging metaphor' rather than a historical 'litmus test' for mass suffering.[51] Unlike historical debates concerned with 'Holocaust uniqueness', Alexander's aim is not to distinguish where and how the Holocaust may be like or unlike other genocides, but rather to demonstrate how the deployment of Holocaust memory, through 'symbolic extension', has been mobilised to lend legitimacy and channel resources to other instances of genocide and mass trauma.[52]

A clear example of the flexibility and power of Holocaust memory in this regard is found in its use in the developing world. If at the United Nations Conference against Racism held in 2001 in Durban, South Africa, the memory of the Holocaust was used to downplay other genocides, so too was its moral authority harnessed in the name of reparations, or utilised to create support for marginalised groups otherwise ignored in the West.[53] This tendency is also apparent in critiques of colonial genocide, where Holocaust memory is generally employed to illustrate the radical nature of genocides perpetrated as part of the European colonial project.[54] As Vinay Lal and others argue, resistance within academic discourse to acknowledging the magnitude of colonial genocides has also had the perverse effect of utilising Holocaust memory to minimise rather than illuminate the nature and scope of previous genocides.[55] While many of these critiques are openly polemical in their approach, their central point – that Holocaust memory is often used as 'screen memory' with regard to colonial genocides – is well taken.[56] What is evident from even this brief examination of the universality of Holocaust memory is that its potential for 'symbolic extension' can be used to include or exclude, to highlight injustice or to screen it from view.[57]

Australian Holocaust Memory: Particular and Universal

Ultimately, whether Australian Holocaust museums utilise the universality inherent in sacred Holocaust memory, or employ its power to screen local traumatic histories, is simply a matter of choice. As the previous examples illustrate, the Holocaust is already a moral touchstone – a 'sacred memory' – beyond the Jewish world. The 'symbolic extension' of Holocaust memory into the non-Jewish world means that any form of Holocaust commemoration must, necessarily, confront how that sacred memory will be transformed as it enters into the public sphere. Thus, while the sacred Holocaust memory housed in the Sanctum derives from a particularistic source, its continued relevance beyond the survivor generation will be dependent on its ability to both contain and transcend its origins.

To achieve such synthesis in Australian museums, those invested with the development and care of sacred memory within spaces such as the Sanctum will need to confront 'uncomfortable' questions with regard to Australia's past and current political climate. For example, as previously noted, the Sanctum of

Remembrance is currently located near the final section of the SJM's permanent exhibition *Long Journey to Freedom*. While this exhibition makes mention of the discriminatory quotas imposed on Jewish migration by the Australian government immediately after the Second World War, the exhibition's emphasis is on the role that Australia played in providing a safe haven for survivors in the post-war period – a place where they have found refuge and been able to rebuild their lives. While this is certainly historically correct, the exhibition's focus on Australia as a safe haven for immigrant groups fleeing persecution – open, welcoming and largely cast in an idealised vision of contemporary 'multicultural Australia' – does serve to obscure 'other narratives'. Beside the panel on quotas, there is no indication of the recurrent xenophobia that has characterised Australia's migration history and the Howard government's rather chequered record on refugees; nor is the fact that while Holocaust survivors undertook the mammoth task of resettling in this country, systematic racial discrimination against Australia's indigenous populations continued to take place. Can such a complex vision of Australia be 'held in tension' within this exhibition space?

The problem remains how to 'weave' such complex and layered issues into largely 'static' displays. This is a complicated curatorial task. The central question of whether this can be achieved with sensitivity, stressing the universality of the 'fight against prejudice, discrimination and racism', while retaining the integrity of each historical instance of such persecution, is more an issue of will rather than workability.[58] In this undertaking, the sacred Holocaust memory inherent in the Sanctum display may yet provide clues as to how to achieve such a difficult synthesis. For example, could not the 'Reading of the Names' ceremony, already deliberately engaging the non-Jewish community and therefore aiming to connect Holocaust memory to contemporary values and behaviours, extend its reach to mention 'victims of other genocides' without losing its emphasis on Jewish communal and personal loss? Would an additional plaque in the commemorative space of the Sanctum acknowledging the original tribal owners of the land (Gadigal clan of the Eora nation) detract from the personal memories housed in this space or could Holocaust memory be retained while simultaneously opening up a space in which Australia's complex past can also be considered?[59] Arguably, such strategies could *add* rather than detract from the Holocaust's powerful symbolic status, allowing sacred Holocaust memory in Australia to 'tell other stories' as well as its own to the greater benefit of all?

At this current point in time such acknowledgements must be made largely by way of 'inference' or additional programming, which the SJM employs in its education and public programmes, and there is now evidence of such an approach being incorporated into temporary exhibitions as well.[60] While it is understandable that Jewish survivors want, and indeed are entitled to, their own commemorative spaces, addressing other victims in such spaces can be achieved if there is a shift in emphasis toward 'displaying empathy'. Sacred spaces and symbols, once placed in public settings, engender such possibilities more than historically bounded displays. In a memorial setting, historical distinctions are maintained but necessarily point beyond themselves as the humanistic elements of sacred memory are emphasised. Empathy is extended and in this process sacred Holocaust memory is both linked to and distinguished from other historical instances of persecution and suffering.

Conclusion

It is evident that an examination of the 'shape' of sacred Holocaust memory in the SJM's Sanctum of Remembrance reveals significant changes in the 'modality of the sacred' both within the Sydney Jewish community and without – and as such provides insight into the current construction and reception of Holocaust memory in Australia. The continued influence of the survivor generation on Australian institutions of Holocaust research and remembrance ensures that particularistic interpretations of Holocaust memory will remain the norm at least for the immediate future. Yet as succeeding generations are now beginning to take on the task of conveying this memory in both private and public settings they must, by necessity, grapple with the implications of this memory for Australia's shifting political and cultural landscape. The survivors' emphasis on the 'exceptional' nature of Holocaust memory may provide a powerful foundation but it will take considerable vision for succeeding generations to endow this particular memory with universal resonance – to engender universality without retreating either into an undifferentiated universalism or a narrow particularism. To not do so, however, to render what may be 'exceptional' as 'exclusive', is to relegate Holocaust memory housed in Australian Holocaust museums to the periphery of Australian public life.

ACKNOWLEDGEMENTS

The author wishes to thank Karen Ades, Robert Aldrich, Carey Glass, Konrad Kwiet, A. Dirk Moses and Jacqueline Ninio for their constructive criticism of earlier drafts. They are, of course, responsible neither for the views expressed nor any errors committed. The views expressed in this article are the author's own and as such do not reflect or attempt to represent the policies of the Sydney Jewish Museum.

NOTES

1. Judith E. Berman, *Holocaust Remembrance in Australian Jewish Communities, 1945–2000* (Crawley, WA: University of Western Australia Press, 2001), p.73.
2. Dan Stone, *Constructing the Holocaust* (London: Vallentine Mitchell, 2003), p.xiv.
3. Emil L. Fackenheim, *To Mend the World: Foundations of Post-Holocaust Jewish Thought*, 2nd ed. (Bloomington: Indiana University Press, 1994), p.14.

4. See David Roskies, *The Jewish Search for a Usable Past* (Bloomington: Indiana University Press, 1999). Roskies argues that each denomination has chosen to commemorate the Holocaust according to its own, pre-existing theological frameworks and that this in itself is a form of response reflective of modern Jewish sensibility. While this is compelling from a praxis point of view, it does not fully confront or account for the effects of the theological crisis evident in the post-Holocaust Jewish world.
5. This observation does not deny the significance of the work of post-Holocaust theologians such as Rabbi Irving (Yitz) Greenberg, Richard Rubenstein and Emil Fackenheim among others; rather it is an acknowledgement that none of these theologies have as yet been fully assimilated into normative Jewish practice.
6. See, for example, David Roskies, *Nightwords: A Liturgy on the Holocaust* (New York: CLAL, 2000).
7. For example, the mourner's *kaddish* is often recited at Holocaust commemorations with the names of the death camps punctuating this otherwise sacrosanct and highly formulaic prayer.
8. See, for example, Alan Mintz, *Hurban: Responses to Catastrophe in Hebrew Literature* (New York: Columbia University Press, 1984); Alan Mintz, *Popular Culture and the Shaping of Holocaust Memory in America* (Seattle: University of Washington Press, 2001); David Roskies, *Against the Apocalypse: Reponses to Catastrophe in Modern Jewish Culture* (Cambridge, MA: Harvard University Press, 1984); David Roskies, *The Literature of Destruction: Jewish Responses to Catastrophe* (New York: Jewish Publication Society, 1989).
9. A corrective to this imbalance is found in Oren Baruch Stier, *Committed to Memory: Cultural Mediations of the Holocaust* (Boston: University of Massachusetts Press, 2005); Oren Baruch Stier, 'Different Trains: Holocaust Artifacts and the Ideologies of Remembrance', *Holocaust and Genocide Studies*, Vol.19, No.1 (Spring 2005), pp.81–106. Stier offers a novel and intriguing review of how post-Holocaust theologies can become 'embodied' in museum displays, but does not extend his study to encompass traditional Jewish responses to destruction existent prior to the Holocaust.
10. Mircea Eliade, *Patterns in Comparative Religion* (New York: Sheed and Ward, 1958), p.2.
11. Ibid.
12. Barbara A. Misztal, 'The Sacralization of Memory', *European Journal of Social Theory*, Vol.7, No.1 (2004), pp.67–84.
13. Ibid., p.68.
14. Ibid., p.67.
15. Jeffrey C. Alexander, 'On the Social Construction of Moral Universals: The "Holocaust" from War Crime to Trauma Drama', *European Journal of Social Theory*, Vol.5, No.1 (2002), p.6.
16. Daniele Hervieu-Leger, *Religion as a Chain of Memory* (Oxford: Polity Press, 2000), p.53.
17. See for example Jay Winter, *Sites of Memory, Sites of Mourning: The Great War in European Cultural History* (Cambridge: Cambridge University Press, 1995).
18. Mark Chmiel, 'The Political Varieties of Sacred Remembrance: Elie Wiesel and US Foreign Policy', *Journal of Church and State*, Vol.40, No.4 (1998), pp.827–52.
19. Ibid., p.29.
20. Interview with Mrs. Marika Weinberger, 31 October 2006.
21. Ibid.
22. This inscription is placed at the entrance to the Sanctum, to the left of the eternal flame.
23. Speech given at the rededication and opening ceremony on *Yom HaShoah* 2005. Dr. Hatfield is a Survivor of Lutsk, where her family was murdered by the mobile killing units operating in 1941–42. The founder and benefactor of the Sydney Jewish Museum, John Saunders OAM, supplied the original funding for the Sanctum of Remembrance.
24. Interviews undertaken at the SJM in October and November 2006.
25. Ibid.
26. Ibid.
27. Ibid.
28. Ibid.
29. Sharon Kangisser Cohen, 'Remembering for Us: The Transgenerational Transmission of Holocaust Memory and Commemoration', this volume.
30. Ibid.
31. It should be noted that this desire is not without historical precedent. After other major destructions in Jewish history such as the Crusades, new fast days and commemorative rituals were enacted in light of what was experienced as 'extraordinary suffering'. See Jacqueline Ninio, 'Out of the Depths

I Cry out to You: Liturgical and Ritual Response to Jewish Communal Catastrophe' (Hebrew Union College–Jewish Institute of Religion, 1998).
32. Irving Greenberg, *The Jewish Way: Living the Holidays* (New York: Touchstone, 1988), pp.326–39.
33. Until recently, in Sydney *Yom HaShoah* was traditionally part of a week of Holocaust remembrance and education planned by the Sydney community under the auspices of the NSW Jewish Board of Deputies. However, as time passes and fewer of the survivor generation are able to be active in these events, the decision was taken in 2007 to 'concentrate' commemoration on one day rather than a week. The day does include ceremonies at Rookwood and other communal sites, but the main events of the day are centred at the SJM.
34. Over the course of the day, survivors, descendants, invited guests and general museum visitors continuously read names of victims.
35. The Arch of Titus was erected in Rome, after the emperor's death, to commemorate chiefly the capture of Jerusalem. Included in the arch are reliefs depicting spoils from the Temple in Jerusalem.
36. See Hans Haacke, 'The Monument Vanishes', in James E. Young (ed.), *The Art of Memory: Holocaust Memorials in History* (New York: The Jewish Museum, 1994).
37. The author is indebted to the designer John Cabello for his generous engagement in discussion and debate concerning the Menorah sculpture, without which this section could not have been
38. SJM vision and mission statement 2007.
39. Berman, *Holocaust Remembrance*, pp.58–74.
40. Ibid., p.202.
41. Neil Levi, '"No Sensible Comparison?" The Holocaust in and out of Australia's History Wars', *History and Memory*, Vol.19, No.1 (Spring 2007), p.125.
42. Ibid., p.128.
43. SJM mission statement 2007.
44. See for example James E. Young, *The Texture of Memory: Holocaust Memorials and Meaning* (New Haven, CT: Yale University Press, 1993); James E. Young, *The Changing Shape of Holocaust Memory* (New York: American Jewish Committee, 1995); James E. Young, *At Memory's Edge: After-Images of the Holocaust in Contemporary Art and Architecture* (New Haven, CT: Yale University Press, 2000).
45. Judith E. Berman, *Holocaust Agendas: Conspiracies and Industries? Issues and Debates in Holocaust Memorialization* (London: Vallentine Mitchell, 2006), pp.34–5.
46. Ibid., p.35.
47. Ruth Wisse, *The Modern Jewish Canon: A Journey through Language and Culture* (New York: The Free Press, 2000), p.19.
48. Alexander, 'On the Social Construction of Moral Universals', p.6.
49. Key landmarks for Alexander are the publication and influence of *The Diary of Anne Frank* and in particular the removal of much of the Jewish content of the book and subsequent play, the Eichmann trial and the screening of the television mini series *Holocaust* to an American TV audience of 100 million viewers.
50. Alexander, 'On the Social Construction of Moral Universals', p.52.
51. Ibid., p.51.
52. For an overview of the 'uniqueness debate' in Holocaust scholarship, see A. Dirk Moses, 'Conceptual Blockages and Definitional Dilemmas in the "Racial Century": Genocides of Indigenous Peoples and the Holocaust', *Patterns of Prejudice: Institute for Jewish Policy Research*, Vol.36, No.4 (2002), pp.7–36; and Gavriel Rosenfeld, 'The Politics of Uniqueness: Reflections on the Recent Polemical Turn in Holocaust and Genocide Scholarship', *Holocaust and Genocide Studies*, Vol.13, No.1 (1999), pp.28–62.
53. William F.S. Miles, 'Third World Views of the Holocaust', *Journal of Genocide Research*, Vol.6, No.3 (2004), pp.371–93.
54. An example of this approach is found in Lilian Friedberg, 'Dare to Compare: Americanizing the Holocaust', *American Indian Quarterly*, Vol.24, No.3 (2000), pp.353–80.
55. Mike David, *Late Victorian Holocausts* (London and New York: Verso, 2001); Vinay Lal, 'Genocide, Barbaric Others, and the Violence of Categories: A Response to Omer Bartov', *The American Historical Review*, Vol.103, No.4 (1998), pp.1187–90; Vinay Lal, 'The Concentration Camp and Development: The Pasts and Future of Genocide', *Patterns of Prejudice*, Vol.39, No.2 (2005), pp.240–43; Jurgen Zimmerer, 'The Birth of the *Ostland* out of the Spirit of Colonialism: A Postcolonial Perspective on the Nazi Policy of Conquest and Extermination', *Patterns of Prejudice*, Vol.9, No.2 (2005), pp.197–219.
56. For example, Friedberg explicitly states that her work is intended to be 'a deliberate transgression of

traditional boundaries in scholarship'.

57. For an example of this dynamic in the Australian context see A. Dirk Moses, 'Genocide and Holocaust Consciousness in Australia', *History Compass*, Vol.1 (2003), pp.1–13.
58. Berman, *Holocaust Agendas*, pp.34–5.
59. This was not considered possible at a 1983 symposium held at the Hakoah Club where survivors actively opposed a similar suggestion by Tony Barta, a historian from La Trobe University. (Interview with Professor Konrad Kwiet, 19 June 2007.)
60. The SJM's education programmes utilise a similar 'particular/universal' approach in a variety of programmes for both students and adults that address issues of other genocides, instances of racial discrimination, and associated behaviours such as bullying in an Australian context. The SJM's most recent temporary exhibition, *Butterflies of Hope*, while centring on the experience of child survivors of the Holocaust also dedicates a section of the display to child victims of other genocides.

Abstracts

'I boxed my way through life!' The Incredible Story of Bully Salem Schott
KONRAD KWIET

This article narrates the incredible story of Bully and Gerda Schott. Bully was one of few Jews to escape Auschwitz, which he did with the help of his future wife Gerda. After escape Bully and Gerda survived the rest of the war, independently of one another, in Berlin. After the war Bully co-operated with the Soviet forces in the tracking down of ex-Nazis. In 1950 he emigrated to Australia. It is individual narratives like these that demonstrate that, despite geographical distance, the Holocaust became part of the history of Australia too. Gerda and Bully became Australian citizens in 1959.

In the Shadow of the Holocaust: The Development of Moriah College, Sydney
SUZANNE RUTLAND

This paper analyses the legacy of the Holocaust in the development of Moriah College, today the largest Jewish school in Australia, and explains why this tragedy led to a determined effort to achieve Jewish renewal as well as academic success. The growth of the College was facilitated first by restitution and later by the generosity of survivors. As a result of survivors' reluctance to talk about their experiences, there was no formal study of the Holocaust until the late 1970s when Holocaust education and memorialisation became part of the College's programme. An analysis of this adds to our understanding of the 'silence', an issue of significant debate in recent scholarship.

Distant Reverberations: Australian Responses to the Trial of Adolf Eichmann
DAVID RITTER

The trial of Adolf Eichmann in Jerusalem in 1961 is widely regarded as one of the principal events in the rise to prominence of a distinct event known as 'the Holocaust' in Western European and American cultural consciousness. This article considers the impact of the Eichmann trial in Australia.

An Early Holocaust Novel: Patrick White's *Riders in the Chariot*, a Critique
JOHN DOCKER

Patrick White's novel *Riders in the Chariot* (1961) can be regarded as a contribution to Holocaust literature, broadly defined. The novel features as one of its main characters

Mordecai Himmelfarb, a Holocaust survivor, who makes his way from Germany, via Palestine, to Australia. In a comparison with Joyce's *Ulysses*, with its anti-essentialising construction of the complex consciousness of Bloom, *Riders in the Chariot* is revealed to be essentialising in its notions of Jewishness. It assimilates Jewish identity to a romantic discourse of attachment to land, highly problematic in a continent where the Indigenous people have been largely dispossessed of that land. The essay also discusses the novel's interest in Kabbalah. Overall, the essay convicts the novel of aesthetic crudity, which has troubling implications for how it perceives its characters, including Jewish characters.

'Remembering for Us': The Transgenerational Transmission of Holocaust Memory and Commemoration
SHARON KANGISSER COHEN

Commemoration has moved from the periphery to the centre of Australian Jewish consciousness, a trend that is also discernable amongst Jewish communities. Over the past six decades the voice of the Holocaust survivor has become increasingly audible, and has been instrumental in establishing a public memory of the Holocaust in Australia. Today, survivors are at the forefront of the commemorative activities and their individual stories, representing a myriad of different experiences, are central to Holocaust education. At present the issue that confronts the Sydney Jewish community is no different from the questions facing other communities. How is memory of the Holocaust to be kept alive and vibrant as survivors' voices begin to recede and as the past passes from 'living memory to history'? This article is based on group interviews conducted with Holocaust survivors living in Sydney, Australia and explores how these Holocaust survivors would like the Holocaust to be remembered in the future. From the discussion groups it was clear that most of these survivors are unsure if the next generation possesses the inclination and ability not only to remember the Holocaust, but to remember it well. There was a clear sentiment amongst all the groups that one of the only ways the memory of the Holocaust can survive is by being cast as a religious act, duty and obligation, to be codified in the Jewish religious calendar.

Memory-Work: Video Testimony, Holocaust Remembrance and the Third Generation
AMELIA KLEIN

This article investigates the responses of grandchildren of Holocaust survivors to Holocaust video testimonies archived at the Jewish Holocaust Museum and Research Centre, Melbourne, Australia. Interviews with the grandchildren show that many have begun to question the existing communal obligations surrounding Holocaust remembrance. As significant sources for Holocaust remembrance, video testimonies have important roles to play in facilitating 'memory-work' for the third generation. Watching video testimony allows viewers to move beyond existing formulaic approaches towards Holocaust remembrance and form their own personal responses. The voices of the third generation emphasise that Holocaust memory in Australia will be shaped by each generation in ways that are meaningful for them.

Displaying the Sacred: Australian Holocaust Memorials in Public Life
AVRIL ALBA

Focusing on the Sydney Jewish Museum's (SJM) Sanctum of Remembrance, this article explores the relationship between Holocaust memorials, the Jewish commemorative tradition and the sacralisation of Holocaust memory in the Australian context. I argue that the building, design and function of the Sanctum reflects a deeply felt need within the Australian Jewish survivor community to develop alternative commemorative forms as a response to perceived 'inadequate' theology. Subsequently, the sacred Holocaust memory housed in this space departs significantly from traditional Jewish responses to destruction. Further, the public nature of the Sanctum has the dual effect of transforming the Jewish commemorative tradition and conveying that tradition to a largely non-Jewish public, explicitly linking Jewish tragedy to broader public concerns. In this progression, a sacred Holocaust memory is created that is at once particular and universal, providing Australian Holocaust memorials with unprecedented opportunities for empathy and identification with other victims of genocide. Yet this powerful dialectic remains, at present, under-utilised. Whether the SJM and other Australian Holocaust museums choose to engage in these opportunities will ultimately depend on the ability of these institutions to grapple with the complexity of Australia's colonial past and contemporary multicultural society. To contend with these issues requires the ability to understand and 'display' the nation as perpetrator *and* resistor of genocidal acts, a complex narrative difficult to assimilate into largely 'static' museum and memorial space. To not do so, however, risks rendering Holocaust memory in Australian museums a solely 'internal', Jewish concern.

Notes on Contributors

Avril Alba is a graduate of Adelaide and Harvard Universities and a doctoral candidate at the University of Sydney. She is currently the Director of Education of the Sydney Jewish Museum.

John Docker is adjunct senior research fellow, Research School of Humanities, Australian National University. His most recent books are *1492: The Poetics of Diaspora* (2001) and, with Ann Curthoys, *Is History Fiction?* (2005). He is currently writing a book entitled *The Origins of Violence.*

James Jordan is lan Karten Research Fellow, lecturer in English and member of the Parkes Institute for Jewish/non-Jewish Relations at the University of Southampton. His current work examines the impact and representation of Jews and Jewishness in post-war British television, beginning with an analysis of Rudolph Carder's 1952 version of 'The Dybbuk' for the BBC. He is also co-editor of *Holocaust Studies: A Journal of Culture and History.*

Sharon Kangisser Cohen completed her doctorate at the Hebrew University of Jerusalem. She currently holds a post-doctoral fellowship from the *Fondation pour Memoire de la Shoah* and is a research fellow at the University of Sydney in the Department of Biblical, Hebrew and Judaic Studies. Her current research explores the post-war experiences of Holocaust survivors in Australia. Her book *Child Survivors of the Holocaust in Israel: Social Dynamics and Post-war Experiences. Finding their Voice* was published by Sussex Academic Press in 2005.

Amelia Klein, PhD, recently completed her doctoral studies in History at Deakin University, Melbourne, Australia. She has been involved in Holocaust education and remembrance programmes in Australia, including making a documentary film, 'Claiming the Memory: Who Owns the Legacy?' (Australian Broadcast Commission Television, 2004), leading the 2004 Adult March of the Living, founding Young Friends of the Sydney Jewish Museum, and teaching an original course 'Reverberations: Generational Impact of the Holocaust' for the Florence Melton School in Melbourne.

Konrad Kwiet (bom in Germany in 1941, resident in Australia since 1976) was made emeritus professor of German Studies at Macquarie University, Sydney in 1999. He was formerly chief historian of the Australian war crimes commission, and visiting professor and research fellow in Amsterdam, Oxford, Washington DC, Heidelberg, Munich, Frankfurt am Main and Berlin. He has published widely on modem German and Jewish history, especially the Third Reich, Antisemitism and the Holocaust. He is currently Adjunct Professor for Jewish Studies and Roth Lecturer for Holocaust

Studies at the Department of Hebrew, Biblical and Jewish Studies at the University of Sydney, and resident historian of the Sydney Jewish Museum.

Tom Lawson is Lecturer in Modern History at the University of Winchester. He is the author of *The Church of England and the Holocaust: Christianity, Memory and Nazism* (2006). He is also the co-editor of *Holocaust Studies: A Journal of Culture and History*. He is currently working on a new study of Holocaust historiography and on an unrelated project on the idea of Europe after the Great War.

David Ritter is a lecturer in law and a doctoral candidate in history at the University of Western Australia. He is the co-editor of *Making Australian History: Perspectives on the Past since 1788* (Melbourne: Thomson Learning, 2007).

Suzanne D. Rutland is Associate Professor and Chair of the Department of Hebrew, Biblical and Jewish Studies at the University of Sydney. She has published widely on Australian Jewish history, edits the Sydney edition of the AJHS Journal, as well as writing on issues relating to the Shoah and Israel. Her latest books are *The Jews in Australia* (Cambridge University Press, 2005) and *Triumph of the Jewish Spirit: Forty Years of the Jewish Communal Appeal* (Sydney: JCA, 2007). She has received a major government grant with Professor Sol Encel to study 'The Political Sociology of Australian Jewry'.